An Invisible Giant

The California State Colleges

Donald R. Gerth
James O. Haehn
and Associates

AN
INVISIBLE
GIANT

Jossey-Bass Inc., Publishers
San Francisco · Washington · London · 1971

AN INVISIBLE GIANT
The California State Colleges
        by Donald R. Gerth, James O. Haehn, and Associates

Copyright © 1971 by Jossey-Bass, Inc., Publishers

Published in Great Britian by
Jossey-Bass, Inc., Publishers
St. George's House
44 Hatton Garden, London E.C.1

Library of Congress Catalogue Card Number LC 79-173855

International Standard Book Number ISBN 0-87589-110-1

Manufactured in the United States of America

JACKET DESIGN BY WILLI BAUM

FIRST EDITION

Code 7137

The Jossey-Bass
Series in Higher Education

Consulting Editors

JOSEPH AXELROD
*San Francisco State College
and University of California, Berkeley*

MERVIN B. FREEDMAN
*San Francisco State College
and Wright Institute, Berkeley*

Preface

In 1960, the higher education community began to be aware of a new effort in California, the development of a Master Plan for higher education in the most rapidly developing and modernizing state. Educators and laymen had long been aware of the University of California, perhaps not as a system but as a single campus at Berkeley with one of the world's great collections of scholars. They were equally conscious of the California junior college (now community college) commitment, with the most campuses and students of any state. Similarly, some outside of California knew of a state college in San Francisco and perhaps at San Diego; these campuses were perceived as having some quality, though limited. One of the coeditors of this volume well recalls the negative attitude of several of his graduate advisors at a prestigious old university toward his becoming a faculty member of a distinguished California state college in the late 1950s. "No one with scholarly interests would move west to a state college." The existence of fifteen state colleges in California was largely unknown in 1960.

The California Master Plan in some sense both formalized and mitigated one of the widely watched and significant experiments in higher education. It committed California to provide access to higher education for all its citizens. The University of California made available education through the doctorate to a highly select student body on its several campuses. The junior colleges were the open door, serving the traditional function of the land grant institutions by providing transfer and technical-vocational curricula. The state colleges were in the middle, with relatively selective admissions standards (then more selective than those of all public campuses in the nation save the University of California and the University of Michigan). The state colleges were in theory liberal arts–professional colleges and in fact were only then emerging from the teachers college–vocational mold. The state colleges were little known nationally, sometimes little known or understood within California, but they were in some ways the key to the eventual success or failure of the California Master Plan. They were assigned the task of educating the great bulk of undergraduates and graduate students through the master's degree. The state colleges were, in effect, asked or told to build one of the largest higher educational enterprises in the world and to do so within a few years to meet the expected tidal wave of students. Thus the invisible giant of the California state colleges began to form during the 1960s. *An Invisible Giant* is a partial review of what happened in the state college system between 1960 and 1970.

Since 1964 higher education has received an unprecedented amount of attention. After the student protest movement focused this interest, scholars began increasingly to study higher education in a variety of dimensions. In addition to such popular concerns as student rights, institutional-societal relations, and the quality of college teaching, scholarly attention was also drawn to questions of organization, governance, and the basic purpose of colleges and universities. These latter subjects are critically important, even though they are less dramatic than disruption and conflict. However, most of what we know about these phenomena is derived from studies of elite liberal arts colleges, usually privately operated; studies of leading universities, state and private; or studies of statewide systems of coordination and control over higher education.

Universities and colleges outside these categories and systems of higher education below the general state level of coordination have been seldom investigated. One type of school in particular—

the state college and regional university—has received less research attention than its significance deserves. *An Invisible Giant* attempts to help fill this gap and to add to the work of such scholars as E. Alden Dunham and Fred Harcleroad. While their work has been on a general plane, this book examines a single system of state colleges and focuses specifically on its organization and problems of governance. Most studies of academic institutions or systems have also tended to be more historical than analytical. Although these works are very important in the development of knowledge about higher education, their emphasis is markedly different from ours. We present an assessment of an on-going educational enterprise, an assessment developed from a variety of perspectives and points of view. *An Invisible Giant* is more than historical in its purpose, and its approach is exploratory. It offers the reader a cross-sectional look at the California state colleges as they have developed since the inauguration of the statewide system in 1960.

Hopefully such an analysis will yield not only a better picture of how a massive state system of higher education functions but also a basis for understanding and generalizing to higher education and its development. Ideally, a comparative study of several systems of public colleges and universities would generate solidly based hypotheses, but our familiarity is mainly with the California system, and we believe that a book such as this represents a necessary step toward broadly based research.

Although many of the specific factors that have gone into the shaping of the present CSC are unique to it by virtue of its size, location, and relationships with other dynamic institutions of higher education, the CSC incorporates virtually all the significant problems that can be found in other higher education institutions. Problems associated with extensive and rapid enrollment growth, with financial strain, with faculty expansion, and with public and political issues are all significant. The ways in which these problems developed and the manner in which they have been addressed are carefully explored in the several contributions that make up the main body of the book.

Persons concerned generally with higher education should be able to gain many insights applicable well beyond the boundaries of

California. Further, college and university administrators, faculty and student leaders, and laymen as well can learn from the experiences of one of the largest systems of public mass higher education.

An Invisible Giant does not represent the final word on academic governance or even on the organization and operation of the California state colleges. The work accomplishes the modest goal of providing a careful assessment of the colleges at a significant juncture in their development. Change will continue, but by critically taking stock of the system we can make a contribution to the knowledge of higher education—a contribution which has general value and application.

We are conscious that throughout *An Invisible Giant* different and sometimes contradictory perspectives are presented. Yet, more important, we also realize and wish to impress the fact that all the writers have contributed out of a deep sense of commitment to the California state college system and the great promise it affords.

Those who have made *An Invisible Giant* possible are the many students, faculty members, administrators, and interested citizens who through their activities, past and present, have constituted the California state colleges. Each of them, from puzzled new freshman to seasoned elder trustee, has helped to make the system the great educational enterprise that it is today. Although the focus of attention in many of the chapters within this book is the array of problems facing the state colleges, the strengths and contributions of the system should not be forgotten; as observers of this system we publicly congratulate all who have been a part of it.

Many of our colleagues and friends have helped in the development of this book. To thank everyone personally would add yet another chapter to a volume already lengthy enough. We do wish, though, to express our gratitude to all of them. We owe a special debt to certain individuals, and we feel that these should be named: Lew Oliver, Sidney Brossman, Morgan Odell, and Edmond Hallberg.

Finally, we owe much to the persons who agreed to contribute to the book. We deeply appreciate the time and attention that each of the authors devoted to his chapter. The contributions that the work may make are clearly a product of their efforts. Any errors of judgment or substance are ours.

We dedicate the book to our wives, Beverly Gerth and Edith Haehn, for the hundreds of hours they have given to the preparation of *An Invisible Giant*. From typing and proofreading the manuscript to the difficult task of providing criticism where it was needed and deserved, they have done an admirable job. We also wish to add our heartfelt thanks to our children for the tolerance they have displayed toward two often too busy fathers.

Chico, California   DONALD R. GERTH
November 1971   JAMES O. HAEHN

Contents

Authors

JOHN D. BACHELLER is associate state college dean of student affairs in the California State Colleges.

ROBERT O. BESS is director of special projects for the California State Colleges.

GEORGE CLUCAS is professor of public administration at California State Polytechnic College at San Luis Obispo.

GLENN S. DUMKE is chancellor of the California State Colleges.

DONALD R. GERTH is professor of political science and vice-president for academic affairs at Chico State College.

JAMES E. GREGG is professor of political science and dean of the Graduate School at Chico State College.

JAMES O. HAEHN is associate professor of sociology and chairman of the Department of Sociology at Chico State College.

LOUIS H. HEILBRON is a partner in the San Francisco law firm Heller, Ehrman, White, and McAuliffe; he has served as a trustee of the California State Colleges from 1960 through 1969, first chairman of the Board of Trustees for three years, president of the California State Board of Education, and member of the California Coordinating Council for Higher Education.

ROBERT G. JONES is assistant professor of political science and coordinator of public administration at Chico State College.

JEROME RICHFIELD is professor and chairman of the Department of Philosophy at San Fernando Valley State College.

WILLARD B. SPALDING is on the faculty at Portland State University; he has recently retired as deputy director and was for some years director of the California Coordinating Council for Higher Education and has been an administrative officer in several major universities.

ROBERT G. THOMPSON is professor of government at Sacramento State College and a member of the Statewide Academic Senate.

JESSE M. UNRUH was a member of the California State Assembly from 1955 to 1970 and served as Speaker from 1961 to 1968; from 1965 to 1968 he served as chairman of the legislature's Joint Committee on Higher Education; he currently is visiting professor of political science at San Fernando Valley State College and Rutgers University.

J. MALCOLM WALKER is assistant professor of business administration at San Jose State College.

KENNETH S. WASHINGTON is special assistant for educational opportunity and human relations with the chancellor of the California State Colleges.

An Invisible Giant

The California State Colleges

1

Overview of the State College System

Donald R. Gerth, James O. Haehn

The California state college system is one of the largest networks of public higher education in the world. Yet, as the title of this book indicates, the system is an "invisible giant"—a complex of colleges rarely noticed by the public or even by scholars in the field of higher education. The anonymity of the California state college system (CSC) is not unique. Other universities and colleges within similar state-supported systems are equally inconspicuous. A wide range of factors contribute to the low visibility of state colleges and universities, not the least of which are their large sizes and rapid rates of growth. As these schools have expanded, they have become the main publicly financed avenue through higher education for an increasing proportion of the population, drawing more and more students from groups who in past years would not have gone to college. The state universities and colleges have thus become what Dunham (1969) has termed "the colleges of the forgotten Americans."

1

The massive growth of the CSC paralleled the general enrollment expansion of higher education following World War II. From
a total student enrollment of less than 2,000 in 1900, the colleges
composing the CSC had expanded to take in more than 12,000
students by 1940, and to nearly 30,000 by 1950. Between 1950 and
1960, however, the mushrooming of student enrollments was such
that close to 95,000 students were attending California state colleges
at the end of that decade. This pattern has continued to the point
that in 1969 the schools within the system enrolled more than
224,000 students. The latter figure is even somewhat deceptive, for,
in addition to the "regular" students, the colleges provided educational services to another 90,000 people in extension and continuing
education programs.

This magnification in enrollment has been accompanied by a
similar and obviously related growth in the number of degrees
granted by the CSC. In the academic year 1949–1950, for example,
the state colleges granted a total of 5,450 academic degrees, while
by 1969–1970 this number had increased to 44,224. The figure for
1949–1950 (the first year that M.A.s were awarded) includes both
bachelor's and master's degrees—5,344 B.A.s and 106 M.A.s. The
data for 1969–1970 also include both levels—37,409 bachelor's
degrees and 6,815 master's (more master's degrees than the number
of total degrees awarded twenty years before).

As the volume of input and output of the state colleges grew
so did the scope and complexity of programs being offered. At first
the colleges focused largely on the training of teachers; later they
broadened their range of courses and majors to include a wide
variety of programs, including many normally associated with universities. In this development, however, the state colleges were always
bound by the restrictions of the Master Plan for Higher Education,
adopted by the California legislature in 1960, which delimited the
kinds of programs the schools could offer and prevented any from
being fostered beyond the level of the master's degree.

Nonetheless, a student can find on one or another of the
state college campuses programs ranging from the traditional teacher
education to majors in environmental design, architecture, winemaking, and religious studies. In addition, during the 1960s virtually
all the schools added majors, minors, and special options in ethnic

studies, various interdisciplinary subjects, and a host of experimental programs.

The press of student enrollment and the demands for new and different programs necessitated the employment of large numbers of new faculty. In 1951–1952 the total full-time faculty in the system numbered just over 1,300. By 1960–1961 this number had increased to a little more than 3,700 and by 1970–1971 to more than 11,000. This growth included a substantial addition of specialists in the new fields being taught as well as many professors in existing disciplines; but to do this the colleges had to recruit larger and larger numbers of part-time and temporary faculty. In 1951–1952 the schools employed 406 part-time faculty; for the 1960–1961 academic year the number of part-time faculty climbed to 970, and by 1970–1971 over 3,500 persons were employed as part-time teachers in the system.

This rapid and extensive increase in full- and part-time faculty brought with it a host of problems. Through most of the 1950s and 1960s higher education institutions generally were expanding and requiring more professors. In competition with other schools the CSC found itself seeking people with specialized training at higher levels of preparation but having to compete in very tight labor markets for these people. One consequence was that during this period there was a decrease in the proportion of new professors coming to the colleges with their terminal degrees. More and more of the faculty were drawn from graduate schools and had little prior experience. Similarly, when full-time staff could not be secured, the colleges turned to nearby industry and government for part-time instructors. The latter brought with them much practical experience and considerable dedication, but they often were unknown by the full-time people in the departments hiring them since most part-timers taught night classes while the full-time staff taught during the day. In short, the growth of the schools constituting the CSC resulted in the transformation of the colleges into highly complex institutions with an increasing range of problems and strains.

Lying behind many of the difficulties was the problem of adequate financing. Nurtured on minimal budgets, the colleges began to receive larger amounts of funding but rarely in quantities keeping abreast of the growth the schools experienced. In the mid-

1960s this source of tension became even more serious, and by the early 1970s the situation had hardly improved. Especially under the governorship of Ronald Reagan, the colleges, along with the state university, became a target of continued proportionate reductions in support. This is not to say the CSC has not obtained greater financial support from the state, but rather that in terms of their growth and the costs faced by the schools, their relative position has declined steadily since 1966.

Each of the nineteen campuses, new and old, has a unique history. Some things are shared among a few, many, or all of the campuses; some things are not shared. Clearly each campus has its own character and educational fix. The bringing together of these nineteen campuses, along with a number of auxiliary and supportive programs, has been one of the major educational ventures of the past decade. A single governing board came into being. The role of a chancellor and his staff was created, and a set of relationships began to emerge among the campuses and with the system. Among the public higher education institutions in California, a distinguishing characteristic of the state colleges has been state agency status; the University of California is constitutionally independent, and the community colleges are based in local districts. The state colleges historically were operated approximately like any state agency, with line item budgets and controls from the Departments of Finance and Public Works and other state organizations. Since the California state college system has come into being however, the issue of state agency controls is far from resolved and has only been redefined. Line item budgets persist; some limited flexibility has been achieved. A whole new set of state agency relationships has emerged with the chancellor and his staff; the individual campuses are no longer centrally involved with state agencies.

Relationships with the other segments of higher education in California have sharpened themselves. In a sense the state colleges are the newest and the oldest in the education complex. While one campus (San Jose) is the oldest public higher education institution in California, the colleges were for years single-purpose institutions and not full partners in the higher education enterprise. The University of California was founded in 1868 and quickly became a major institution, and the community colleges came into being as junior colleges with clear responsibility for and early acceptance of their roles in providing lower division work. The state colleges emerged as partners in the 1920s, 1930s and 1940s, and in a sense are still emerging. Relationships among the segments of public higher education and competition for resources were at the heart of the Master Plan. Key issues, going well beyond resource allocation and including responsibility for programs, especially graduate and professional degree programs, selection and admission of students, and support for research, have continued to divide the various sections of higher education. Articulation of academic programs among the segments, despite an organized articulation conference, continues to be troublesome. At the end of the 1960s the provision of space for all eligible applicants, particularly the acceptance of community college graduates by the state colleges and university, became an important issue.

In planning the book we had to make a number of critical decisions about its composition. One of these was to approach the subject by asking several highly qualified people to write about topics in which they have expertise. This approach poses problems of integration and continuity, but it also strengthens the volume by presenting the direct comments and insights of those best informed on a particular subject.

The scope of the analysis was the second basic issue. Every effort was made to ensure that a thorough and balanced body of articles would appear on the principal aspects of state college operations and problems. Still, some subjects proved to be either too broad to explore in a single article or too removed from the general direction of the book as it took shape. No chapters have been included, for example, on the relationships of the state colleges to the other segments of higher education in California. These relationships have been so vital to the development of the California state colleges that we felt a distinct and separate study should be made of them.

Among the subjects omitted for the sake of cohesiveness were the academic programs offered in the state colleges; problems associated with student placement, housing, and counseling; and questions of educational planning and experimentation. We are not implying that these topics are less important than those included, but rather that as the book emerged their inclusion would have detracted from the main thrust of the analysis.

What has emerged is a book focused primarily upon the structure and governance of the California state college system. Such an emphasis is not unwarranted, particularly now that the Master Plan, largely centered upon matters of structure and governance, is being questioned. Further, the rash of student unrest and public discontent has in large measure revolved about issues of organization and control.

Part One provides a general history and background of the state colleges before we move to the chapters in Part Two on the administration of the system. Having established a context in which to view the colleges, we present the roles and problems of those charged with the official operation of the system, including the trustees and the chancellor.

Governance in the state colleges is not just the result of actions within official hierarchies but also involves various auxiliary structures. Key among these are the statewide academic senate, the independent faculty organizations, and statewide and local student governments. In Part Three each of these is given attention, with a special eye to their effects and problems on the systemwide level. Part Three is also devoted to certain major problems of the colleges —specifically, ethnic and racial pressures, and faculty perceptions of governance. Clearly, these do not exhaust the range of strains and conflicts taking place within the California state colleges, but they are some of the most important issues.

In Part Four, we present our conclusions and an analysis of the prospects for the future of the California college system. The tone of many of the articles is critical, almost negative. Nevertheless, all the contributors have written out of deep concern for the California state college system. Criticism, in some cases anger, is more the product of these concerns for the betterment of the system than an example of sheer emotional negativism. All organizations, academic and nonacademic, are beset by problems. By focusing attention on these problems and by stimulating critical assessments of them, we can take a major step toward finding the causes and eventually the solutions. Only through this often difficult pathway can the long-run strengths of the California state colleges be fostered.

We do wish to emphasize, however, that taking this approach does not and should not detract from the generally excellent job that has been done in the California state colleges. For more than one hundred years the state colleges, in one or another form, have provided liberal and vocational education for the young people of California, a service which has benefited the students and the state. Much of this education has gone on with the restrictions of limited resources and marginal status, but in the face of these obstacles the state colleges have performed well and consistently. This book is a minor tribute to the system and its many accomplishments.

2

History of the California State Colleges

Donald R. Gerth

The California state colleges had their formal beginning in 1862 with the founding of the State Normal School in San Francisco. They are in origin teacher-training institutions, sharing this characteristic with many state universities and colleges in the nation.

The California constitution of 1849 provided for the encouragement of a system of schools and created an elective office of superintendent of public instruction. No provision was made for schools other than the common or traditional public schools and a university. In 1853, Superintendent J. G. Marvin in a report to the legislature stated, "No apparent necessity for a normal school has yet arisen. The supply of competent teachers in California is more than equal to the demand" (Ferrier, 1937, p. 327). In 1857, the San Francisco Board of Education established a Weekly Normal School to train elementary teachers. In 1861, Superintendent Andrew J. Moulder reported to the legislature that he had frequently called attention to the need for some kind of normal school to meet a rising demand for teachers.

Every year this necessity is becoming more apparent and more urgent. It is rare, indeed, that the educated man possesses the art of teaching. He may be as learned as a collegiate education can make him and yet lack the ability to impart this information. Long experience in other states has established the great superiority of those teachers who have received a normal school education. They are always sought for and, other things being equal, always receive the highest compensation. In all other professions and trades a long apprenticeship is considered necessary; but in our state, it too often happens that the impudent pretender who has failed in all other pursuits betakes himself to teaching as a last resort to avoid hard labor. Of this, the state superintendent has had frequent proof in the wretched chirography and equally wretched orthography and grammar of the communications addressed to him [Ferrier, 1937, pp. 327–328].

Moulder went on to suggest a small appropriation to the San Francisco Normal School, heretofore municipally supported, to make it available to the state as a whole. Later in 1861 the State Teachers Institute, a private group, met in San Francisco and endorsed Moulder's plan.

These and other pressures brought action from the legislature; on May 2, 1862, the legislature passed an act creating the California State Normal School in San Francisco. Applicants were to be admitted from the various counties in proportion to their representation in the legislature and were required to state in writing their intention to teach permanently in California. The trustees were the members of the State Board of Education, the state superintendent, and three educators; they were known as the Board of Trustees of the State Normal School.

The normal school opened later in 1862. The trustees fixed the admissions quota at sixty students; up to the date when the school was to open with an entrance examination there was only one applicant for admission. Five others came on that first day. By the end of the first year, registration had increased to thirty-one. By 1866, enrollment had increased to 384, and there were 108 graduates; and by 1870 consideration was being given to a new site, for the old one was overcrowded. Principal W. T. Luckey reported, "Surely the time has come when representatives of thirty-five counties preparing to become the teachers of thousands of our children may reasonably expect to have classrooms in which their health will not be endangered and to which they may invite their parents and friends without a feeling of mortification" (Ferrier, 1937, pp. 329–331). Superintendent D. P. Fitzgerald reported this need to the legislature in 1870 and recommended San Jose, then a small city at the southern end of the San Francisco peninsula, as a new site. "San Francisco is not the place, for all experience proves that a school of this character cannot flourish in a great commercial city. To locate the normal school in San Francisco would be dropping a piece of literature into an ocean of mammon. Neither Oakland nor Berkeley is the place; in either of these towns the normal school would be so overshadowed by the state university, with its magnificent endowment and huge proportions, that it would be like a sickly little plant in the shadow of a great oak. San Jose is . . . the proper location for the state normal school" (Ferrier, 1937, pp. 331–332). Later in 1870 the legislature reestablished the state normal school in San Jose and appropriated $12,500 for its annual budget. Thus was the first and embryonic California state college founded in San Francisco and moved to San Jose.

Population growth in southern California brought the need for a branch of the state normal school, which was opened in Los Angeles in 1882; in 1886 this branch was separated from the parent institution and became Los Angeles State Normal School. At the same time the governing structure was revised so that each institution had a board composed of local citizens and each functioned within the administrative jurisdiction of the superintendent of public instruction. The framework for the development of a number of institutions was established. In succeeding years, Chico State Normal School opened in the northern part of the state in 1889; San Diego in 1897; San Francisco (again) in 1899; Santa Barbara in 1909; Fresno in 1911; and Humboldt, also in the north and on the coast, in 1913. California State Polytechnic Institute at San Luis Obispo, opened as a coeducational state vocational high school in 1903, also functioned within this framework.

As this network of institutions was being developed, some

reorganization was taking place at the state level. In 1913 the legislature created a State Board of Education composed of lay individuals to exercise limited powers of governing and to give advice on all state educational operations except the University of California (a constitutionally independent entity) to the governor, the superintendent, and the legislature. The elected superintendent was still the administrative head of all education for the state. In 1916 the new board commented on the normal schools in a report to the governor: "California has reason to be proud of her normal schools and of her generosity in providing, equipping, and supporting them. Our eight California Normal Schools represent an investment of $2,696,149. Their total annual budget for 1915–1916 was $995,-508.98. Their faculties numbered 267" (Ferrier, 1937, p. 333). During World War I, support developed in Los Angeles for a southern branch of the University of California, and this enthusiasm soon turned to support for changing the Los Angeles State Normal School to a branch of the university. This move had the backing of the Los Angeles faculty and Board of Trustees as well as the community; in 1919 the Los Angeles State Normal School became a branch of the university. In 1921, the legislature reorganized policy and administrative structures for education. A State Department of Education was created specifically to succeed to the responsibilities of the State Board of Education; the director of the new department was to be ex-officio the superintendent of public instruction, a constitutional and elected officer. The State Board of Education was to continue as the policy board for the new department and the normal schools and had the authority to approve the superintendent's nominations for presidencies and the faculty. A system of dual or shared authority was created which was to persist until 1961. The legislature also redefined the role of the normal schools as constituting the first two years of college or university level instruction, an act which provided a base for further changes and the renaming of the institutions as state teachers colleges. In 1923 the institutions were authorized to confer the bachelor of arts degree restricted to teacher education.

By 1935 the state teachers colleges enrolled more than 7,000 students, and they were each developing strong identifications as regional institutions. The legislature again changed both their names and functions, and they were designated as state colleges, each named for its location; the institutions were authorized to go beyond teacher education and offer undergraduate liberal arts majors, as long as these majors were in fields which were also major teaching areas in the secondary schools. Enrollment grew in succeeding years to more than 10,000 in 1940, declined during the World War II years to a low of 3,800 in 1943, and then began the post-war expansion. In 1938, a second campus of the California State Polytechnic College was established at Kellogg-Voorhis, now Pomona.

During World War II, the Santa Barbara State College campus became part of the University of California, the second and final (to this date) transfer of a campus from one system to another —though the concept of separate systems of public higher education in California did not emerge until some years after.

In 1945, coincident with the end of the war and the return of the veterans, the program and enrollment expansion which is still underway began. The legislature authorized in 1945 a fifth year of study leading to a secondary teaching credential. In 1946, programs leading to a liberal arts degree, without reference to teacher education, were authorized. In 1947, the master of arts degree in programs related to the preparation of teachers was authorized; also two new campuses were established, in Los Angeles (again) and in Sacramento, followed in 1949 by another new campus in Long Beach. The year 1955 saw the start of master of science degrees in vocational fields. In 1957–1958, four additional campuses were begun at Fullerton, Hayward, Stanislaus County, and San Fernando Valley, followed two years later by three additional campus authorizations at Sonoma, San Bernardino, and the Los Angeles south bay area (now Dominguez Hills). Since 1960, only one additional campus has been authorized and established, at Bakersfield in 1967, although three other sites were under active consideration.

In 1947 the legislature authorized "a comprehensive survey of the system of publicly supported higher education in California," and the report of this survey, commonly known as the Strayer Report, was issued in 1948 (Department of Education, 1948). This was not the first statewide study of higher education; previous studies had been made in 1899, 1919, and 1931–1932. The 1947 survey was recommended to the legislature by the Regents of the

University of California and the State Board of Education. The important conclusions of the Strayer Report for the state colleges were several. This report urged a definition of functions among the three segments of public higher education in California: the university, the state colleges, and the then-named junior colleges. The hope of the authors of the report was to promote orderly growth. The report also urged the creation of a central office for the state colleges, beyond the person of the state superintendent of public instruction, and this change was accomplished in 1948 with the establishment of the Division of State Colleges and Teacher Education in the State Department of Education. Thus for the first time there was a single office staffed with a small number of people and charged with some planning and coordinating responsibilities.

The years after 1945 were ones of constant stress on public higher education in California, although the stress induced by growth and program development was not accompanied by any lack of public or legislative support. The three groups within public higher education were expanding; new campuses were being added; and the expansion was competitive, both for numbers of students and for program. Each segment, most notably the university and the state colleges, sought to protect itself from the other two. The Strayer Report represented an initial effort at differentiation. Even prior to that the Liaison Committee was formed, in April of 1945, between the Regents of the University of California and the State Board of Education; by 1951, this committee was supplemented by a joint staff. In 1953, the Liaison Committee urged another study (Department of Education, 1955) which was completed between 1953 and 1955. The Restudy, as it is commonly known, was carried out by a group of educators who made 140 recommendations; the Liaison Committee adopted eighty-nine of these, the State Board in turn approved seventy-eight, while the Regents approved thirty-five.

All the while the state colleges continued their growth and program development. The University of California sought to reach an agreement to stabilize the state college programs, but to no good result. By the late 1950s, the state colleges were in essence regional liberal arts colleges; most had completed the change in character from the old teacher-training function. The new state colleges, founded since 1947, did not even share the teachers college history.

By 1958, the state colleges were authorized to offer master's degrees without reference to teacher education, and some were suggesting the development of doctoral programs on three of the campuses.

Governance of the state colleges had not developed in pace with growth and program development. While the campuses were nominally governed by the State Board of Education, which had the power to approve presidential and faculty appointments as well as curricula, the campuses were largely semi-independent fiefs of the presidents. The Division of State Colleges and Teacher Education had only a very small staff, with an average of four individuals concerned with programs on the campuses. Each campus was relatively independent, subject to the controls of a line item budget from the legislature and the resulting agency controls carried on by state departments such as Finance, the Personnel Board, and Public Works. The most important governing process for the campuses was the monthly meeting of all the presidents, organized in the Council of State College Presidents, and supplemented on occasion by the business managers from the campuses or the chief instructional officers and deans of students. The presidents were appointed by the state superintendent of public instruction with approval of the State Board of Education; subsequent to appointment presidents were relatively free agents. Each established his own lobby in the state capital. While faculties and administrations complained loudly in the 1950s of a lack of autonomy and of central controls from state agencies, the perspective of time suggests that there then was a relative measure of moving room and independence for the campuses, though each campus was subject to the almost absolute power of its president. Beyond the work of the monthly meeting of presidents and the Liaison Committee of the two segments, there was little in the way of orderly and systematic planning for the development of state college programs on a statewide basis.

The selection and admission of students have always been central to any college or university. Historically, the state colleges used a variety of patterns, emphasizing secondary school achievement and recommendations. While the University of California is the land grant institution for the state, it has never been open generally to all high school graduates and has become increasingly the most selective public university in the nation. The state colleges were also not open generally to all high school graduates and were single purpose institutions down to 1935. Thus it has fallen to the community colleges (then junior colleges) to be the open door institutions in the state. In the late 1940s, the state colleges admitted about 60 per cent of all secondary school graduates. In the early 1950s, based on a study done internally among the campuses, standards of eligibility for admission common to all of the campuses were defined with roughly 45 per cent of all secondary graduates eligible for admission, based on a wide spectrum of secondary school curriculum and not emphasizing traditional college preparatory subject matter. (The University of California then accepted approximately the top 15 per cent.)

By the late 1950s, the state colleges had experienced substantial uncoordinated growth and expected explosive expansion in the 1960s because of the coming tidal wave of students; their programs were developing in a way which might indeed threaten the University of California. The agreements reached after 1945, most often in the contexts of the Strayer Report and the Restudy, concerning differentiation of function between the university and state colleges, were becoming attenuated. Still the environment of public support and even legislative enthusiasm for higher education persisted. Pressure was growing in the legislature for the development of additional campuses, for these were political prizes to be brought home by legislators to and for their constituents. Competition for state funds between the university and the state colleges was growing. In the 1959 session of the California legislature, twenty-three bills, three resolutions, and two constitutional amendments were introduced calling for new campuses and for changes in the structure of public higher education.

This was the background for the Master Plan for Higher Education in California (Department of Education, 1960). A legislative resolution in 1959 called upon the Liaison Committee "to prepare a master plan for the development, expansion, and integration" of higher education in California (California Legislature, 1959). The California Master Plan has been widely used throughout the nation as a model; it has served as a landmark in the governance and planning of higher education in the world. Like most public documents, it represented some substantial compromises.

It has been interpreted by some in California as a ratification of the status quo and by others as a peace treaty. The latter characterization is the more adequate, for the Master Plan was an agreement among the segments and with the state government about principles for the planning, governance, and development of the segments of higher education. For the California state colleges, the Master Plan marked a major turning point in the character and development of the campuses.

The California state college system was established under an independent Board of Trustees on July 1, 1961. The post of chancellor was created, and the concept of a system of public higher education institutions was implemented. In addition, the Master Plan defined more clearly than before the differentiation and overlapping of functions among the three segments of public higher education and created a Coordinating Council for Higher Education as a voluntary coordinating body composed of segmental and public representatives to advise the governor, legislature, and segments.

The functions of the California state colleges were defined to include undergraduate and graduate programs in the liberal arts and sciences and in applied fields and professions leading to baccalaureate and master's degrees and to joint doctoral degrees under certain circumstances with the University of California. The selection of students for the California state colleges was redefined to set eligibility for freshmen at the top 33⅓ per cent of secondary school graduates, and the system was to limit lower division enrollment to 40 per cent of undergraduate enrollment, thus diverting substantial numbers of lower division students to the community colleges.

The Master Plan team recommended that the structural changes creating a Board of Trustees for the state colleges and a Coordinating Council for Higher Education be incorporated in the constitution. California has a relatively lengthy constitution, with many of the details of government in it. The legislature declined to incorporate any more than provision for eight-year terms for trustees (in contrast to sixteen-year terms of office for the Regents of the university). Thus the state colleges were more nearly subject to legislative and state government control than was the university with its constitutional status. Legislators clearly wanted to retain some access to the system on matters of budget, the creation of new campuses, and general development.

The implementation of the plan was no small feat. The state colleges were almost one hundred years old when on July 1, 1961, the Board of Trustees and the first chancellor, former President Buell Gallagher of the City College of New York, took the responsibility for the new system. Unlike the University of California, which essentially grew as a complex from the expansion of a single campus, the state colleges were federated into a system from a series of campuses that had been relatively independent for most of their history; indeed, a principal internal faculty drive for the Master Plan had been made to gain greater independence from state government. The birth of the system was slow, but it was not easy.

The first task was to create a chancellor's office and staff. The board located the office in the population center of Los Angeles, away from the state capital. Gallagher inherited a small planning staff that had been created the previous year by Governor Edmund G. Brown's former education secretary, a San Diego State College professor, Don Leiffer, who became executive vice chancellor of the California state colleges and a major figure in the new system. Others were appointed to the staff including President Glenn Dumke of San Francisco State College, who had represented the state colleges in the Master Plan effort, as vice-chancellor for academic affairs. The Board of Trustees undertook regular meetings, and the atmosphere within the system was tense, with all participants exploring the new relationships. Gallagher never took hold of his responsibilities; he devoted much time to responding to attacks from the far right about his alleged radical past. For personal reasons which have never become publicly clear, Gallagher resigned by phone from New York in February 1962 and returned to his former presidency. Under considerable pressure to keep the system moving, the trustees selected Dumke in April of 1962 to become chancellor. This was not a popular choice with all portions of the faculties, for Dumke, who had come to San Francisco in 1957 on a wave of great popularity and support and had made pioneering reforms on that campus in faculty governance and curriculum, had by 1962 also made some enemies as a result of presidential decisions and appoint-

ments at San Francisco and in the pressures of his participation in
the Master Plan survey team. It is not an unfair assessment that
Dumke initiated as chancellor the real beginnings of the life of the
state college system, activity which has brought him some support
and substantial criticism. The passage of time makes clear that much
of the faculty support for the Master Plan at the time of its consideration was based on an anticipation of autonomous campuses,
with the board and chancellor insulating but not necessarily governing the campuses in detail. Conversely, the board and chancellor
were determined to build a system. Three key organizational moves
were made early by Dumke. The first was to build the chancellor's
staff, largely from within the system, with faculty in most areas of
administration; the second was to appoint presidents for campuses
largely from outside the system to act as change agents; and the
third was to support the development of a statewide academic
senate.

In the fall of 1961, at an early meeting of the board, building plans were under consideration for several of the campuses.
Individual trustees questioned particular building proposals, both
in terms of the development of the campuses on which they were to
be located and also in terms of the interrelationships of programs
among the several campuses in the system. Out of this discussion the
board declined to act on the building proposals until each campus
submitted an academic master plan, something no campus had, for
until then the campuses had planned programs and buildings (some
faculty would allege that the order was reversed) on an ad hoc basis.
The presidents who were present at that board meeting in 1961 were
not kind about the desire of the board to have academic plans. The
faculties almost without exception were outraged at this board interference with local autonomy. Nevertheless, each campus faculty
and administration went to work to develop an academic plan. In
1962 the board adopted a plan for "The Broad Foundation Studies
for the California State Colleges," spelling out academic programs
which would be common to the campuses. In 1963 the first "Master
Curricular Plan for the California State Colleges," developed by the
campuses and the chancellor's staff, was approved by the Board.

The academic plan seeks to define for each campus the scope
of its instructional program for the present and the next five years;

they are updated each year. After the initial outrage, which few now remember, the academic planning process itself has become one of the genuine positive accomplishments of the system; three skillful state college deans of academic planning on the chancellor's staff were largely responsible: James Enochs, now vice-president for academic affairs at Sonoma State College; Ellis McCune, now president of the California State College at Hayward; and Gerhard Friedrich, the incumbent dean of academic planning. Academic planning in the California state colleges could well be the subject of a separate study.

Another early issue was the selection of students. The Master Plan called for the reduction of the zone of eligibility for freshmen from 45 per cent to 33⅓ per cent of high school graduates and suggested greater emphasis on traditional academic subject preparation in admissions requirements. Holding action was taken by the board for the fall admissions cycle of 1963, based on rough statistical calculations made by a special study group, and then the largest admissions study ever attempted in the United States, of some seventy thousand students, was initiated. This resulted in new admissions standards which did not emphasize traditional academic subject matter in the secondary schools, for this requirement had been found to be not crucial. The admissions cutbacks of the early 1960s in some measure contributed to the tensions of the late 1960s, for, unplanned, they tended to reduce access for minorities and the poor to state college freshman classes. The values of the higher education community changed dramatically from a traditional academic emphasis to one focusing on access and a concern for race and poverty.

The first ten years of the California state college system were years of intense feeling on the part of the higher education community generally, and the state colleges not only did not escape this intensity but were among the chief centers of politicization and tension on American campuses. Issues attendant to student and faculty activism, the role of the chancellor and board, budgets, and autonomy for the campuses were often in the center of an arena of tension. But the real issue in the California state colleges, most often unspoken, has been and is the dual and often conflicting need to create on the one hand a system of state colleges responsive to the educational needs of the state and, on the other hand, to maintain and develop separately the educational vigor of each campus. The life of an educational endeavor lies in the relationships between faculty and students and between them and the character of their campus.

3

⊓⎍⊓⎍⊓⎍⊓⎍⊓⎍⊓⎍⊓⎍⊓⎍⊓⎍⊓⎍⊓⎍⊓⎍⊓⎍⊓⎍⊓⎍⊓⎍

Chancellor of a
Multicampus System

Glenn S. Dumke

⊓⎍⊓⎍⊓⎍⊓⎍⊓⎍⊓⎍⊓⎍⊓⎍⊓⎍⊓⎍⊓⎍⊓⎍⊓⎍⊓⎍⊓⎍⊓⎍

W hen the Master Plan team gathered in 1959 to plan the re-structuring of California higher education, every member of it, in-cluding representatives from the universities, the state colleges, the junior colleges, and private institutions, came with a preconception that a single board to supervise higher education in California was the logical solution to the problems then being confronted. After nine months of effort and investigation, the team ended up with exactly the reverse opinion. Every member of the team concluded that a single board simply would not work effectively in the Cali-fornia situation.

There were many reasons for this conclusion, but the basic one was that the university had a constitutional shield and the state colleges were directly responsible to the legislature. Any attempt to merge the two would require that the state colleges acquire the con-stitutional shield which the legislature was not at the moment disposed to grant or that the university relinquish it and become a regular state agency, which the university was unwilling to do. Moreover, those members of the team who had studied what had happened in other states where single boards existed were well aware that the research institution ordinarily was the favored unit in any such system, and the state or community college which emphasized teaching usually played the role of second-class citizen. It was generally agreed, therefore, in the interest of effective operation and also in the interest of dignifying the role of the state colleges and giving them advantages which they had not previously possessed, that the state colleges should have their own Board of Trustees, have their own systemwide government, and stand as an integral and equal unit in the tripartite system of California public higher education. There was much talk of the overworked State Board of Education, which had not only the elementary and secondary schools and junior colleges but also the state colleges to supervise. Everyone more or less agreed that this task was much too large and that the state colleges were simply not being given the attention they deserved.

Accordingly, the Master Plan recommended that the state colleges establish their own board, modeled somewhat on the Board of Regents of the university but given a different title, and that systemwide governance be set up under a chancellor who would be the executive officer of the board. These recommendations were accepted and put into law in the form of the Donahoe Act of 1960.

The chancellorship of the California state colleges, therefore, immediately became one of the most important positions in higher education in the nation, controlling as it did sixteen campuses with an enrollment of 95,081 (fall 1960) students. Moreover, expansion plans and the existing rate of growth forecast even wider responsibilities in the very near future.

There were obvious advantages in an independent board and government for the state colleges. In the first place, the colleges could be certain that their administration would be higher education oriented and would look to the requirements of the state colleges per se. In the past, the colleges had had an administration which was beset with problems of the lower schools and the junior colleges. Second, the existence of a central academic government was in direct response to the then strong demands of the legislature and other state agencies for unified representation and response from the state colleges. The presidents of the various colleges had customarily battled one another in the halls of the legislature for their annual budgets in the same way that they had battled the university and other state agencies. The legislature was weary of the complex and time-consuming process of dealing with each college on an independent basis. Third, it rapidly became apparent to the perceptive leadership of the colleges that if the state colleges could unite on programs, they could be an exceedingly powerful and effective force in the state of California. Lacking the strong alumni association of the university and its influence in the legislature, the state colleges had instead a much broader geographical base and a larger and less selective population base. They were graduating, then as now, the people who controlled the economy of California, who moved out into business, public service, teaching, corporate farming, and other activities which put them in the mainstream of the active life of the state. With this foundation on which to build and with a unified approach, the state colleges could expect to speak in a loud and clear voice which would have to be listened to by the state of California.

A fourth evident advantage of their own government was the possibility of establishing quality controls and upgrading the general level of the state college operation. One problem had overwhelmed all others in the early history of the colleges—that of quality, consistency, and maintenance. Several of the colleges were under serious criticism for the level of their academic achievements; few state college programs were accredited by national groups; and even where creditable experimentation and innovation had been attempted, little attention had been paid to articulating the results with other institutions, to the detriment of students trying to transfer. One of the prime responsibilities of the chancellor, therefore, was to devote attention to quality. And this became a major goal during the first years.

Finally, systemwide government opened the prospect of engaging in planned development. Growth had always been a serious problem for the state colleges. The colleges were experiencing an avalanche of students, and to have sixteen institutions meeting this pressure of numbers in sixteen different ways seemed hardly the most efficient method of answering the needs of the state. As a result, planning activities, in relation to both physical plant and academic programs, became an early concern of the chancellor and the Board of Trustees. A first step was to insist that the error common to so many institutions of higher education—building buildings without relating them to a planned academic program—would not be repeated, and physical plant planning was delayed until academic program planning had its foundations securely laid.

The role of the chancellor was somewhat different from that of the president of the university. The university had emerged from a single mother institution, and all the university campuses started as branches of Berkeley. As a result, the university had quite naturally developed a tightly centralized system with a large central staff and much power in the hands of the president. The state colleges had an entirely different history. They had not emerged from a mother institution but found themselves suddenly organized in a system composed of sixteen ruggedly independent and somewhat diverse institutions, each with a president who was protective of his own autonomy and who demonstrated considerable reluctance to sacrifice any authority to the central government. The university, in other words, was built using centrifugal forces, while the state colleges were based on centripetal forces.

Consequently, the chancellor early announced that no attempt would be made to jam the state colleges into a tightly centralized organization which paralleled that of the university. Rather the goal would be a federation, not an empire, in which the campus presidents would retain much authority. Despite the high degree of local autonomy thus retained and the large amount of authority delegated to the campuses and their presidents, the issue of local autonomy has been a serious one and constitutes one of the chief problems of the central office.

These problems of the center versus the component parts were to be expected. They exist, in fact, in parallel form in almost every similar historical attempt to unify segments of an organization into a single structure. Indeed, an interesting parallel can be drawn between the thirteen colonies and the sixteen California state colleges and the process which each group went through in the organization of a central government. The state colleges experienced nearly every difficulty that the thirteen colonies experienced in organizing a nation. They had their constitutional convention (the Master Plan and the Donahoe Act). They had their tensions between local autonomy and the establishment, which balanced the forces of regionalism and "states' rights" with the necessity for central organization. They even had their "Whiskey Rebellion," which took the form of a San Francisco faculty revolt in 1964. The task of any chancellor is to keep firmly and clearly before the constituent units of his organization the advantages of acting in unison in critical areas; he must also remind them that unity brings with it many more advantages than appear on the surface.

The organization of the central government of the California state colleges follows more or less traditional patterns of academic organization in that the chancellor, the chief executive officer, is responsible to the trustees for the operation and maintenance of the system, and his line authority is delegated to the presidents of the now nineteen campuses. The presidents have much power. They are not absolutely autonomous, nor should they be, but they are certainly powerful officers and have a tremendous amount of responsibility and a broad range of authority. They are real presidents, not provosts. At the same time, they are responsible to the chancellor and through him to the board, and systemwide policies and programs must be carried out in accordance with systemwide procedures.

The staff of the chancellor's office was originally organized into three major divisions—a vice-chancellor for academic affairs, a vice-chancellor for business affairs, and a vice-chancellor for external affairs. This last included relationships with the citizen constituencies via the advisory boards, the legislature, and the press. Developments in the state college operation have altered this arrangement somewhat, and there was subsequently established an executive vice-chancellor who is responsible for the internal operations of the office and for much of the internal operating mechanism of the system. The position of vice-chancellor for external affairs has been abandoned, and his duties, which were so diverse as to be almost impossible to perform by a single individual, have been dispersed among several officers of the central staff. The vice-chancellor for academic affairs and the vice-chancellor for business affairs are still in control of their rather large areas of concern. An assistant chancellor for faculty and staff affairs directly responsible to the chancellor has emerged as another position of high level. The general counsel has been made a vice-chancellor for legal affairs, and the former chief of facilities planning was promoted to a vice-chancellor. To sum up the major responsibilities of each of these officers briefly is not easy, but it may be said that the executive vice-chancellor is in charge of operations, the academic vice-chancellor deals largely with planning and academic quality, the business vice-chancellor concentrates on the fiscal responsibility of the system to the state and the budgeting process, and the assistant chancellor for faculty and staff affairs is chiefly concerned with the quality of the faculty and staff, recruitment, grievances, discipline, and related matters.

The mechanics of governance are focused primarily in monthly meetings of the presidents with the chancellor and his staff. These are usually one- or two-day affairs, and the work is controlled by an agenda committee elected by the presidents. A consistent attempt is made to have the presidents work together in helping the central office structure the trustees' agenda. The presidents also deal with many administrative problems which require joint discussion.

The chancellor also meets fairly regularly with the academic senate. He is an official member of this body, although he does not chair it, and his primary role is to discuss with the senate the major issues before the system. I urged the faculties, as one of the first acts of my administration in 1962, to set up a statewide academic senate so that they could be represented completely and fully without recourse to dues-paying membership organizations which had sprung up in past years in the state colleges as a result of the historic lack of faculty representation in policy formulation. The membership organizations were not ready to be displaced, and the senate became a cockpit for a power struggle among some of the organizations which from time to time gained control of the executive structure. The relationships between the chancellor and the senate during the first several years of its existence, therefore, were largely concerned with a resolution of this power struggle. The senate attempted, largely because of the influence of the membership organizations, to move into control of various administrative procedures. As time passed, however, the mood changed somewhat, and it is to be hoped that the senate will henceforth concern itself with those matters appropriate to faculty governance, which are very numerous and which for several years have been ignored in favor of controversial areas of lesser importance. Just as the chancellor should receive from the presidents their advice and counsel on matters of administration and general policy, so he should receive from the senate its opinions on policy matters concerning curriculum and faculty.

The chancellor relates to the students largely through the council of student body presidents, which, except for one brief hiatus, has had an executive committee structured to maintain relationships with the central office and with the trustees. Just as the chancellor receives guidance from the presidents and the faculties, he should also receive advice from the student government on matters concerning student welfare.

The chancellor is concerned with the alumni, and a constant effort has been made to encourage the establishment of a statewide alumni organization. In addition, the chancellor maintains, through the presidents, relations with the advisory boards, which currently constitute the most important and effective citizen constituency of the state colleges. Annually or biannually the chancellor calls a meeting of delegates from the advisory boards to acquaint them with systemwide problems. These periodic conferences have proved to be most useful and effective in broadening the understanding of the citizen constituency so that they can effectively support the state colleges in the legislature and throughout the state.

The chancellor also speaks for the system to outside groups and to the public. His responsibilities in this respect include a considerable number of speeches and public addresses to widely varied groups, representations to the press in connection with state college affairs, and the taking of public positions on state college policy and program matters.

As executive officer of the Board of Trustees, the chancellor's prime responsibility is to the board. He must maintain contact and communication with the board, serve it by presenting its views on program and policy, and be constantly aware of the board's position on various matters. He must also acquaint the board with problems facing the state colleges and lead it in the establishment of policies appropriate to the educational structure. Under the Donahoe Act, the chancellor is an ex-officio member of the Board of Trustees. I have abandoned the vote voluntarily, feeling that it mitigates against the effective carrying out of the executive officer's position.

One of the most important responsibilities of the chancellor is appointing an acting president when a vacancy occurs and recommending candidates to the trustees for regular presidential appointments. The quality of the individuals who hold presidencies is a key to the quality and effectiveness of the entire state college operation. Weak presidents confront the chancellor with the necessity of handling in the central office crises and problems which should instead be handled on campus. Presidents who are not fully willing to work within the system confront the chancellor with the task of reconciling ill-advised local policy with the policy of the trustees. The ideal president, from the chancellor's viewpoint, is a strong leader willing and able to handle campus problems on campus and to lead his institution in appropriate directions, but one who is also aware of his responsibilities to the chancellor, the trustees, and the system as a whole. Although the usual presidential tenure is eight or nine years, which compares favorably with the national average, it still becomes necessary to appoint, on the average, two presidents per year. Therefore, selection procedures have been developed out of the considerable experience of the central office. These procedures emphasize background qualities based largely on success in comparably responsible positions. A constant search is made for names appropriate for consideration, both within and outside the system.

Another responsibility is to maintain effective relationships with the other units of higher education in California. The chancellor works with the Coordinating Council for Higher Education, which, although periodically changed in structure, consists of representatives from the public, the three segments of public higher education, and the private segment. Because of the considerable recommending authority of the council in matters of system growth and program extension, these relationships are important and require attention.

The chancellor and his colleagues in the central office also answer for the system to the legislative analyst, the legislature through its various committees, the Department of Finance, and the governor. This obligation is tremendously time consuming and occupies a large amount of staff time. Although the university system is only half as large as the state college system, it early established a much larger central staff. One of the on-going problems of the chancellor's office is to maintain a relatively small central staff based on the federation principle, which at the same time acquits itself effectively of all of the responsibilities placed upon it. This task is especially difficult because of the prevailing hostility toward anything that smacks of bureaucracy.

The chancellorship and the government of the California state colleges were established at a critical moment in higher education history. The European concept of higher education involved an elite approach to the responsibilities of the state. It concerned relatively small numbers of people and a small and exclusive professoriat, which produced the community of scholars concept of academic governance. This concept meant that campus matters were discussed by the faculties as a whole or in large committees, and solutions were reached on the basis of widespread faculty involvement in decision making. The administration of most European universities consisted of rectors elected by the faculties, with lesser permanent civil service–type officials doing the administering. This democratic and professional approach to higher education administration was transplanted to the United States. The procedure was immediately complicated by the establishment of the open door philosophy, giving opportunity to much larger numbers of young people. As a result, institutions in the United States grew rapidly in size, and the concept of solving problems of administration or policy by large group discussion no longer worked very well. Accordingly, college and university administrators in the United States came to possess authority and permanence to a degree not evident in European institutions. Tension developed between faculty members who wanted to apply the European concept of participatory democracy and administrators and boards who realized that this system was not practical in the American context. This struggle and these tensions have created a more or less consistent adversary relationship between administration and faculty in the United States. And before the recent campus unrest began, this long-term struggle was constantly resolved by compromises and concessions on both sides but with considerable weight being placed on the faculty as the nuclear group in academic governance.

The era of campus turbulence, however, which started at
Berkeley in 1964 and reached its peak at Columbia and Kent State,
climaxed in the California state colleges in 1968. These campus
tensions brought about fundamental changes in the concept of academic governance and started a series of trends which are still in
progress. Widely dispersed decision-making procedures which had
worked reasonably well in earlier days now simply did not fill the
bill, and the authority of the administrator was recognized to be of
great importance if stability were to return to the campus. As a
result, there has been considerable movement away from the model-
ing of campus governance on the political state, with the faculty
acting as a legislature and the administration serving merely as an
executive to carry out its policies. Emphasis has been placed on the
development of a management hierarchy in which the administrator
assumes an active role of leadership and responsibility. The federation concept, although maintained in principle, was modified to give
the central office much authority, and although every effort has been
made to maintain the power of the presidents and as much local
autonomy as possible, there has been a clear trend away from decentralization toward a more administration-oriented power structure.

The chancellorship and the presidency, therefore, have increased in significance in the total governance picture. Although no
attempt has been made closely to model state college government on
business or industry, much emphasis has been placed on management competence and managerial authority and responsibility.
Student and faculty grievance and discipline procedures have been
modified to restrict local decision making, and a just and equitable
system of academic due process has been established. Faculty members who look back to the peaceful past, and even farther to the
European model, regret this change and in many cases oppose it,
but as long as the majority of college and university administrators
emerge from the faculty ranks, there is little danger that the process
will intrude upon the integrity of academic tradition.

Higher education is now big business involving large numbers of people, many millions of dollars, and large physical plants.
The management principles necessary to operate any large institution are now required in higher education. A realization of this fact

should be to the advantage of the state colleges and to higher education, and definitely not to their detriment.

The basic question that has to be answered is whether the new government of the state colleges under the chancellor and the trustees, in accordance with the Donahoe Act, has benefited the colleges, their students, and their faculties. The record in this regard seems quite clear. The system has more than doubled in size, serving in 1970 nearly a quarter of a million students on nineteen campuses throughout California. The breadth and richness of curricula have improved considerably, including a wide range of undergraduate and graduate instruction in the liberal arts and sciences, applied fields, and the professions. Schools of engineering, business, nursing, teacher education, and all the offerings of a general university except medical and legal training and advanced doctoral and postdoctoral work have been undertaken. A joint doctoral degree was worked out with the University of California; certain campuses establish working relationships with counterpart campuses of the University of California so that a small number of doctoral degrees are now sponsored by the state colleges.

Superior teaching has been recognized and rewarded through funded awards programs. Curricular planning has been refined, and degree requirements have been strengthened. At the outset of the Master Plan, only seven programs in the California state colleges were accredited by national professional accrediting agencies. Today, the number approaches one hundred. As the interest in economically deprived groups and ethnic minorities developed, courses and programs were offered in these fields. Honors and advanced placement programs have been developed for superior students. An international study program with nearly five hundred students in many countries of Western Europe and Asia has been established. The library resources, always in short supply and a source of some criticism by accrediting groups, were subjected to scrutiny, and a long-range plan was set up which is annually funded, in whole or in part. Faculty sabbatical leave programs have been improved and broadened. And faculty travel, primarily for the purpose of recruitment, has been expanded and funded to a much broader extent than previously. Summer session and extension salaries have been aligned with those during the academic year.

Salary increases have been a matter of great concern, especially in relation to university salaries. In 1961–1962 the average weighted all-rank salary for the regular faculty at the University of California was 18.7 per cent above that for the California state colleges. By 1968–1969 this differential had been reduced to 6.9 per cent. In the American Association of University Professors (AAUP) salary scale, the average compensation of 1961–1962 was rated C. In 1968–1969, it was rated B overall, while the pay scale for instructors, assistant professors, and associate professors received an A rating. Personnel rules and regulations and grievance procedures have been developed with the cooperation of the faculties.

Master plans for physical plant growth were developed on each campus, and the architectural planning process emphasized the educational functions to be served by the buildings, along with consideration of cost and esthetics. The method for selecting architects devised by the state colleges has been emulated and praised by many government agencies. Criteria and procedures for site selection were established, and three locations were chosen for future state colleges on the basis of a legislative provision enabling advance purchase so as to avoid the cost of inflation. Year-round operation was instituted and pilot programs were started. A residence hall program was developed with both public and private funding, and a college union program was begun. Construction of college unions has been completed at five campuses and is underway at four others. State college foundations have increased in size, numbers, and scope; they provide services many times as great as those in 1960. A statewide lecture series, the first systemwide cultural program, has also been set up.

These achievements indicate that the governance of the state colleges has been effective in improving their service to the students and citizens of the state, as well as in maintaining and improving their academic quality. In 1960, the state colleges were seriously criticized in certain instances for the level of their academic work. At the end of the decade, the California state colleges were recognized as the outstanding state college system in the nation and, in the view of their own national professional association, ranked at the very top of similar institutions throughout the country.

The chancellorship of such a large system, therefore, is a

significant position of leadership, and in the present period of rapid transition it attains even more importance. The chancellor has clear obligations to the people of the state of California and also to the integrity of the academic process, and although these duties do not appear to be always immediately reconcilable, he must bring about that reconciliation to the best of his ability.

4

⊔⊓⊔⊓⊔⊓⊔⊓⊔⊓⊔⊓⊔⊓⊔⊓⊔⊓⊔⊓⊔⊓⊔⊓

Faculty Views of the Role of State Government

James E. Gregg, Robert G. Jones

⊔⊓⊔⊓⊔⊓⊔⊓⊔⊓⊔⊓⊔⊓⊔⊓⊔⊓⊔⊓⊔⊓⊔⊓

How do members of the faculty of the state colleges view state government in California? Obviously in many different ways and from a variety of perspectives. For some professors state government is a distant bureaucracy which constantly interferes in the professional relationships between student and teacher and whose most positive function is to provide a monthly paycheck. For others state government is synonymous with politics with all the negative connotations of that term in the eyes of those who are apolitical or apathetic.

To have two professors present "the faculty view" of state government is presumptuous. As the history of the relationship between state college faculty and state government proves, there is no single view on virtually any matter inside the California state colleges. Therefore, what follows is highly personal and limited by the biases and unique experiences of two political scientists currently teaching at a California state college. We have chosen to write subjectively about our topic, reflecting upon our work in state government while we were absent from academia. One of us spent a year in the state capital serving as staff secretary for education to former Governor Brown. The other served for a year as a staff consultant to the assembly education committee. We bring a unique perspective to our writing. Our career is teaching in a state college, but we also have had an opportunity to view our subject firsthand in the state capital. Thus, we can empathize with our colleagues in the state colleges who view state government and politics from a hostile and distant viewpoint, but we can also empathize with those bureaucrats and politicians who labor in the political environment of Sacramento.

Many factors affect the faculty view of state government. A faculty member is more than a teacher and a scholar with selfish occupational interests. He (or she) is a citizen of a small town or a metropolis in northern, central, or southern California with all that regionalism implies in California politics. A professor's outlook on government and politics may be further complicated by a hostile relationship between town and gown in some communities where state colleges are located. Since 1965 the colleges have been embroiled in statewide political controversy over campus unrest so that now the town and gown problem is in reality statewide. The anti-intellectual attitudes of large numbers of citizens and politicians threaten some professors. Other professors thrive on the challenge, which in some cases only deepens and continues the hostility. And many state college faculty have feelings of inferiority because of what they consider their second-class status compared to university faculty. For years state college faculty have resented a state government that has perpetrated a system of lower pay, higher teaching loads, and fewer research opportunities in comparison with those of UC faculty. A common campus saying goes: "Junior faculty on state college campuses ride bicycles to work, eat sack lunches, and do weekend research!" State college faculty are frequently hostile toward state government bureaucracy with its myriad personnel regulations which make professors feel like state employees rather than highly regarded professionals. Finally, most state college faculty teach on campuses which are growing very quickly, and the resulting tensions for their professional lives border on the destructive. A rapid influx of young junior colleagues, overcrowded physical facilities, a high turnover of administrative personnel on the campuses, and a lack of faith in the trustees and in the chancellor's office to make the case for state college needs to the governor and the legislature have all led to negative views by state college faculty.

The relationship between state government and state college faculty was probably never poorer than at the end of the 1970 legislative session. Hostility toward professors was summed up best when the budget included a general cost of living pay raise for all state employees (including college presidents and nonacademic staff), but none for professors at the colleges or the university. State college faculty returned to their campuses in the fall of 1970 know-ing that the custodians, the secretaries, and some administrators had received pay raises denied faculty.

The plight of the state colleges was discussed by *Sacramento Bee* education writer James Wrightson on July 23, 1970, in a col-umn entitled "Rendezvous at Last Chance." Characterizing the bud-get struggle as a card game of budget blackjack, Wrightson said simply, "The guys from the state colleges lost." Over thirteen mil-lion dollars in appropriations were lost to the colleges in the last several days of the legislative session. Cut from the governor's budget for the state colleges were cost of living salary increases for faculty, $9,100,000; one half of all sabbatical leaves, $746,897; one half of all creative leaves, $295,000; forty-four janitor positions, $250,000; library allocations, $3,000,000; and complete laboratory schools on the campuses of Fresno, Chico, Humboldt, and San Diego state colleges. Wrightson said of the budgetary actions, with tongue in cheek, that the University of California situation is considered serious but not critical, while at the state colleges the situation is critical but not serious.

The faculty view of state government is further complicated by a conflict inherent in the governance of state-supported institu-tions of higher learning in California. Faculty see themselves as professionals who know best how to accomplish the goals of higher education. Most faculty have the somewhat politically naive notion that taxpayers and politicians ought to leave professional educators alone. For years education professors taught aspiring young teachers that education was apolitical and that the public schools were above politics. Nothing was further from the truth, and in the 1960s education and campus unrest became exceedingly controversial political issues.

Faculty members may not want their colleges to be involved in politics, but they cannot escape it. Some faculty persist in believing they are not accountable to governing bodies such as the trustees or regents, nor are they accountable to politicians and bureaucrats who claim to represent the citizenry who pay the taxes that make possible the very existence of the institutions in which faculty teach. Far too many faculty think of state government as a nuisance that must be tolerated in order that paychecks arrive on payday. Faculty members, for the most part, deserve an F for failure on their political report cards. They have never learned that, as C. P. Snow once wrote, successful politicians push on unlocked doors and failures push on locked doors. State college faculty found more and more locked doors in state government as the decade of the 1970s began.

Certainly the doors to the governor's office and the legislature were not easily opened to state college faculty during the first term of Governor Reagan. There were openings during the two terms of Brown, however, and several state college faculty members served on the governor's staff in a number of capacities. Most faculty realized that the Brown years brought major changes in the governance of the state colleges, six new campuses, and moderate increases in budgetary support for operations. Still, by 1966 many faculty were bitter about Brown. Some thought he was too supportive of forced conversion to year-round operations and the quarter system. Still others felt that he paid too much attention to the needs of the university and too little to the needs of the state colleges. He was considered too willing to listen to his fiscal and political advisers instead of to his educational advisers about college budgetary needs. Faculty also resented some of Brown's trustee appointments and particularly felt aggrieved by his reappointment of Charles Luckman. Luckman had long been a faculty nemesis, and his reappointment was vigorously opposed by faculty representatives, but to no avail.

Some politically naive faculty advocated a "catastrophic theory" of state government by 1966. Their thesis was, "Let's dump Pat Brown for Ronald Reagan and then the people of California

will get the kind of state government they deserve." After the catas-
trophe, according to this group, the people would turn to leadership
that would lavish loving care on the state colleges.

The election of Reagan as governor has proved a mixed
blessing for the state colleges. Some have said that Reagan has been
kind to the state colleges in order to punish the university. It is a
fact that the governor's policies have hurt the colleges less than the
university, but this action has been offset by the governor's harsh
words about faculty. On the issue of budgetary support, the pattern
of the Reagan administration has been to call for massive cuts in the
college proposals early in the process of state budget planning. Those
associated with the colleges bitterly assail the proposed cutbacks, the
governor then relents, and a budget figure somewhere between the
college requests and the governor's proposals is finally approved by
the legislature.

Reagan has used his item veto power on occasion to cut back
programs that faculty thought were vital, as well as salary increases
voted by the legislature. During the 1970 session state college faculty
were hit hard by three items. First, the 5 per cent cost of living salary
increase which the governor had included in his original budget was
cut by the legislature. There was little evidence that the governor
fought for restoration. Second, the faculty work load credit for graduate teaching was raised from ten to twelve units, the same as for
undergraduate teaching. Third, as has been noted above, the
faculty's sabbatical leave and creative leave programs were slashed
by 50 per cent. Regardless of what the truth may be, many faculty
thought Reagan willingly let the legislature cut his budget whenever
it directly affected faculty.

Reagan's appointments have included some moderates, but
the overall faculty assessment of his appointments has been negative.
Such outspoken right-wing trustees as Dudley Swim and Robert
Hornby frighten and anger faculty. Indeed some faculty wonder
whether Reagan must not regret having such outspoken and bitter
men on the Board of Trustees at a time when his office has made
efforts to build a bridge to the faculty through meetings with faculty
representatives. Even these attempts at improving relations between
the faculty and the governor's office have failed because of the narrow spectrum of faculty represented. It is ironic that under the

Brown administration attempts by the governor's office to set up such meetings were opposed by the trustees and Chancellor Dumke. They believed their authority to run the system would be undermined. Brown reluctantly acceded to the protests, and the faculty were shut out of the governor's office at that time.

Obviously the governor is not just another trustee. He frequently finds himself in conflicting roles when acting as a trustee on fiscal matters and then making executive decisions in the context of other state priorities. The governor is likely to be better briefed than other trustees since he has staff representatives other trustees lack. His position of political importance makes his utterances on college matters very influential among the public and fellow trustees. His presence at a trustee meeting often turns it into a three ring circus, complete with intense mass media coverage, elaborate security precautions, and protesting delegations of students, faculty, and citizens. Certainly the highly charged atmosphere under which trustee meetings have been held is not conducive to wise deliberations on matters of serious educational policy.

While any governor can command public attention by virtue of his position, the circumstances surrounding trustee meetings have added to that power. As a result, the governor is in a position to set the tone of public opinion regarding the state colleges. Some would say that Reagan has heightened negative public reaction to the colleges, but in many instances he has just been responding to conditions beyond his immediate control. However, in other circumstances the governor has further complicated matters by making stern and uncompromising statements that limited options open to state college officials.

The public and most faculty misunderstand the power of any governor in California. He works under a number of severe constraints. On budget matters the governor can make cuts and effectively control about one dollar out of three that is appropriated by the legislature. The governor's maneuvering room is severely restricted by earmarked funds for highway, welfare, and public elementary and secondary education. Thus it may often appear that the governor and the Department of Finance are unduly harsh on college budgetary proposals. Once the legislature has approved the budget the governor has another opportunity to influence the fiscal decisions of the state by use of his veto to reduce or eliminate items. Given the problems of budget balancing and the options available to any governor who is limited by a rigid position on new taxes, he may have little choice but to take apparently antieducational actions.

In the gubernatorial campaign of 1966 Reagan said little to indicate any antieducational program bias. His general stance was that of cutting back state expenditures, but during the campaign he did not specify where he would make cuts. Once in office his budgetary decisions took on the appearance of program bias against higher education and mental health in particular. But it is precisely in these areas that any governor must cut if he hopes to have a major impact on the budget. Budgetary decisions can be viewed two ways. Such decisions can be thought of as purely administrative and subject to careful judgments as to objective values and priorities; or they can be viewed as political decisions designed to attract votes or to reward or punish segments of the bureaucracy or the public. State college faculty have viewed Reagan's actions in these matters as being punitive and part of an antieducational bias of his administration. When some of the faculty's cherished budget hopes did not materialize under Brown, the faculty felt they had at least a sympathetic hearing. Under Reagan college faculty have not appreciated some gains in fiscal flexibility and have been perhaps overly sensitive about the motives of the governor in his budgetary decisions.

On the matter of appointments to such key educational bodies as the state college trustees, the university Regents, the Coordinating Council for Higher Education, and the Board of Governors of the community colleges the governor does not have as free a hand as many might think. Most of the less than two thousand appointments he can make offer little or no salary. The governor's ability to appoint people to such posts is limited by the need to appoint wealthy individuals who can devote time and money to the work. This limitation means that such appointments frequently go to wealthy contributors to the governor's last campaign. Probably no post is more sought after in state government than that of Regent of the university. Whether they like it or not, state college trustees are "second-class regents." This hierarchy was shown during the Brown years when former Brown campaign aide William Coblentz was "promoted" from the trustees to the Board of Regents. Regents are almost always wealthier and politically more important than trustees, but one seldom finds men of only average wealth on either board.

One must add that a governor is limited in his impact on the state colleges by the conservative views of educators about education. As Clark Kerr has commented, college professors are most liberal about other people's affairs and most conservative about their own. The governor can make life uncomfortable for the educational establishment, but in the final analysis he is limited in any all-out attacks. Events have focused much of his attention on higher education, but faculty need to remember that a governor has much to do in Sacramento besides making darts to throw at college professors.

The most important but frequently ignored political link in this enormous system of public higher education is between the teaching faculty and the elected members of the California state legislature. The faculty, because of their unique social roles and their participation in the governance of the colleges and university, in large part determine the quality of higher learning. The scholarly community expects the state legislature to usually do nothing more than annually appropriate the financial resources to carry the research and instructional functions forward. Besides exercising direct control over the annual appropriations process, the legislature also, however, plays a critical role in shaping the general character of public higher education through the creation of statutes governing, among other things, capital outlay programs, faculty working conditions, student recruitment, and curriculum.

The future of public higher learning in California constantly rests on the fragile and frequently unstable relations between the faculty and students and the legislative spokesmen for the people. Although the university and the state colleges have lay governing boards with broad authority to set policy and manage their respective systems, the legislature can and does intervene directly in the determination of administrative and educational matters. Besides amendments or additions to the state codes, legislative initiatives often take the form of constitutional amendments, resolutions, investigations, and specific control language attached to the annual budget bill specifying the conditions under which state funds are to be expended.

Current faculty opinion regarding state government is, in

large part, attributable to Reagan's effective and continuing political use of campus disturbances in California and elsewhere. Reagan was elected by a margin of more than a million votes over Brown and had made the University of California at Berkeley and higher education in general one of his leading campaign issues. In his first inauguration speech Reagan made it clear that public higher education was of special importance to his administration by declaring that he did not think it political interference to ask the university to "build character on accepted moral and ethical standards." During the governor's first term in office he was able, unlike his predecessor, to publicly deplore campus disruptions and directly intervene without assuming responsibility for the results.

The governor's early proposal to end the tradition of tuition-free public higher education was the first of many initiatives contributing to the emergence of faculty disaffection with his administration. Tuition was sought by the governor to partially compensate for a proposed across-the-board state budget cut of ten per cent. Both Kerr, then president of the university, and Dumke, chancellor of the state college system, expressed general faculty opinion when they opposed tuition as providing insurmountable obstacles for poor but capable and qualified students. In the governor's first televised "Report to the People" in January 1967, he suggested that if the state colleges and university would carry out a 10 per cent cut in their budgets without reducing the quality of their programs, he would not push for the tuition charges. Actually the state colleges and the university were being asked to contribute almost half of the general fund savings sought by the governor.

Anticipating concern from the academic community, Assembly Speaker Jess Unruh warned faculty members to stop walking in picket lines protesting the governor's action. "An irrational, emotional reaction to the governor's tuition plan," he said, "is likely to enhance the possibility of the adoption of tuition rather than impede it" (Unruh, 1967). Although this prediction was not immediately verified, his assessment of public reaction to the street approach to political influence was later reflected and confirmed by the major newspapers. Between the governor's tuition proposal and his reelection in 1970 an incredible array of issues was seized upon

and manipulated by political and social extremists to further separate the citizens of the state from their institutions of higher learning.
These included public unrest over the academic appointments of
Richard Flacks, Herbert Marcuse, and Angela Davis; political
murders at UC–Santa Barbara and UC–Los Angeles; fire bombings
at San Francisco and Berkeley; and faculty and student walkouts at
almost all of the university and college campuses. Most serious of all
was the indiscriminate violence and destruction which engulfed
first Berkeley over the People's Park incident and then Santa Barbara over issues which still remain unclear and confused.

The governor's mobilization of the National Guard and the
subsequent street violence over the People's Park in Berkeley had a
traumatic and conclusive effect on faculty opinion. As a result many
faculty declared that they refused to accept the men responsible for
such actions as the representatives of the system of law and order
envisioned in the Constitution merely because they are in positions
of power, and they would never cooperate with any forcibly imposed
peace.

Faculty have been drawn into statewide political struggles
only to be repeatedly humiliated because of what appears to be a
fundamental misunderstanding of the character of political institutions. State legislators and the governor are accountable to the voters,
who are, in turn, often insensitive to the fragile values which govern
the academic community. When public disenchantment, or for that
matter enchantment, with higher education becomes evident, it
would be politically irresponsible for an incumbent legislator or
governor to turn away from this interest; it is a requirement of their
respective roles that public concern be articulated and if necessary
be given legitimacy in law.

Public interest in the management of higher education has
been evident for several years. Among a surveyed cross-section of
Californians, 74 per cent supported the view that "the taxpaying
public should have more to say about how the state university and
college system is being run" (Field Research Corp., 1970). At the
same time 64 per cent of the respondents endorsed the belief that
public higher education "must stay independent of political control
by the governor or the legislature." While these findings are clearly

incongruent, it would appear that the public has at least a rudimentary understanding of the importance of institutional autonomy and its relevance to educational quality.

Also straining relations between legislature and faculty are the clearly divergent characters of their respective roles. Legislators must be responsive to a broad set of public issues and needs and may not, therefore, always agree with the faculty on the annual distribution of state resources or the most pressing state social problems. Most of the teaching faculty in California are political spectators; whatever understanding they have of the legislative process is largely conditioned and mediated by faculty organizations and the public press. While the character of legislative-faculty interaction is somewhat unusual, its form is not; faculty organizations, like other interest groups in the state, delegate substantial discretionary authority to small executive staffs whose role is to inform and influence state legislators, administrators, and their own members. Even though the legislative advocates from the state and community colleges and the university struggle to keep their systems abreast of the hundreds of relevant measures annually introduced in the state legislature, general faculty attention to the day by day legislative process is extremely low and often ill informed. University faculty, as distinguished from the Regents, have not had an organized and effective input into legislative decision making. The state college faculty, on the other hand, have suffered from inconsistent representation from at least four independent organizations. During the 1970 session of the state legislature all faculty groups, including spokesmen for the Regents and trustees, appeared to be particularly incapable of coping with a Republican margin of control on several key committees.

If a collective faculty opinion exists, it contains unmistakable elements of arrogance and contempt, covered with a veneer of aloof professionalism. The professional bias, while accepted as legitimate within the scope of an individual's training, often strenuously resists any lay involvement in decision making that affects the character, quality, or quantity of professional services. As a result members of the academic community are constantly on the alert, ready to indiscriminately rush to the defense when programs and professional perquisites are publicly examined by members of the state legislature or administration. In higher education, nonacademics are generally considered by faculty as incompetent to assess the quality of various academic activities. Members of the academic community, from the legislative perspective, seek shelter from public ire by claiming that legislative inquiries pose explicit threats to academic freedom. Like so many other fundamental concepts in American society, academic freedom is becoming devalued from overuse by those whose activity is dependent upon its maintenance. Because of indiscriminate and casual usage the faculty may be losing its ability to signal real and cumulative dangers to public higher education. The current estrangement between the lay and academic community can, in part, be attributed to the academic community's failure to recognize that the conditions for its survival are no longer clearly understood by the public or the legislature. When the necessary conditions are unclear to the faculty members themselves, it is unreasonable to expect the public's view to be more informed. State Controller Houston I. Flournoy (1969) characterized the problem as an "understanding gap," asserting that "there is no more reality in the attitude of some faculty members that the state colleges or the university are really no concern of the public or, if you will, the politicians than there is in the attitude of many citizens that individuals who hold views alien to their own ought not to be allowed to set foot on any campus."

Exacerbating the current public disaffection with higher education is faculty reaction to the legislative process. The basic currency in American politics is the simple majority of votes confirming a candidate's ability to symbolically aggregate community interests. Besides frequently bringing together ideologically incompatible social sectors, symbolic aggregation often leads to bogus legislative behavior. Legislative activity of this sort will not and is not intended to result in statutes. Products of such behavior are speeches on the chamber floor, legislative resolutions, news releases, and ad hoc or interim investigations. Such actions, if uniform and cumulative, can signal real intentions; often, however, they only serve to periodically confirm the issue-loyalty of the incumbent and ensure that his coalition remains intact. Even if misunderstanding were eliminated, faculty, like other citizens, would still be politically disabled by their inability to distinguish the real from the unreal threats and by their frequent diffuse and unselective reaction to symbolic output from the legislature or the governor's office.

The faculty's positive impact on legislative decision making has been remarkably insignificant. This lack of impact is particularly unfortunate now that there is unmistakable legislative uncertainty over the current organization and management of higher education in the state. The role of the faculty was, for example, clearly put into perspective when the Republican chairman of the Joint Legislative Committee on Higher Education convened, during the 1970 session, an advisory committee of students on higher education matters but avoided seeking faculty advice.

One prominent issue that brought the 1970 legislature and the faculty together was the enrollment capacity of the institutions of higher education. Several legislative hearings were held on the enrollment and admissions issue. The investigations were specifically designed to reveal the extent of the alleged student overenrollment, the impact of this condition on other segments of public higher education in the state, and a consideration of long-range solutions. This was the second year that the state colleges, in particular, had been accused of turning away or redirecting substantial numbers of qualified applicants and the second year that the legislature had considered the matter through special hearings.

State college and university faculty were generally conspicuous by their apparent ignorance of the extent to which qualified students were being denied educational opportunities. They were also ambivalent about altering the utilization standards for campus facilities as one way of handling additional students. When the instructional day was extended into the evening hours, faculty complained to the state legislature that they had no place to rest and no place to eat in reasonable peace and comfort. Instead of giving positive guidance to an efficient utilization of the campuses, faculty representatives called into question the fundamental intention of the legislature by speciously suggesting that the rate of use could be increased by providing services for twenty-four-hour days, paying premium salaries for off-hours teaching, and permitting free education from ten at night to seven in the morning. Such an approach is a public insult to the men seeking solutions and is hardly conducive to increased faculty-legislative understanding.

The faculty generally considers the legislature and the governor responsible for any deterioration in the institutions of higher learning while routinely attributing to themselves responsibility for acknowledged higher levels of quality. This attitude gives rise to some humorous inconsistencies. Faculty, for example, continue to emphasize the deteriorating working conditions and low salaries as compared to those in other major systems of higher education. This position results in the rather ironic assertion from currently employed faculty that it is almost "impossible to hire or retain qualified faculty members." Faculty groups believe, in short, that it is legislative penury that has caused a decline in the quality of education.

Some faculty have tried to seize the political initiative by utilizing the tools of the politician. As many have discovered, politics is an activity for which their abilities or at least instincts are frequently irrelevant. The unfortunate result has been the loss of whatever moral or intellectual suasion the academic community once possessed. Even when faculty groups have attempted to expose important educational data, the results have been disappointing and have often been presumptive evidence for legislative charges of sloth and selfishness. Recent faculty emphasis on slowly increasing student teacher ratios is illustrative. An increase from a low of 15.76 to 1 in 1961 to 18.13 to 1 in 1969 is to the potential undergraduate or his parent hardly a compelling reason to deplore legislative or gubernatorial leadership, particularly in view of the governor's rebuttal that one of the several law schools of the university has a student-teacher ratio of 35 to 1.

Faculty, when they collectively choose to take the political offensive against the governor and the legislature, are simultaneously moving against the people of the state. This is their right and responsibility as citizens, but public higher education cannot survive a condition where those most closely attached to its institutions implicitly declare war on those who support them. Clearly, significant portions of the public distrust the academic community, and without the confidence of the public the faculty can do very little to protect the special prerogatives that are fundamental to the quality of their work.

Faculty are often incapacitated by hostility toward representative institutions, particularly when these institutions turn their

attention toward the academic community. The faculty have therefore sought autonomy and discretionary powers from the state
legislature. Unfortunately, the exercise of this very discretion has
partially contributed to many of the problems. For example, no clear
and unambiguous statement on enrollment policy was ever incorporated into law. Had enrollment and admissions policies been given
statutory recognition, appropriate levels of support would perhaps
have been automatically forthcoming from the legislature. Since the
creation of the Master Plan for Higher Education, the state legislature has provided generous budgetary support under the assumption
that all qualified students seeking to enter public institutions of
higher education should be admitted. If the legislature or the governor's administration deviates from this pattern of support, the state
colleges and university cannot find immediate relief in the existing
law because they have essentially made a virtue of its absence.

The diffuse faculty hostility toward the current Republican
administration has made it particularly difficult for faculty to convince people of specific instances of administrative malfeasance. In
reacting to charges that ten to forty thousand qualified students were
turned away from state colleges for the fall 1969 semester, the
governor asserted that there was no evidence that any had in fact
been rejected from the system and that "it would be a crime" if it
were true. The current Republican administration and selected
members of the legislature emphasize underutilized instructional
facilities and suggest that students are found at the bottom of the
faculty priority list. In their view, faculty seek only to "protect their
comfortable little niches." The academic community shouts back by
attributing their problems to a "handful of know-nothing legislators."

In 1969 the bipartisan Assembly Select Committee on
Campus Disturbance issued a finding that too little emphasis was
being placed on the needs of students and too much on faculty
prerogatives, research activities, and institutional status. The committee report, signed by four Democrats and five Republicans, also
charged that administrators and the governing boards of the university and the state colleges failed to develop effective channels of
communication with students, faculty, and the public and were often
unreceptive to and disdainful of public opinion. The bipartisan
character of the report put to rest the frequently expressed faculty

view that their political difficulties were mainly ascribable to the Republican leadership.

The faculty position on political interference within the university and state colleges has been unstable and inconsistent. Reagan's attitudes continue to be seen by the faculty as antithetical to public higher education; yet great faculty tolerance and ambivalence were demonstrated when the educational process was violently disrupted by dissident students and faculty. The state legislature has never curtailed academic freedom to the extent that it has been abrogated by those most intimately related to higher education. This has not gone unnoticed by the public, nor is the public ignorant of its power to make decisions on the fate of higher learning in California. The usual tensions between legislature and faculty have been growing and now seem to be beyond that threshold which promotes constructive change. Should this trend continue new forces may give life to serious repressive consequences for the system of public higher education.

5

Roles of Trustees

Louis H. Heilbron

The role of state college trustee was created out of administrative and legislative necessities, in approximately equal parts. The twelve state colleges existing in 1960 were under the loose supervision of the State Board of Education, a public body of ten members, appointed for four-year terms by the governor, with the consent of the senate. The Education Board had jurisdiction over the public elementary and secondary schools of the state, purchased all of the textbooks for the elementary schools, administered teacher credentials (granting and revoking licenses) and generally controlled teacher training, directly operated schools for the deaf and blind, had broad guidance relationships with the then seventy junior colleges, and "supervised" the state colleges because of their historical development from normal schools.

The overloaded Board of Education devoted comparatively little time to the state colleges until 1960, but the increased effort made then still was not sufficient. The superintendent of public instruction handled most of the college relationships. Problems of admissions standards, new curricula, faculty authority, and relations with the University of California demanded more attention than this board could properly give or be expected to give.

The legislature had its special concerns. Each of the state colleges, through the locally interested legislators, was seeking enlarged budgets for expanded curriculum and administrative support. The lobbying race for funds between the colleges and the university was becoming hard and swift. Most of the legislators were tired of the pressures and fearful of unnecessary duplications. The legislature and the governor insisted that higher education put its house in order, gave the educators six months to do so, and thus the Master Plan was developed and embodied in the Donahoe Higher Education Act of 1960.

The plan allocated general education functions and emphases to the three segments of higher education. From an organizational standpoint the new State Board of College Trustees paralleled the Regents of the University of California, with two exceptions. There were the same number of appointed trustees (sixteen), the same principal public ex-officio members (governor, lieutenant governor, superintendent of public instruction, and speaker of the assembly), and the chief executive officer (chancellor) was made a board member. The governor made the appointments. The powers of governance were couched in much the same language. But the terms of the appointive trustees were eight years, compared with sixteen for the Regents, and the operational authority was embedded in statute instead of the constitution.

The Master Plan recommendations had contemplated more exact parallels than these. Longer terms were requested (twelve years, if not sixteen) on the theory that such terms immunized the educational institution from politics. For a time, the constitutional issue threatened the entire enterprise. The educators wanted the Board of Trustees to have the same autonomy as the Regents in fiscal and in academic affairs. The university was particularly eager that the entire Master Plan be included in the constitution in order to nail down the limits of state college academic functions, especially in research and the authority to grant the doctorate with university approval. The legislature was determined to keep the terms of appointees short compared with those of the Regents and to prevent the details of the untried Master Plan from becoming frozen in the constitution or to create another board with the juridical independence of the Regents. It took the governor (Brown) himself to bring the educators (from the Regents, the State Board of Education, and the Master Plan Committee) to agree to accept the statutory rather than the constitutional route to reform.

Unquestionably, some of the operational problems later encountered by the trustees stemmed from the failure to achieve the constitutional goal. But the concept of constitutional immunity has been exaggerated considerably. There is considerable turnover of board membership due to deaths and resignations, even in the case of sixteen-year terms; over a period of sixteen years, earlier and later appointees may reflect the same political viewpoints and respond similarly to the same political pressures; and, finally, a governor and other public ex-officio members can exercise considerable influence over either type of board if they give their time, attention, and effort to it. Moreover, the budgetary and appropriation powers of the executive and legislative branches of government are formidable and can be used in a manner that neutralizes the apparent independence guaranteed by constitutional status. A board, constitutional or legislative, may prefer free or minimum tuition, but budgetary cuts may provide no alternative to the imposition of substantial tuition fees in order to support viable operations. (The purpose here is not to evaluate tuition but simply to point out the power of the purse.)

Perhaps the fundamental issue is the place of elective public officers on higher education boards. The original theory was that the educational cause would be well served if certain of the highest officials of the state were kept informed by participating in the university and college boards. These officers, by direct contact with academic programs, presumably would support them in the political arena and paradoxically (in view of their offices) keep them out of politics. For approximately a hundred years in the case of the university, this theory worked out quite well. But the expenditures of higher education have become so high and visible, the students so numerous, the utterances and acts of many so strident, and, on occasion, faculty statements and complaints so widely directed that education itself, particularly higher education, has become the subject of politics. It is not surprising that elected ex-officio officials attempt to take the lead and to influence decisions at the board level. In political terms, they may feel they have no other course. In terms of board structure and action, this effort has proved unfortunate. The governor and other high public officials have easy access to the public media, know how to use corridor television while their appointed colleagues are busy handling routine matters, enjoy the inherent influence of their offices, and generally are in a position to weight unduly the deliberations of educational boards. This is not to say that such public officers should refrain from exercising their legitimate powers on the educational scene. The governor, for example, must support or modify or veto educational budgets; he may have to send in the National Guard to handle a campus riot; but these are functions he exercises as a constitutional officer, not a board member. The temptation of any public officer on a board is to take a popular position, one calculated to be accepted or hailed by the majority of the electorate, while the great educational need of the moment may be to support or explain an unpopular issue. Such support may be essential to the preservation of the educational process, of freedom of inquiry, of the pursuit of truth. In the interests of all concerned parties—the elected public officials themselves, the rest of the board, the educational program, and the public—it would be preferable if higher education were restructured to eliminate the membership of the ex-officio members. Such a procedure would not usher in the millennium but would afford the lay boards the opportunity to reflect their independent judgments after appropriate consultation and communication with the administrative, faculty, and student segments, depending on the problem involved. Most policy recommendations originate in one of these segments and are dependent upon effective administrative presentation. The trustees (or Regents) would have the continuing responsibility to implement their decisions and be accountable, but the decisions would have been made clearly in the educational context.

Another problem facing the original board was the location of state college headquarters. The State Board of Education was established in Sacramento; should the state college administration be elsewhere? Should the headquarters be built on an existing college campus or adjacent to one on the theory that central administration needs physical association with the academic program in order to avoid becoming an impersonal bureaucracy?

The board was almost unanimous in its view that the educational capital should be away from the general capital of government. In this way the day to day pressures of the legislative and other executive agencies could be minimized. In light of current higher education budgets, campus unrest, and other academic problems occupying the center of the political stage, this original viewpoint may seem unimportant or erroneous. Wherever the chancellor and his staff may be, they cannot escape political realities. Nor are these necessarily hostile—informed and sympathetic legislative committees, particularly education committees, can be most helpful when the going is rough. Nevertheless, geographic separation does tend to reduce the times and the intensity with which political interests are asserted against the educational process.

There was another and more persuasive reason for the choice of location. Most of our colleges were situated in Southern California and most of the projected expansion was planned in that area, where the people and the students lived. The interrelationships between the central administration and the college planners and administrators would be considerable. It would be economical to place the headquarters in the center of the area in which the greater part of its business would be conducted. This was the contention that ultimately produced the reluctant cooperation of the Department of Finance and the legislature in locating the headquarters in Los Angeles.

The decision on a campus or independent location was easy. A central headquarters situated on a campus tends to overwhelm it—to substitute state administrative considerations for local ones and to reduce the importance of the local campus personnel and problems. Moreover, it can easily involve state personnel in the campus situation. Some detachment in work can be achieved in an independent location; but since daily contact is required between the headquarters and the campuses in field consultations of one kind or another, the headquarters need not become isolated or bureaucratic. What is lost is the close, continuing impact of the student scene. On balance, the separate headquarters seemed clearly desirable. (No campus invited us!)

In order to provide an orderly transition from the State
Board of Education to the state college trustees, the members of the
state board were made trustees until their respective state board
terms expired. The trustees decided initially on the same officers,
and for a year I and Thomas Braden served, respectively, as president and vice-president of the Board of Education and also as
chairman and vice-chairman of the trustees. At the end of the planning year I resigned from the state board in order to devote all possible time to the trustees, who became operative July 1, 1961.

Our most immediate and pressing personnel matter during
the planning period (July 1960 to July 1961) was the choice of a
chancellor. The selection committee, composed of Braden, Theodore
Merriam, and myself, compiled a list of 180 names most carefully—
using recommendations and suggestions from all the national university and college foundations (Carnegie, Ford, and so on), university and college presidents, administration, faculty, and interested
citizenry. Our committee screened the nominees, with the help of
experts, including the general secretary of the American Association
of University Professors (AAUP) and went to the Midwest and the
East to interview the top candidates. Finally we brought back three
names (one of whom the board selected), a president of a great
urban college, a president and a vice-president of distinguished mid-
western universities. The quality of all was unquestioned. Of the two
not selected, one subsequently became president of his university and
the other has risen to a position in the federal cabinet. Buell Gallagher, president of the City College of New York (CCNY), became
the first chancellor.

Gallagher served for about eight months. During his short
term, he gave a lift to the entire system. Although he was frequently
attacked by certain rightist elements as too much of a liberal and
too soft on communist influences, he was able to show a long history
of dealing forcefully and affirmatively with extreme leftist elements.
It was unfortunate that so much of his energy was diverted to
establishing his position; however, his forthright expositions won
him the devotion of the faculties and impressed students and trustees.
In the end, he resigned to resume his presidency at CCNY for
personal reasons. There was no rift between him and the trustees.
A primary economic factor was that his years of accumulated retire-

ment benefits, which he had mistakenly thought would be transferred intact from New York to California, could not be thus protected under California law. The manner of his going, however, left much to be desired. While arrangements were being made for his formal inauguration, he announced his resignation when on a trip to New York. The trustees were left to pick up the pieces in an atmosphere charged with rumor.

Gallagher had selected Dumke, president of San Francisco State College, to be his vice-chancellor for academic affairs. Dumke had been closely associated with the development of the Master Plan for Higher Education and was most familiar with the history, administration, and purposes of the state colleges. The board was inclined to make an immediate appointment but decided to extend its investigation for nearly two months. The faculty insisted on a right of consultation, and a trustee selection committee, with several faculty members added, reviewed the options and made its recommendation, with the result that Dumke was appointed chancellor at the board meeting of April 1962. The trustees concluded that it would take another chancellor two years to learn about the system as much as Dumke already knew.

Certain elements of the faculty protested that there had been insufficient consultation with them, although there had been much less when Gallagher had been appointed to their satisfaction. They thought it unwise to elevate or appoint any person from within the state of California, believing that only an outsider could be sufficiently objective. The trustees considered this idea preposterous— that there was no one worthy or able to be chancellor out of a population of seventeen million people. However, this thrust toward faculty participation in important decisions that affected them was important. Subsequently, almost all college presidents have been appointed after recommendation by either a faculty committee or a "rainbow" committee on which faculty, administration, and trustees are represented. This participation was unique in public higher education.

During the long period when the colleges were normal schools, the superintendent of public instruction, with the consent of the Board of Education, appointed the college presidents, who were accustomed to administering with the control and independence of a high school principal. When the colleges were formed into a system, the faculties felt that their institutions had come of age and must recognize a strong faculty voice. The trustees concurred in the creation of a statewide academic senate and of local campus senates where these had not yet been formed.

As the trustees contemplated the role of faculty in the governance structure, their statutory obligation was clear: they were to govern. While government of a large enterprise necessarily implies delegation, the trustees have always been sensitive to the legal fact that the ultimate responsibility is theirs for whatever of consequence happens in the college system. The trustees choose a chancellor, the chancellor selects a staff, but whatever they do and how they do it reflects on the board. Since the chancellor serves at the pleasure of the board and the presidents are appointed and removed with board approval, accountability is a fair result.

However, the board saw its primary function as determining policy rather than entering into the details of administration. (And when the trustees have strayed from this concept, they have run into trouble.) Much of this policy must deal with educational matters: curricula, admissions, transfers (consistent with the Master Plan), calendar, and so on. These are areas traditionally within the professional competence of faculty. The board immediately recognized that it should not act to define or control course content; it could decide whether to establish a school of engineering or a graduate program in social work at a given college but should not determine the curriculum thereof. Budgetary considerations underlie many academic decisions, and many areas, such as admissions, student discipline, and the objectives of a college program, are of direct concern to the board. To deal with all these matters the board requires faculty and administrative points of view. It therefore welcomed and encouraged the formation of the statewide faculty senate.

The board took literally the provisions in the academic senate constitution that senate participation in policy making would be advisory. Not long after its creation the senate took a different view of its function and considered that its recommendations, particularly in matters involving educational policy and faculty affairs, should be almost conclusive. In this position the senate was supported by several college faculty organizations which functioned outside the system. These different interpretations were destined to cause a number of misunderstandings between board and faculty. Many had no substantial basis because in most instances the board did act in accordance with senate recommendations.

Another matter facing the trustees almost at the outset of system operations was that of educational objectives for the state colleges. The trustees were aware that the constituent colleges had their own histories and traditions and that these should not be forfeited in order to establish systemwide conformity. The colleges were not to be all things to all students. Humboldt naturally had developed an effective program in forestry and in the study of marine life; such specialization should be preserved. It was not necessary for San Diego to establish a sophisticated program in forestry. Similarly, San Francisco State College had a nationally known record in the creative arts and San Diego State in the field of public administration. California Polytechnic was outstanding in agriculture, animal husbandry, architecture, and, in particular, a methodology which emphasized practical instruction in the lower division years and theory in the senior years. For the good of the state and in order to avoid needless duplication, these areas of emphasis were to be supported.

As a corollary, the general foundation courses in all the colleges should exhibit the same high quality. Substance, not form, was to be the chief criterion of quality. Needless duplication was to be avoided and eliminated. The tendency to proliferate courses and excessively fragmentize knowledge was to be curtailed. The mission of the colleges, as indicated in the Donahoe Act, was to teach, and the trustees had occasion to reiterate this emphasis from year to year. Research was authorized as a supplement and aid to better instruction and not as "pure research" or for meeting arbitrary standards of publication. Each college was to submit a five-year master plan for its own development, including its graduate program. Building and expansion should follow and meet academic requirements and not precede them. Although most of these fundamental policies were declared before the establishment of the statewide academic senate, the senate, once it came into being, did not recommend any material changes in these objectives.

Faculty and trustee relations were frequently not so smooth, however. On occasion, the board modified or took action contrary to a faculty recommendation. In an early instance the board adopted the principle of year-round operation on the quarter system, which had previously been recommended by the statewide education Coordinating Council and adopted by the University of California. The college senate had made a study of the proposal and had recommended a trimester calendar or an arrangement with two semesters plus a special session. The board considered the contentions of the faculty (regarding efficiency, faculty preference, academic considerations) but submitted to time pressure from the Coordinating Council and the legislature without examining in detail the lengthy faculty report. In retrospect, this action proved to be a costly error—not so much in dollars, but in a loss of credibility that trustees' intentions regarding cooperation with faculty were entirely honorable.

By the mid-sixties, faculty salaries in the state colleges, which had been above salaries paid in competing universities and colleges in the rest of the country, began to lose their lead. The faculty, supported by the chancellor, pressed for compensation that always would be at least fully competitive. Moreover, the faculty representatives considered that they were entitled to the same pay as their colleagues at the University of California and that it was not equitable to pay a professor of the same subject a different and higher amount simply because he was employed by the university.

This demand presented the trustees with collateral problems. Faculty at the university had much lighter teaching loads, but the research and publication demands were far higher. Tenure at the university was acquired on the average after seven years; at the state colleges in four years. Salary raises even within grade at the university were given primarily on a merit basis but were across the board in the state colleges. The university competed principally with the Ivy League institutions for its faculty, and, by and large, the state colleges did not. Nevertheless, the trustees supported the principle that the teaching mission was certainly as important as the research function and that the gap between the salary scales should be closed in most subject areas. Definite gains have been made since the Board of Trustees was established but not quickly enough to satisfy many faculty elements.

Since the trustees deemed the teaching mission preeminent, they were slow to reduce or adjust the traditional twelve-unit teaching load. Toward the latter part of the sixties they did make substantial adjustments in favor of faculty who were teaching graduate courses. They would not commit themselves to a nine-unit load, however, although pressed to do so by two of the leading faculty organizations and the statewide senate. The trustees did adopt the policy, however, that their overall teaching load should be competitive with that required in similar institutions. (The list of fifteen or more institutions, used for comparison purposes by the trustees, the Department of Finance, and the legislature, included a number of prestigious universities throughout the country.)

One thorny salary problem which still leaves unhappy memories concerned the "1.8 debacle." In fiscal 1964–1965, the legislature had authorized certain salary raises for the following year which the trustees passed on to the faculty. Since the trustees were required to operate on a line by line budget, they were compelled to limit the total raises to the ceiling established by the legislature. Due to a miscalculation in the chancellor's office, which was not caught by the Department of Finance in review, it was learned in November of the fiscal year that the salary increases, if paid to the end of the year, would produce a deficit in the increase fund. There was plenty of money in other budget categories available for transfer to meet the deficit, but it would take a legislative act to authorize the transfer. After conferring with the chairman of the principal legislative committee involved, the chancellor believed that the authorization for such transfer would be given in January, provided that the whole matter was not made an issue of consequence. When the time came, however, it was evident that the legislature would not authorize the transfer since they believed a poor precedent would be established for other state agencies. The trustees learned that they would be criminally responsible if they did not readjust the salaries so that there would be no deficit. In a public meeting attended by representatives of official and unofficial faculty bodies and many individual faculty members, the problem was discussed. The board finally decided to cut salaries of senior faculty and administrative officers for the remaining period of the year (March 1 to June 30) 1.8 per cent. At the same time the Board of Trustees promised to make every effort, to the very last day of the legislature, to try to reinstate the salaries established the previous July.

The legislature stood firm to the end. It was their view that no salary cut was involved because every faculty member (after the 1.8 deduction for the spring months) received the raise that he would have received had the original computations been made without mathematical error. A great many faculty continued to hold the trustees responsible for an unwarranted and vicious cut. Some accused the trustees of being immoral because they would not elect to go to jail. Unquestionably, the right action, consistent with sound business practice and with moral commitment, would have been to pay the full amounts of compensation with legislative authority. But since this was not forthcoming, the trustees took the only course available to them. As noted, the money was there. If ordinary business practice had been permissible, allowing a transfer of funds between general categories when an error had been made in good faith, an error which in the total budget was not substantial, there would have been no problem.

Faculty grievance and disciplinary procedures were another source of difficulties. "Interim" procedures in these areas were established in 1961 but prevailed for nine years. The academic senate, administration, and trustees were unable to agree on permanent regulations. Draft after draft contained proposed procedures of such complexity that academic due process threatened to become endless. (Grievances deal with complaints by faculty members who claim that they have been deprived of rights to appointment, reappointment, tenure, promotion, or the like. Disciplinary proceedings arise from acts alleged to be in violation of statute or of unprofessional conduct and may result in penalties such as discharge, suspension, or reprimand.)

Finally, in January and February of 1969, procedures in both areas recommended by the academic senate and supported by most faculty bodies were adopted by the trustees. The national AAUP was favorably impressed with these new procedures which made faculty committees the chief agencies for faculty discipline, including the appellate level. However, after a relatively brief trial, these regulations were superseded in September 1970. The discipline procedure now requires outside hearing officers (attorneys) as fact finders; faculty committees decide, in view of the findings, whether there have been violations of conduct or professional ethics and recommend the penalty. The final decision rests with the president or chancellor. There are no outside hearing officers in the new grievance procedure, but administration has the final word. While these developments represent an erosion of faculty authority, probably they would not have occurred if the faculty had been willing to adopt effective self-discipline and performance controls by the mid-sixties and these had been tested by experience.

Admissions represented another area of trustee concern. The charge to the state colleges was to consider as eligible students the top one-third of the high school graduating classes. The courses which established eligibility were largely college preparatory courses. In the interest of being fair to the greater number of students, the trustees, upon recommendation of the chancellor and the faculty senate, approved an admissions program which considered the total record of the student in all courses. In practice the quality of the student body was improved, although eligibility had been broadened. In 1968, the trustees expanded the exemptions from regular admission requirements from 2 per cent to 4 per cent of the new enrollment to provide liberal opportunity for minority groups.

A number of problems arose in the late 1960s with respect to minority students, particularly black students and Third World (Mexican-American, Oriental and Indian) students. The movement to establish black studies and other ethnic studies programs reached some of the colleges in 1967 and 1968. The matter came before the trustees in the form of a proposed master's degree in black studies for San Francisco State College. The degree was approved subject to the condition that the program meet with quality requirements on course content and procedures.

In late 1967 campus violence became a central issue. All official bodies—trustees, chancellor, faculty organizations, student councils—passed strong resolutions against the use of violence as a tactic for reform or for any other purpose. But violence took root and continued on several campuses—at San Francisco, San Jose, Long Beach, San Fernando, Los Angeles, and Fresno. Occasionally, activists manhandled or attempted to attack employment recruiters from Dow Chemical Company. In San Francisco, the particular objective was to compel the college to accept a black studies program which would have been substantially under the control, both as to curricula and as to personnel, of the Black Students Union. Violence was also directed toward achieving an open-admissions policy for minority students; one crisis arose when a group of students desired to eliminate ROTC from the campus. In short, these occurrences were typical of unrest throughout the country, but it arrived a little later at the state colleges than in many other institutions.

The trustees, almost from the beginning, sought immediate reliance on police intervention and protection. After a day of turmoil at San Francisco State when the police stood by but the president did not call them, a day's hearing was held before the board in order to determine the propriety of the president's acts. At the hearing the president demonstrated that his forbearance was at all times advised by experts in crowd control made available to him by the San Francisco police department and that he had been following the counsel of police officers. Notwithstanding the proof, which also satisfied state legislative committees, the board directed an investigation of the stewardship of the president (predicated on his conduct on that critical day) and passed a strong resolution which denied college presidents flexibility in calling the police and required automatic expulsion or suspension of students for engaging in violent acts.

The majority of the board considered that a hard line was essential in order to control campus violence. The minority agreed that there had to be firm control but that the president of the college should have some choice concerning use of police because frequently the presence of police on the campus escalated rather than reduced the violence. A majority of the board also held that penalties should be automatic, while a minority again believed that it was necessary for the president to have a range of action regarding first offenders, young students under older student influence, and the evaluation and conditions of the specific acts involved. This flexibility was restored at the next regular meeting, but the underlying issue continued to plague board deliberations.

Moreover, the board was divided on the question of entering into any discussions with students during a period of violence. Beginning in November 1968 and continuing until March of the following year, the San Francisco campus was in a state of siege and violent unrest. Black students had presented a series of nonnegotiable demands, including those for open admissions and an autonomous black studies department under student control. Certain members of the board could not believe that the word *nonnegotiable* was literal and that no adjustments meeting real concerns were feasible. Even though the board prohibited discussions with the students during this violent period, the president of the college made himself available for any communications and faculty committees did the same. The theory was that even during a time of war peace negotiations often occur and produce constructive results. Many trustees felt that any such efforts toward settlement amounted to appeasement.

The three-month student strike or boycott of classes accompanied by violence at San Francisco State also involved a partial faculty strike initially undertaken by the American Federation of Teachers local in support of student demands and quickly expanded to include faculty demands. The faculty strike was finally ended when a trustees' committee through discussion with representatives of organized labor and a mediator caused the striking faculty (close to one quarter of the total) to return to teaching. The college had not agreed to any substantive curriculum or personnel changes or to any of the fifty-two demands, but the majority of the trustees' committee had stated (individually) that they would recommend a minor change in the faculty grievance procedure already proposed by the academic senate. The students soon followed the faculty group in ending their obstructive tactics and boycott. Without communication the result could not have been achieved. At the time of the so-called settlement and return, the college was 20 per cent operative.

Firmness in relationships is not a quality that can be isolated; it may be used to best advantage in direct relations between the parties and in developing a formula for the resolution of issues. Talk with determined destroyers will be of no avail, but talk with many of the opposed and the alienated may be the simplest way to avoid destruction. Any overall view must recognize that quiet and dedicated faculty in all the colleges have done noble work in causing students to "cool it" in time to prevent them from boiling into an unruly mob.

Unquestionably, growth and expansion were primary concerns for the trustees during these ten years. Full-time equivalent student enrollment increased from 70,000 in 1960 to close to 200,-000 in 1970; full-time faculty, from 3,589 in 1960 to 10,235 in 1970; and part-time faculty increased more than proportionately to 4,000 in 1970. Buildings were needed to accommodate the educational requirements, and the trustees successfully called for the financing and expended the moneys necessary (about half a billion dollars) to perform the work within the allowable time. Campus master plans were developed, aided by an architectural consultant for each campus. Private architects were introduced for the first time and competed with the public division of Architecture to plan approximately half the buildings. The trustees approved the master planning and the individual plans to the considerable advantage of all concerned. The physical appearance of six new colleges and all the existing colleges was materially enhanced. In spite of temporary overcrowding in certain colleges the challenge of growth did not intimidate the state college system.

The Board of Trustees had to develop special relationships with the chancellor, the Coordinating Council, the University of California and the legislature. The chancellor by law is a trustee. However, he is primarily the chief executive officer of the trustees and the college system. The trustees expected the chancellor to present the most important policy matters and implement policies by operating through the college presidents and the official faculty organizations. Any chancellor tends to protect his board from handling too many difficult or disagreeable issues at one meeting. At times the board considered its agenda too tepid, but someone was always available to turn on the heat.

The chancellor is in the best public position when an educational policy issue developed by his administration or by the faculty has their joint approval. He is subject to many pressures not only from his own staff, including the college presidents and the trustees, but also from conflicting faculty and student groups and from influential external agencies, such as the governor, the Department of Finance, and the legislature. It is a nearly impossible job. He is never going to please everybody at any time: if he did, he would be conservative, liberal, bold, cautious, hard, flexible, an inspiring leader, and a loyal follower. A chancellor cannot be all of these things at the same time or different times; he simply has to be himself.

The trustees related to the University of California mostly through the Coordinating Council. Under the Master Plan (Donahoe) statute, each of the systems appointed three representatives to the council. For the most part, this association with the university was most cordial and cooperative. The university repeatedly supported the trustees' budgetary demands for research funds; for equivalent salary scales, especially at the undergraduate teaching level; for funding sabbatical leaves; and for a number of other items. Conflicts arose only when the university felt threatened by efforts to accelerate the timetable for building new state colleges (competition for capital funds) or to change the names of the colleges to California State University (competition in prestige) or to authorize the state colleges to grant their own doctorates, even in limited fields (departure from the Master Plan). In most cases, the respective representatives found their problems and approaches to solutions substantially the same. This phenomenon caused the legislature to increase the number and proportion of public members and recently to reduce the college and university representation to one member each.

Thus, the idea of a Coordinating Council, created primarily so that the two great segments of public higher education (and subsequently a third, the community college board) could resolve their differences and coordinate their activities in a public forum, has undergone a change. The public members are clearly in a dominating position numerically (the new ratio is seven to three) and the council could become a superboard if it were ever given operational authority. Such a result would require a constitutional amendment. In the meantime, reducing the voice of the colleges and the university to a minimum may restrict the chances of effective coordination since the actions of the council are only advisory and the three segments have a long tradition of independent action.

The trustees' relationship with the legislature has always been vitally important. If the legislature is not satisfied with college operations, appropriations suffer. Evidence of fiscal irresponsibility, campus disruptions, or weak discipline adversely affects legislative attitudes toward funding and stimulates proposals for legislative controls. The trustees have been fairly sucessful in opposing legislation which would involve detailed restrictions on campus administration or on their own authority. After years of effort, they succeeded in obtaining legislation which removed many of the obstacles of line budgeting, thus making possible transfers within and between certain categories. Toward the end of the sixties they obtained, for the first time, substantial research funds to support better instruction. Most trustee communications with the legislature are made in written form or are presented at interim committee meetings; the chancellor and his staff give testimony at the session committee hearings. The trustees have taken many firm budgetary positions but have been less willing to act as a buffer when individual colleges have come under attack for derelictions in academic matters—for example, by pointing out that criticism may have been justified but involved a miniscule part of the college program or that any academic program worthy of the name must allow a margin for error.

Many of the state colleges are universities, in fact if not in name; they are small cities in population, in diversity of enrollees, in the problems they reflect and must face from day to day. A board of trustees meeting nine or ten times a year over two-day periods can deal effectively with only the broadest problems that come to the surface and compel overall attention. The center of attention has shifted in a decade from administrative structure to faculty authority to student aspirations and conduct. The one constant is that the trustees always have plenty to do.

The obvious question is: Where are the colleges headed during the next ten years? What are the likely developments? The following is an attempt to evaluate some trends, and the future tense is used only to suggest my best estimates.

After almost tripling in the 1960s, student enrollment will probably go up at least 50 to 60 per cent again by 1980. There will be continuing pressure for faculty recruitment and building expansion. Appropriations will continue to increase in total dollars, but such amounts may still fall short of adequate monies to provide for growth enrollment, essential pay raises for faculty and nonacademic staff, plant maintenance and equipment, capital improvements, and inflationary factors. Public and private colleges and universities throughout the country are facing budgetary crises which threaten serious dislocations in curricula, reduction of the quality of teaching and research, and demoralization of personnel. A reordering of priorities in government spending and in private giving and probably increases in taxation will be necessary to prevent serious damage to California and, generally, to American higher education.

Voters will continue, at least in the early seventies, to be wary about supporting expansion by large bond issues. The resulting congestion will invite new devices to cope with student needs. We can anticipate cutting down on lecture time and increasing the opportunities and requirements for independent self-study. A student's attendance on a campus will not be as important as his demonstrating, through comprehensive examinations or other evaluative programs, his knowledge and intellectual capacity. There will be an emphasis on tutorial teaching for the disadvantaged and for top students. Proposals to cut matriculation time to three and a half or three years and to teach partially from a university without walls have been made by the chancellor of the state colleges and others, but these plans will take time to develop and adjust. The initial costs of these innovations may be high.

Pressure will continue to admit culturally disadvantaged students irrespective of deficiencies in their high school records or standard college preparatory tests. As an adjustment to overriding social and economic needs, such a procedure may be required, provided it is subject to commensurate tutorial support in the first two years and upper division education then becomes genuinely competitive. Much of the liberalization in admissions should be at the junior college level. In short, the admissions policy should guarantee educational opportunity, and the retention policy should assure educational quality. Black and other ethnic studies will be adjusted to meet substantive needs, to remedy the injustices of past omissions but not at the price of distorting history This result, in part, will be brought about by the minority students themselves who want to be prepared to live in the real, competitive world and who do not want to receive second-class degrees derived from the study of dubious subject matter.

Nonresident fees should be reduced at least for exceptionally qualified applicants since most of this group continues to live in and contribute to the welfare of this state after graduation. A shift to year-round operation and expanded night classes in the urban colleges will enable the system to serve more students than it now does.

Mass higher education will cost considerably more, not withstanding innovations, economies, and the reduction of unnecessary duplication. The emphasis on teaching should not decrease money for research, including the appropriations of the university. If err we must, it should be on the side of academic adventure as against static knowledge, of development as against the status quo. The energies of higher education should be partly directed to assisting and counseling the secondary and elementary school systems on improving their educational programs so that higher education itself does not become a frustrating experience.

The greatest problem of higher education will be to be true to itself, to seek the truth with reason and skepticism and be the servant of no institution or segment of society—government, industry, political powers, ethnic groups, or students. This task will not be easy. Some forces in society want the college institution per se to become the instrument of social reform and revolution. Once the colleges become activist and teaching and learning are directed to the achievement of specific political results, their value is seriously imperiled. The sanctity of the classroom must remain inviolate; it must remain open to the expression and testing of all ideas and principles relevant to the subject; it is no place for indoctrination or the sharpening of activists' axes. A great danger in certain branches of the university and in several of the state colleges at the end of the sixties was that fear itself had begun to enter the classroom; that extremist students attempted, at times successfully, to destroy the educational process. At the moment there is evidence that the mass of students is prepared to insist upon the right to an education free from disruptions or coercion by other students. Once the vast majority asserts its right, the hard-core destroyers can be identified, isolated, and speedily removed from the campus. They may still constitute a community problem, but the community is a far more formidable and diversified target than the college or the university by itself.

Students will continue their efforts to accelerate change on the outside, particularly for the purpose of assuring survival in a liveable environment. Progress in the solution of some of the great inter-

national and national issues—Vietnam, the control of nuclear arma-
ments, racial equality, pollution—will reduce tensions on the
campus. Visible and constructive achievements in these areas should
greatly reduce the incidents of violence. Stricter disciplinary regulations, speedily and justly enforced, should provide acceptable controls, but the campus will properly continue to be greatly disturbed
by the struggles of men to maintain viable relationships with their
fellow men and with their environment. The warning of the President's Commission—that student violence and violent overreaction
speed up the vicious cycle—should be heeded. When students have
faith in the future, the campus will be at peace, whatever its intellectual ferment.

Teaching will be more innovative, imaginative, and direct in
the seventies as a result of the students' protests in the sixties. Field
and apprentice work in public and private social agencies, as part of
the curriculum, will be a common phenomenon. Student evaluation
of teaching will be an accepted input in connection with faculty
promotions and reappointments. Student participation on faculty
and trustee committees will be quite usual (the practice is widely
accepted already), but enthusiasm will wane when it is discovered
that most committee meetings are not very exciting. Students will
not gain the decisive role in hiring faculty.

Faculty is faced with the necessity for internal reform. They
will be expected to do a better job in evaluating and rewarding (or
withholding rewards for) their own performance and to be more
demanding in the maintenance of professional standards; for example, in connection with retention, promotions, tenure, and controlling efforts to politicize the classroom. The acceptability and
operation of the trustees' disciplinary policy, which assigns fact-finding in faculty cases to outside attorneys (generally selected by bar
associations), will be interesting to observe.

There are signs that one or two faculty associations may
make another attempt at statewide organization for collective bargaining to establish their prerogatives and economic position. Most
faculty members find the bargaining concept foreign to their experience and are confused as to what it involves. It does not seem to be
the natural or desired expression of the members of an individualistic

profession. The drive for collective bargaining could be successful if: the faculty loses faith that their official bodies are effective; some serious issue affecting their welfare (such as the continued refusal to raise salaries) or academic freedom can be expanded to fighting proportions by union organizers; faculty members are willing to suffer economic loss or discharge in the event of strike, legal or illegal; the legislature is overwhelmed by the strength of the movement and authorizes collective bargaining for college personnel or public employees generally; the present climate of public hostility to any unrest in the academic world changes to one of sympathy or at least neutrality with respect to the particular cause. In 1967 the Board of Trustees adopted a resolution favoring the principle of shared responsibility as the alternative to collective bargaining; it should be noted that the board's salary recommendations to the legislature in 1968 and 1969 were arrived at after extensive consultation and exchange between the chancellor's office and the senate and faculty organizations. (The New York law which provides for an adapted form of bargaining for public employees, involving complex administrative and legislative fact-finding machinery and outlawing strikes, has not evoked interest in California.)

Changes may also be expected in board membership and in application of the Master Plan. The trustees will reflect the demands for younger appointees and more diversified backgrounds, including some from the academic world and minority groups. More women will be appointed. The Master Plan of 1960 will continue to be criticized on the ground that it makes state colleges second-rate institutions. Many people argue that so long as major research opportunity is reserved to the university, so long as salaries are not equal for the academic classifications and the university is given the right to draw from the top one-eighth of the high school graduates, the status of the state colleges is bound to be secondary. However, the new stress on teaching will affect the university as well as the colleges during the coming years. In a vast mass program of higher education, it will not be possible for any participating institution to become purely research oriented. The state college share of the top students is bound to increase on the basis of presently scheduled campuses. In due course university status should be accorded to a number of the state college campuses, although they would remain in the present system. The junior colleges are already the major lower division institutions of the state.

Clearly, pay scales should be equalized for the same kind of teaching, the same academic load (however distributed), and the same kind of qualifications. But the variety of the tripartite system in California still seems preferable to one monolithic bureaucratic system. The Master Plan should be modified where necessary to meet educational needs, but its broad lines of authority should be preserved at least for most of the next decade and not scuttled for some scheme of gigantic merger. As the present institutions fill up and new ones are created, the requirements of quality may be served better by a program of decentralization in each of the systems than by a pyramiding of bureaucratic controls.

Students, young and old, credit and noncredit, will continue to receive higher education. Substantial beginnings in lifetime education will be made. The secluded and elitist educational institutions which succeeded the monasteries will be institutions of the past. Much of the charm of their leisurely way will be gone, and there will be nostalgia for the old ways among the old professors and the old alumni. Mass higher education with its millions, largely guided by personal assignments and self-education and aided by technological devices in the library, classroom, laboratory, and home, will be here. In the interest of equity and fairness, notwithstanding their discomfort, these changes will be good for California and America.

6

⊔⌐⊔⌐⊔⌐⊔⌐⊔⌐⊔⌐⊔⌐⊔⌐⊔⌐⊔⌐⊔⌐⊔⌐⊔⌐

Problem of Money

George Clucas

⊔⌐⊔⌐⊔⌐⊔⌐⊔⌐⊔⌐⊔⌐⊔⌐⊔⌐⊔⌐⊔⌐⊔⌐⊔⌐

For the California state colleges the decade of the 1960s opened with great promise. Under the new Master Plan for Higher Education, the colleges were formed into the largest single system of higher education in the United States in terms of numbers of students in attendance. Although certain gains had been made, the financial outlook in the early 1970s was somewhat less promising.

After the 1970–1971 budget was signed by the governor, a leading state newspaper conducted a survey of the nineteen-college system and devoted a front-page article and an editorial to the crisis period caused by funding problems (Los Angeles *Times,* 1970). One major budgetary cut appeared punitive in nature: the granting of a 5 per cent cost of living increase to all state employees except faculty at the university and the state colleges which triggered an appeal to the state supreme court. However, concern over this particular action by the governor and the legislature should not divert attention from two fundamental fiscal problems confronting the state college system. To appreciate the nature of these two problems requires some understanding of the history and role of the three segments of public higher education in California.

Under the constitution of the state, the University of California was constituted as "a public trust to be adminsitered by the existing corporation known as 'the Regents of the University of California,' with full powers of organization and government, subject only to such legislative control as may be necessary to insure compliance with the terms of the endowments of the university and the security of its funds (California Constitution). The excellence of the University of California today rests in good measure upon the foresight and leadership of those most responsible for providing and maintaining this constitutional prerogative. By and large, successive governors and legislatures have been willing to appropriate sufficient funds to keep the university among the top five universities in the country—a significant achievement for any state. Although this high level of support is not guaranteed by the constitution, the unique structural arrangement provided by the constitution has been a major factor in achieving widespread acceptance of this support level.

Giving control of the university to the Regents has empowered them to operate essentially within a two-tier structure—the statewide university operations, headquartered in Berkeley, and the administration on the individual campuses. There is continual debate within the university concerning centralization versus decentralization, an issue which at times has created major stresses. The significant fact, however, is that the university's two-tier system has operated successfully over a long timespan. While a succession of legislatures and governors has generally respected the language of the constitution, erosion would have set in if periodic attempts at encroachment emanating from both branches of government had not been confronted and resisted by the Regents and a long succession of capable administrators at the university.

This unique structural and operational relationship between the state and its university, established over approximately a century of experience, has not been modeled by the California state colleges. The reasons are many and complex. Egalitarian pressures probably bear more heavily upon the state colleges than the university, and certainly the self-preservation instincts of the executive and legislative branches make it unlikely that a drive for constitutional status for the state college system will emerge from either branch. So the California state colleges have been, and are likely to remain for some time in the future, a three-tiered state agency, with all this status implies.

The top tier, consisting of the state control agencies in Sacramento, is very much in evidence and control. The middle tier is governed by the trustees through the headquarters staff headed by the chancellor in Los Angeles. The bottom tier is located in the administrative staff headed by a president at each of the nineteen campuses.

Before the Master Plan created the middle tier in 1961, local campus administration was very active in the struggle to gain support at the state level. As Kennedy (1966) describes it:

The presidents were not prevented by the State Board of Education, the state director of education, nor anyone on the administrative staff of the State Department of Education from dealing directly with their respective state assemblymen and senators; nor were they prohibited from going to Sacramento to lobby for legislation which they individually wanted for their respective colleges or to lobby against legislation which they thought might be detrimental. Because the State Department of Education did not have, during this pre-expansion period, sufficient staff to help expedite for each state college necessary approvals for other state control agencies, state college presidents, deans, and business managers frequently went to Sacramento to walk-through important documents or requests requiring multiple state agency approvals.

Although state college governance was strengthened by the creation in the mid 1950s of the Division of State Colleges in the Department of Education, other state agencies continued to play an important role in controlling the colleges. A review of the state college administrative manual, July 1960, reveals a fifteen-page list of major state agencies or state officials with powers directly affecting the operation of the state colleges (Kennedy, 1966). After a decade of operation under the Master Plan many of these governmental agents still have a policy and operational involvement with the system. Certainly some changes have been made, but gains have been offset largely by new agencies such as the chancellor's office, the Co-ordinating Council for Higher Education, and the Department of General Services, which came into being in the 1960s.

The bureaucratic three-tier structure insures the maintenance of state-prescribed policies, procedures, and standards throughout the system. Those who seek a two-tier arrangement for the colleges have resistance to overcome from outside the system and entropy from within, as many officials and employees have become pre-occupied with administering rules and regulations.

Shortly after the trustees officially took over their respon-sibilities in 1961, a decision was made to locate system headquarters in Los Angeles. This move was not well received by the legislature, and each year since Sacramento has attempted to force a return to the capital where all state agency headquarters are expected to be located. By and large, this decision to relocate was favorably ac-cepted within the state college system as it provided definite advan-tages in the academic realm of operations. However, distance from the Sacramento control agencies introduced additional delays into a fiscal operation not known for being prompt and efficient. The establishment of a strong chancellor's staff which would be favor-ably received at two levels, on the campuses and in the capital, required systemwide decision making and a relinquishment of Sac-ramento controls. While some transfers of decision making were effected, in 1965 a report of a special ad hoc committee created by the trustees in a crisis situation charged that "The growing pressure on tax dollars causes the Department of Finance to exercise tight control over virtually all state college fiscal matters." The commit-tee, which included trustees, the chancellor, college presidents, and academic senate leaders, concluded: "If there is any one position that all segments of the state college system agree upon, it is that these controls must be eliminated or moved to the trustees if the state college system is to operate satisfactorily" (California State Colleges, 1965, p. 36).

The ad hoc committee then set forth a series of suggested changes for consideration, and the one recommendation concerning fiscal operations read as follows:

The Department of Finance [should] permit the Board of Trustees, within broad state fiscal policies to: (a) transfer funds between budget categories; (b) establish a contingency reserve fund to cover costs of excess enrollment and other unanticipated expenses, with authority given to the trustees to transfer funds into this fund from any other account; (c) authorize one or two colleges to operate under a program budget during the 1966–1967 fiscal years; (d) establish the state college operating budget under a single appropriation for the entire system; (e) reduce salary-savings requirements to a reasonable level; (f) approve budget transactions relating to appointment of personnel and establishment of new positions; (g) delegate to the colleges decisions relating to sabbatical leaves, appointment of faculty at advanced salary steps, and reclassifications of positions within available funds (when adequate guidelines are developed); (h) operate within the guidelines on administrative reorganization adopted by the Board of Trustees and approve adjustments in staffing and in position level indicated by these guidelines, within available funds; and (i) enter into contracts in excess of $1000 (the existing limitation) involving procurement of services and/or materials when such contracts have been previously approved as to form or general content. (Some of these changes may require legislative action.) [California State Colleges, 1965, p. 38].

By the end of the 1960s further progress had been made in effecting some changes by the Department of Finance and the Department of General Services. However, in a special report prepared at the request of the legislature, the legislative analyst took the following position.

The basic reason for the existing system of budget administration is to be found in the fact that under the state constitution the governor is held responsible for the general and continuing management of the fiscal affairs of the state. In order to carry out this responsibility, the Department of Finance, as the governor's fiscal agent, is given broad statutory powers concerning the financial policies of the state and such specific powers and duties as have been found necessary to the exercise of that authority. The authority of the Department of Finance to approve or disapprove budget revisions, use of salary savings, and initial development of capital outlay projects, as well as the authority of the Department of General Services to approve or disapprove contracts and purchases, is related to their broad responsibility for financial

management. To limit the governor and his administrative agencies to
the review and approval of proposed budgets could restrict greatly their
ability to carry out their general responsibility for the management of
state expenditure [Legislative Analyst, 1970, p. 18].

The conclusions reached by the analyst indicate that the state colleges will have to continue seeking delegations of authority from the
state bureaucracy.

In contrast to the state agency role of the state colleges, the
community colleges operate under provisions of the state constitution
as part of the public school system. These two-year colleges are
under the jurisdiction of local school boards, which means a simple
two-tier arrangement for governance—the board and the campus
administration. Unlike the university, the community colleges do
not constitute a system. The newly created Board of Governors of
the California community colleges is not designed to disturb local
autonomy; rather, the governors will provide a statewide coordinating mechanism and a voice for the community colleges in matters
affecting higher education in the state.

The community colleges have relied upon the local taxpayers as their basic means of support. Reliance has not been placed
upon the governor or the legislature to provide supplementary state
funds. Rather, community college representatives and other public
school officials have jointly sponsored periodic initiative measures to
increase the basic General Fund guarantee in the state constitution.
The amount to be provided from state funds for each pupil in
average daily attendance (a.d.a.) is written into the constitution.
Approximately three-fourths of this money has to be assigned as
aid on a per-a.d.a. basis. The remaining one-fourth, distributed on
an equalization formula, provides basic support for community colleges which do not have sufficient assessed wealth behind each pupil.
This constitutional approach has assisted in maintaining local control over the community colleges. The governor and the legislature
are therefore not centrally involved.

The fiscal effect of these differences between the segments
can be highlighted further by describing the method each used in
the 1950s to obtain appropriations. The printed budget of the university, in a form prescribed by the university, was taken to Sacra-

mento in early October by the president and a special meeting was held with the governor and the director of finance. By early December the university budget request received approval for inclusion in the governor's budget for presentation to the legislature. Typically, several broad policy reductions were shown in the governor's budget as evidence of the impartial role of the governor and the Department of Finance in controlling the state budget. It was commonly understood at the working staff level that decisions reached on reductions were relayed downward to the budget analysts who were responsible for the technical presentation of the figures. The university-prescribed budget format—additional evidence of the special constitutional status of the university—was then accepted and printed in the governor's budget.

In contrast, each state college was required to use Department of Finance budget forms for its annual budgetary requests. A dress rehearsal presentation was first made in a general meeting in which presidents, business managers, and representatives of the Department of Education met with the director of finance and his staff members. Subsequently, individual meetings, which included a representative from the Department of Education, were set up in the Department of Finance for each college to go over its line items in the budgetary request. These meetings were detailed and exhaustive and formed the basis for subsequent higher-level decisions within the department prior to budget adoption. The accounting-oriented emphasis was upon enrollments and related work load formulas, individual positions, line-item operating expenses, and individual items of equipment. In reality, the Department of Finance performed as a department of bookkeeping and accounting. Budgetary hearings were not held for the community colleges since, as mentioned earlier, they receive state funds through public school apportionments.

This pattern in the segmental approach to obtaining General Fund support in the governor's annual budget was largely repeated in the subsequent legislative hearings on the budget. The university hearing dealt with broad concepts and programs. Reductions were rare, and quite often special items for agricultural research were added as university representatives graciously acceded to demands emerging from agricultural members of the state legislature. On the other hand, in the state college hearings concentrated attention was paid to policies that could be delineated as line items in the budget of each college. Not infrequently, lengthy discussions would ensue over an individual position, an operating expense item, or a piece of equipment.

Clearly, specific provisions in the California constitution have served both the university and the community colleges well. Lacking constitutional status, the state colleges find themselves on dead center. The university receives significant amounts from the federal government and from private endowments while the community colleges realize more than half of their support from local tax sources. The state colleges remain a state agency and must rely almost exclusively upon General Fund support. This historical precedent weighs heavily against the state colleges, who find themselves not unlike an underdeveloped nation with a single-crop economy.

California has always used the number of students as a basic measure for the level of support granted to higher education even though the method of counting students varies, and so it is not possible to accurately compare the three segments. The university has relied upon an enrollment head-count; the state colleges utilize a full-time student equivalent count based upon units of credit; and the community colleges use an average daily attendance figure based upon hours of attendance in the classroom. The best common basis for comparison developed thus far is the total and full-time enrollment figures published by the Department of Finance. Despite the availability of these figures, they are not used in the budget building process for the three public segments.

The governor and the legislature have little or no control over the level of support for lower division programs in the community colleges. This support is determined by local tax rates and by statewide voter initiative measures which are periodically placed on the ballot to establish a new level of General Fund support for each pupil in average daily attendance. As a consequence, the wealthier community college districts can and often do offer salaries in excess of those offered at either the university or the state colleges. In contrast, the governor and the legislature exercise complete con-

trol over the state colleges, and full-time equivalent figures are almost the exclusive basis for determining the annual level of support.

A student enrollment count has not been used as the primary
measure for support for the university. The university generally has
assumed all students in attendance were taking full programs, and
the budget presentation by the university has not separated instruction and research functions. In addition, the university operates
many specialized facilities and professional schools. Because their
budgets are developed differently, the university and the colleges
cannot be compared in terms of instructional costs. The level of
General Fund support for the university has always been higher
than that accorded to the state colleges, and this differential has
usually been accepted.

What has really widened the funding gap between the university and the state colleges has not been the conscious and delib-
erate attention to the budget by the governor and the legislature.
The major cause is the special relationship that has developed between the university and the federal government. In a real sense,
the university is as much a federal university as it is a state university. Federal funds have come into the university in increasing
amounts and for the more exotic programs and research. Significant
federal money, placed upon a state-financed base, has not provided
funds for students but rather for research and particular programs.
Large-scale disparities have been permitted to occur in federal
financing of public higher education in California. Even excluding
the atomic energy installations managed by the university, federal
funds to the university ($150.1 million in 1966–1967) were almost
five times those given to the state colleges ($32.9 million), while
the latter segment handled over two times the total number of students. This 10:1 ratio seriously skewed any reasonable balance in
financial support for the university and the state colleges. In the
federal pecking order, the community colleges ($12.1 million),
which enrolled almost twice as many full-time students as the state
colleges, received one-third as much money, or a 6:1 ratio. This
federal impact upon higher education in California has largely by-
passed the governor and the legislature. The partnership of the
university and the federal government has on the one hand moved

the university into a position of eminence in the country and the world. On the other hand, the fiction of equitable levels of support for public institutions in California continues in the annual budgetary review process.

The cornerstone of the federal-university partnership has been the magic word *research,* and its implications deserve close scrutiny. In 1968, the Coordinating Council for Higher Education commissioned Louis T. Benezet, then president of the Claremont Graduate School and Center, to study and report upon faculty research in the California state colleges. His report, submitted to the Coordinating Council in October 1968, has some strong statements on behalf of the state colleges. For example, commenting upon the language in the Donahoe Act, the report stated, "It is unfortunate that the state colleges, the largest higher education system in the world, operates in the shadow of legislative provisions which encouraged, however inadvertently, a sense of mediocrity. . . . The task, then, is to redefine research functions for the state college faculty so that we can reduce the second-class status (*logically* founded or not) inherent in the teaching-only orientation of the Donahoe Act" (Benezet, 1968, pp. 26–27).

The strongest statement came from a former chairman of the Coordinating Council for Higher Education, Arthur G. Coons, who reflected upon the language he wrote into the Donahoe Act:

The wording chosen at the time was the best possible compromise. I was determined, as my book on *Crises in California Higher Education* states, to get the privilege for faculty research into the state colleges. I was opposed by Kerr who was representing the monopoly of the university in this regard. I took the position that faculty should be allowed to carry forward research even if it were not on state funds but supported by sponsoring organizations, that nothing under these circumstances should prevent the possibility of a faculty man going forward with some type of research that was substantive. I still think that it is appropriate in the state colleges for such research to be conducted with the released time charged to the project. The University of California at the time very strongly resisted this interpretation, but it never got into words except in the way which it is in law which primarily relates to the utilization of state funds [Benezet, 1968, Appendix H].

Meanwhile, the U.S. Office of Education still presents enrollment data on institutions of higher education to support increased federal funds. Allocation of federal money simply is not premised upon enrollments, and neither the state colleges nor the community colleges have been well served by the U.S. Office of Education or other federal agencies dispensing funds to higher education. Federal money has been sent to the more prestigious institutions without regard for imbalances thus created within the states and particularly in California.

The fiscal "coordination for higher education" that is conducted in California revolves primarily around numbers of students and the demands upon the General Fund, while the arrangement between the university and the federal government remains a largely private affair. Large-scale federal support has also come into the state to bolster the private universities and colleges. This development has not been a central concern of the governor and the legislature, who are undoubtedly relieved by not having also to provide funds to the private segment of higher education. California assists the private institutions only through tax exemptions and the indirect device of providing scholarships for tuition and fees.

The Carnegie Commission on Higher Education study of federal funding stated, "At various times in history, the federal government has exerted a substantial influence on the development of higher education. But the enormous role it now plays in the financing of colleges and universities is a phenomenon of the past decade" (Wolk, 1968, p. 1). Although Chairman Clark Kerr commented in his prefatory remarks, "The way the federal government provides funds is as important as the money itself," and "the method of funding bears directly on the distribution of power and money," there is no reference in the commission's findings to disparities created within a state by federal support only for the universities and the private sector. This problem of segmental balance has been left largely unresolved and there simply is no viable plan or mechanism on the horizon to redress this imbalance of funding.

Private giving by corporations and individuals adds to the pattern of unequal support. In the year 1966–1967, the University of California endowment had a market value of $271,254,000, and voluntary support received for the year was $30,128,408 (American Alumni Council, 1969, pp. 34–35). Comparable data are not available for the state colleges or the community colleges, but it is not likely that the combined totals would reach 5 per cent of the university figures.

Awareness has grown concerning the effect of federal funding. In 1965, the state assembly requested the Coordinating Council for Higher Education to examine the magnitude and scope of federal assistance and to recommend organizational changes required to coordinate such programs. The council's report merely suggested that the council should be involved where programs concern two or more segments. More significantly, the report also asked the council's director "to review the advantages and disadvantages of a policy by the federal government of making institutional grants to institutions of higher education and to fully inform the council of this matter no later than the March 1969 meeting" (Coordinating Council for Higher Education, 1968a, p. 95).

Perhaps the most comprehensive congressional bill on federal funding, which reflects a move toward an institutional grants approach, has been the Miller-Dadario effort. In a special report on the bill, the formulas and estimates for colleges and universities throughout the country were set forth (U.S. Congress, 1969). Thirty per cent of the funds made available would be based upon the projects which research institutions had conducted during the prior three years. This provision accommodates the institutions that had benefited the most from federal assistance. Forty per cent of the funds would be awarded according to numbers of undergraduate students enrolled. This feature of the formula recognized the needs of two-year and four-year colleges. The remaining 30 per cent would be distributed according to the number of advanced science degrees awarded. This figure was weighted to favor sustained graduate programs in the sciences. The application of the formulas was calculated and set forth by state as well as by institutions within the states. The University of California system would receive $31,518,000 as compared to $20,585,000 for the California state colleges. While this ratio would represent an improvement in relative consideration given to the state colleges, the federal fund flow would continue to be the single most important factor affecting support disparities. The imbalance is of such severe proportions that major corrective action is badly needed. Large-scale institutional grants which recognize student enrollment appear to be the best course of action for restoring a semblance of fiscal balance to higher education in the state.

On another tack, Reagan sought information from the Coordinating Council and recommended that the council study nationwide financing of higher education in the hope that they would discover some unique or creative approaches. The findings, published in May 1968, reviewed a series of less-than-consequential sources of revenue and concluded that "the traditional income sources remain the basis for financing institutions of higher education" (Coordinating Council for Higher Education, 1968b, p. 17).

The governor and the legislature will probably continue the classic pattern of using the General Fund to support the university more than the state colleges, and the state colleges more than the community colleges. The liaison between the university and the federal government has permitted the university to become a truly great institution and this gravitational pull of federal dollars has been out of the purview and control of the state of California. Pride in the achievements of the university exists with an uncomfortable realization that neither the governor, the legislature, nor the Coordinating Council for Higher Education has been able to bring about significant fiscal equity in public higher education. The burden rests heavily upon the state colleges because of their almost exclusive reliance upon the General Fund for support. The community colleges are also in trouble with a financial base resting on the local property tax and the General Fund. The California state colleges are an "invisible giant" when federal funds are distributed, and this invisibility is a basic problem which has been left dangling.

Identifying fiscal problems is an easier task than coming up with their solutions. Nevertheless, priority attention must be given to these important issues facing the state college system. Dependence upon the General Fund also means continued administration as a state agency. The two problems are interrelated, and unless significant changes are made the system will continue to labor in a cumbersome and unresponsive way with its resources. The funds available and the flexibility to use them simply do not match the role assigned to the California state colleges.

A search for alternative sources of funding does not reveal many choices for the system. The regionally located colleges have not sought local tax support, and they are not likely to do so without some state plan for local tax relief. High tuition rates meet with formidable resistance as they would destroy the concept of low-cost higher education within the state. Private sector giving has not been of major proportion in terms of the need, and these funds will probably continue to be directed to the private universities and colleges, as well as the University of California. Clearly, then, the General Fund will have to serve as the base, much as it does for the university. But this foundation needs a strong supplementary flow of funds, and the state college system should look for federal help. Although seeking federal funds may not be a popular move, the options are limited. From the state point of view, federal aid may be an acceptable alternative to increasing state support for the colleges.

Securing financial resources is a basic need of all higher education; the problem of the California state colleges, viewed in this context, is not unusual. The establishment of the state college system has not produced substantially more funds or altered significantly the administration of available resources. While the state colleges made financial gains during the 1960s whether or not they advanced within the context of higher education in California is not clear. I believe they did, though the gains have been at high cost to the participants. The achievements of the sixties may be difficult to sustain in this era of public disenchantment with student dissent and political exploitation.

7

New Management for Higher Education

Jesse M. Unruh

In 1961 California began a full-scale experiment with voluntary coordination of public and private higher education.[1] This experiment was undertaken in response to the recommendations of the 1960 Master Plan for Higher Education and with the blessings and cooperation of the legislature, the governor, the three segments of public higher education, and the principal spokesmen for the private colleges and universities. The vehicle for this experiment has been the Coordinating Council for Higher Education, a body originally made up of fifteen members, three from each public segment, three from the private institutions, and three representatives of the public, to which three additional public members were added a few years ago. Most recently, the council membership from the segments has

[1] This chapter adapted from "New Management for California's Higher Education Enterprise," *Compact,* June 1969, 4–8.

been decreased to one representative from each segment; the substantial balance is now the public members.

I think the results of this experiment are now fully evident: Voluntary coordination has failed. Interestingly, there is general agreement on this fact among all who have taken a close look—all except those officials who have always opposed effective statewide coordination as an infringement upon their essential freedom. A survey conducted by business leaders at the behest of the governor, a study sponsored by the Coordinating Council itself and undertaken by the Academy for Educational Development, and the report of a two-year staff study for the Joint Legislative Committee on Higher Education all have found that there is inadequate planning; continuing needless duplication of programs, facilities, and functions; an absence of cooperative effort and other clear evidence of a lack of effective coordination among the various segments of public and private higher education in California.

The late Arthur Coons, president of Occidental College and one of the principal authors of the 1960 Master Plan, wrote the following about the period 1965–1967 in a recent book entitled *Crisis in California Higher Education* (Coons, 1968).

Within each segment there has been some struggle between and among institutions, but the main struggles have been between and among the segments themselves as major "corporate" estates vying for advantage, favor, and finance. At times these segments have sought or have found common ground. At other times, and much more characteristically, they have been vying vigorously for their own interests, often with not much evidence to support the idea of a commonly respected profession, manifesting bitter animosity, charges, and counter claims.

In sum, the system of voluntary coordination established under California's Master Plan has done little to foster the orderly growth of higher education.

In California the term higher education embraces at least three separate statewide educational systems. The University of California operates nine campuses and some thirty other facilities under the direction of the Board of Regents. The California state colleges are nineteen liberal arts colleges joined together under the administration of the chancellor and his staff and governed by a

Board of Trustees. Since July 1, 1968, the public community colleges, of which there are more than ninety campuses maintained by local districts, have been linked together to a degree yet to be determined under the Board of Governors of the California community colleges. There are also forty-nine independent institutions which are members of the Association of Independent California Colleges and Universities, plus thirty-one other accredited private institutions spread up and down the state. In addition, there is a State Scholarship and Loan Commission which administers the state scholarship and fellowship programs, the California Maritime Academy, and the Coordinating Council for Higher Education.

As these facts suggest, California's higher education structure is at once highly stratified and highly fragmented. No single agency has authority and responsibility for statewide policy development, the establishment of new institutions, the approval of new programs, or comprehensive financial planning. In past years each of the three public segments has been able to add enrollment, develop new programs and activities, build new facilities, and budget available funds with little attention to similar activity and expansion in the other two public segments.

No agency below the level of the governor and the legislature has the authority to reallocate resources among the segments according to changes in statewide needs and objectives. The Coordinating Council was intentionally denied such authority when it was established in 1961 as a voluntary body controlled by segmental representatives. The Master Plan Survey Team explicitly rejected the idea of a single board with effective governing powers. Instead, it recommended the establishment of an agency which is more like a protective association than a coordinating board and which cannot serve a more significant role without substantial overhaul of its powers, duties, and composition and without some curtailment of the constitutional autonomy of the University of California.

New programs such as equal opportunity programs, computer-assisted instruction, educational research and data processing centers are established within each segment with little regard for what is being done within the other segments. Except for isolated informal arrangements between individual institutions with a strong common interest, the three segments are operated as if they were in three different states. The consequence is duplication of effort, needless competition and, most seriously, lost opportunities for productive cooperation in teaching, research, and community service activities.

It is increasingly evident that the state can no longer afford a laissez-faire attitude regarding the organization of higher education, that California must now begin to bring together her educational resources so that they may be employed more efficiently on the one hand and with greater freedom from needless constraints on the other. California, like other large states, must now look for new forms of organization and governance of higher education which will make it possible to achieve these goals.

Unfortunately, the 1960 Master Plan for Higher Education in California was not really a master plan. It might have been described more accurately as a temporary negotiated settlement between opposing interests as to their shares of the educational market, or, more simply, a cease-fire agreement. I suspect that this statement may be received with mixed feelings of surprise and pleasure by legislators and officials of other states who have been bombarded for years with propaganda about California's achievements in this sphere. Nevertheless, it is true: California has just begun to establish true educational planning and an effective structure of coordination for higher education.

The principal objectives of statewide coordination or governance of higher education are fairly simple: to see that the primary educational needs of the people of the state are being met throughout the state and in as efficient and effective a manner as possible. Programming and fiscal planning on a comprehensive basis and with broad participation are the principal methods of achieving these objectives, along with evaluation, cost-benefit analysis, and continuing experimentation, dissemination, and encouragement of new ideas as to how the educational needs of the state can best be met. The coordinating or governing agency cannot become involved in the administration of individual campuses or programs. Rather, each institution, according to its resources, experience, special characteristics, and motivation, must manage its affairs so as to contribute most effectively to the educational needs of the state and the nation.

Basically, the goal is to create an organizational environment which fosters responsive and creative diversity.

The best way to make this happen is much less clear, although I think we have learned something from past mistakes. At the state level the issue may be described as one of coordination versus integration. Coordination has been and must be voluntary. The Coordinating Council was recommended as a way to bring the segments together to discuss their mutual interests and to give an appearance of unity of purpose without endangering their basic sense of independence. Accordingly, the powers and duties of the council were written in very general terms, and the council was limited for the most part to advising the governing boards of the segments. Appropriate to these objectives, the public was given a very small place in the council's membership.

The few achievements of California's Coordinating Council can be listed quickly. It has succeeded in restraining the university and the state colleges from succumbing too easily to pressures for the establishment of new campuses. It has played a significant role in the annual determination of faculty salary increases. The council has been a very useful agency in the allocation of new federal aid funds. In recent years it has been, on occasion, a forum for discussion of several important policy issues. But beyond these activities the council has not had a significant impact upon public or private higher education in California.

One reason for this ineffectiveness is that the council has rarely stepped beyond the bounds of the Master Plan with respect to problems of enrollment distribution, state funding, and the expansion of educational opportunities. It has not attempted to develop short- or long-range programs and fiscal plans for higher education. A solution to the problem of the state college drive for university status has not been found. It has had little impact on the growth and development of the community colleges. Because of the minor role the council has played, membership has not been elevated to the level of the university's Board of Regents or the Board of Trustees of the state colleges.

I am convinced that these failures are inevitable for a voluntary coordinating agency which is simply added to an existing

pattern of interests and which lacks the authority to override the
decisions of constituent members. As long as these constituent
organizations or segments remain as the basic structural units of the
system they will remain paramount, and the governing board and
administrators of each segment will continue to give first priority to
the interests of that segment. This would also be true, I believe, of
some form of "mandatory" coordination with the coordinating
agency's powers and duties carefully spelled out.

Perhaps I can best illustrate what I consider necessary to
organize higher education in a large state by describing the principal
elements of a new proposal for California developed by the Joint
Committee on Higher Education. Under this proposal the university and state college systems would be merged into a single unified
system of public higher education; the new structure would also ab-
sorb the powers and duties which have been assigned to the Board of
Governors of the community colleges. This new system is to bear the
name of the University of California. A single governing board
would be assigned statewide responsibility for the general governance
of the unified system, for the allocation of state and federal appropriations, and for the development of long-range program and fiscal
planning. Although the community colleges would retain their basic
relationship to their local boards and districts, they too would come
within the jurisdiction and policies of the proposed new board. The
existing Coordinating Council, of course, would be eliminated.

Below the level of the statewide board there would be an administrative and coordinating body for each major region of the
state. These regional units would be responsible for focusing the
various public higher education resources on the needs of each
region and for monitoring the implementation of statewide and
regional policies. Within each region the individual institutions
would function as university (graduate) centers, liberal arts colleges,
community colleges, or specialized institutions according to the needs
of the region and their own capabilities for service. The individual
institutions would be expected to function within this structure
with no less freedom than they now enjoy within the existing
systems, and in some cases much more.

In its organizational aspects this proposal has the general
characteristics of a federation and follows the basic pattern of

government within each state. In this sense the proposal would substitute a form of federalism for a very loose form of confederation among the existing public institutions of higher education. Higher education in California has become much too large an enterprise to operate effectively and efficiently in a disjointed, segmented manner. Although some opponents of consolidation point with alarm at the sheer size of the enterprise which would be created, the sheer size of the present enterprise makes almost intolerable the existing stratification and fragmentation.

There are four basic objectives behind the proposal. The first is to eliminate the organizational barriers that have been built up between the University of California campuses, the state colleges, and the community colleges, so that all the resources of public higher education can be employed with maximum effectiveness. The second is to free individual institutions from the unnecessary constraints upon their development which now result from inclusion in one of the segments. The plan is intended to foster educational pluralism, to reopen the channels of development which, intentionally or otherwise, have been closed under the segmental form of organization.

The third basic objective of the proposed reorganization is to insure that planning, financing, and evaluation will be done continuously, comprehensively, and in a manner which permits informed review by the governor and the legislature. By bringing fundamental responsibilities for planning, financing, and evaluation within the compass of a single board, the public will have some assurance, for the first time, that all aspects of higher education and its links with the public schools are systematically considered in the largest possible planning context. I am persuaded that by no other organizational means can the full values of a large, complex, and highly differentiated educational system be developed and rationally managed.

This structure will also permit important changes in the method of allocating state funds for current expense and capital outlay. The creation of a single statewide agency to deal with all of public higher education (and with any state aid to private higher education) will enable the legislature and the governor to delegate greater authority to deal with the many competing interests which now converge at the state level. At the same time the legislature would gain a much more comprehensive and understandable view of higher education, its functions and financing, during the budget process. With the development of comprehensive long-range fiscal and program planning by the statewide board, individual institutions can be given substantially greater responsibility for their current financial operations. The new board will be expected to develop a system of allocations to the individual institutions based upon unit costs and performance standards rather than detailed budget approval. The proposed regional bodies will be expected to assist the state board by monitoring the equity and efficiency of the allocation system within each region.

Obviously, this proposal represents an attempt to gain the benefits of centralized planning and governance at the state level and the benefits of decentralized administration and operation at the regional and campus levels. In this I believe it is responsive to the point made by current critics in regard to what they call the "sickness of government"; that is, the failure of government to perform effectively those functions for which it is suited and to keep out of activities in which its intervention is marked by waste, confusion, and public disenchantment. The attempt to combine governing and doing, two essentially incompatible functions, will paralyze decision making, whether in a buisness corporation or, on a larger scale, in state and federal government. The cure is not simply recentralization, which implies a weakening of the central agency. Top management must be freed from operating responsibilities so that it can concentrate on decision making and direction. Operating responsibilities must be given to the principal operating units, nongovernmental institutions and agencies, whether they be colleges and universities or hospitals, businesses, labor unions, and so on. The guiding policy, in economic terms, should not be a return to laissez-faire but a restructuring toward a greater institutional specialization of labor.

In California, the governing of higher education has become highly fragmented. Governors and legislators are called upon or pushed into the direct exercise of governing powers in times of crisis. Under the pressure of events and not being accustomed to this responsibility, they frequently become entangled in the basic operation of the institutions with a destructive and demoralizing impact. Such occurrences would be much less likely, it seems to me, if there were already a statewide governing body for higher education (or perhaps, where feasible, for all education) which could be held responsible and accountable for carrying out the broader policies of the state as they concern higher education, research, and other related public service.

Of course, no organizational structure however carefully devised will guarantee necessary and desired changes in educational policies and performance. It can, however, make change possible and even encourage movement toward an improved management and operation of educational institutions. Some of the changes which I hope for in California include the following: greater coordination and cooperation of programs and policies between public and private institutions of higher education, both statewide and regionally; a strengthening of individual campus advisory boards so that they take on some of the community relations functions which segmental and statewide governing boards are unable to perform well; the development of regional service centers to provide specialized high-cost services in such areas as data processing, the storage of specialized resources, admissions processing, and purchasing; the development of special purpose institutions, particularly on campuses which may not otherwise draw a sufficient number of students; the development of jointly sponsored instructional programs and the joint appointment of faculty, especially in new areas of instruction in which each institution does not have sufficient resources of its own; the establishment of research and development centers which utilize talent from the community colleges and four-year liberal arts colleges as well as the university campuses.

Finally, there may be the possibility of developing a regular channel for strong new ideas as to the nature and content of instruction, research, and other public service so that these ideas do not go unheeded until the demand behind them erupts into a crisis which threatens the whole structure. Our concepts could be revised as to the composition of governing boards, opening those boards to membership for faculty, student, and administration representatives. Perhaps an independent commission or office might be established to perform both as a kind of ombudsman on a statewide basis and as an open channel for new ideas. Whatever the solution, we have got to find a way to make higher education more responsive on a continuing basis to students, faculty, and community groups who still see higher education as a major force for freedom and enlightenment in our society.

8

‌⌐⌐⌐⌐⌐⌐⌐⌐⌐⌐⌐⌐⌐⌐⌐⌐⌐⌐

Politics and Purse Strings

Robert G. Thompson

‌⌐⌐⌐⌐⌐⌐⌐⌐⌐⌐⌐⌐⌐⌐⌐⌐⌐⌐

Before looking into the California state colleges, one must first glance at the big scene. These are nervous times for educators, for things are happening all over the country that reveal some deep disorders in both the academic and the political communities. Thoughtful members of both groups are seeking solutions to the many legitimate demands for change. Most disturbing, however, to those who seek understanding of these complex problems are the simple solutions gratuitously offered by the more excitable portions of our society who demand immediate action to quell all campus unrest, whether legitimate or not. When these demands create a political reaction against the colleges, trouble threatens.

The gap is increasing between our nation's youth and its elders who control the political power apparatus and the educational bureaucracy. The immediate future will probably determine whether this gap will be closed or whether each side is going to give up on the other and arm itself for political warfare. If the latter happens, higher education can only suffer, for publicly controlled colleges and universities are so widespread in our nation that what happens to them sends reverberations through the whole academic world.

There is today a growing hostility between public higher education institutions and the communities which support them. California became a focal point of national attention when the discontent of a significant number of students in its public universities and colleges erupted into disorder to the point where the political community has reacted vigorously against its educational system. To get to the root of the animosity one must be aware that the academic functions of institutions of higher learning in the United States have always created a tension with the general public. Occupied by "people who think otherwise," universities and colleges are, or should be, skeptical observers of everything they survey as well as creators of new ideas which often challenge the "conventional wisdom" of the times. When this traditional tension is compounded by student and faculty upheavals against the higher educational apparatus itself for not doing more to goad the community into changing its traditional practices, dark suspicions are raised about an already tense situation. In California the political hysterias of the past have had a noticeable effect on higher education. The loyalty-oath controversy of the late 1940s is a good example, and its scars are still apparent.

The current political crisis in higher education is an extension of the traditional argument over what an institution of higher learning should be doing. Modern universities and colleges are often vast enterprises governed by educational executives whom Thorstein Veblen described as "captains of erudition." Some of these institutions have tried and largely succeeded in making peace with society's powerful interest groups and even have received entry into the political establishment in some areas. Many large, public-supported institutions have contented themselves with supplying the corporate and professional communities with a continuing supply of trained human material to man their bureaucracies and to practice professional arts and sciences. These trained products are well received and given corporate blessing if they can do their jobs without rocking the various boats on which they ship out upon graduation. As "students" this collection of human raw material has been quantified, classified, and categorized with scientific dispassion and pumped through the educational machinery at the lowest possible cost, like crude oil through a refinery. Students are expected to be diligent, serious, and grateful to the political authorities who have provided them their great opportunity.

Trouble began, however, when some of the students, encouraged by some faculty, began to resent the impersonal efficiency of their training and demanded that their education do more than equip them for a box in an organizational hierarchy. Free speech movements, teach-ins, love-ins, drop-outs, freak-outs, protest literature, and "new left" politics began to overshadow the traditional and publicly accepted good clean fun of beer busts, pep rallies, football, and inebriated old grads at the fraternity bash. A shocked community resented this student and faculty irascibility and the radical political and social criticism emanating from the colleges and universities. It was a betrayal of the taxpayers' generous support—a vicious biting of the hand—that caused the most bitter political reaction. In California, the whole thing became such an important issue in the 1966 gubernatorial campaign that one observer could comment without gross exaggeration that candidate Reagan won the election over University of California student Mario Savio of the free speech movement. The abrupt dismissal of university President Clark Kerr shortly after the election and the Reagan administration's proposed tuition charges at both the university and the colleges underscored the political reaction to disorders. The tension has not abated, nor is the quarrel over the purpose of higher education resolved. Students have discovered political power and seem bent on using it to make their educations more significant.

The governing authorities of higher educational institutions have rarely included students, with the result that a student's perspective of his education has seldom affected institutional policy. All too frequently regents, trustees, or other governing bodies have regarded the universities and colleges as service industries to commercial interests they represent. Faculty tend to look upon their institutions as providers of career opportunities in which they can advance themselves professionally. Contact with students has become increasingly reduced and remote as research and consultative opportunities make more demands on professors' time. In short, the whole purpose of most universities and many colleges has moved

away from a concern for the enlightenment of students to a preoccupation with the prestige of its faculty and its place in the hierarchy of "great institutions of higher learning."

The students want a voice in the educational policy governing their institutions. The demands range from getting a seat on
policy-making committees to the more radical call for a complete
change even if it means "grinding the university to a halt" or "bringing it to its knees." The public and its politicians view these demands
with alarm and see a dangerous move toward the "European" concept of student activism where, as one California politician put it,
"the universities become staging areas for violence and revolution."

The whole California political scene has been rocked by
student power. For a while the state colleges were little more than
nervous observers of the difficulties which burst upon the University
of California. Their hopes for continued tranquility and a political
gain over their unadmitted rival were dashed, however, when San
Francisco State College was confronted with an outburst of student
protest. Student unrest has opened the political bag, but its contents
must be examined in a broader perspective.

Politics in lush and bountiful California has always had its
flamboyant dimensions. The state has been the spawning ground for
bizarre political schemes such as "Ham and Eggs," The Townsend
Plan, and End Poverty in California. Then, too, all kinds of political
cults flourish in the fertile ground of a rapidly expanding population
—Birchers, Nazis, Communists, Free-lovers, Christian Anti-Com-
munists, and mystics of various sorts find California a comfortable
home. Its politicians have ranged from progressive Republicans like
Hiram Johnson and Earl Warren, through the moderate Democrats
such as Edmund G. Brown and Jesse Unruh, to the frugal and
photogenic Republicanism of Ronald Reagan. Swingers and squares
have all made the political scene, yet California has managed to
build a good state government and an exceptional higher education
system.

These have developed because there is also much more sober
dimension to California politics. Beneath the almost continuous
political spectaculars produced by campaign management firms well
schooled in Hollywood techniques of show-biz is the apparatus of
government which does the job. Included are a well paid and
equipped legislature that employs an unusual number of experts to

advise it, a vast, well paid, and comparatively highly skilled bureaucracy which enjoys one of the most protective merit systems in the nation, and probably the best judicial system of any state in the union. Higher education is right in the thick of things with its lobbyists, who are referred to by such impressive titles as vice president–educational relations or director of governmental affairs. The function of these people is to get what they can for their institutions. For many years the representative of the University of California was one of the most skilled lobbyists in the state. During this period the state colleges had no such agent and relied on college presidents, faculty, and a host of professional organizations to represent them. The result was a cacophony of voices often contradicting one another on the desires of individual colleges as well as the whole system. The university enjoyed the discordant voice of the state colleges and even resisted their transition from teachers colleges to general liberal arts institutions.

Higher education in California is a highly competitive undertaking. The university is number one and plans to stay that way (Tool, 1966). The state colleges are number two, with all the complexes of second-class status, but are pressed by number three, the community colleges. All three want money and lots of it. The university gets most of it in the form of salaries, teaching loads, research support, and Nobel Prize winners on the faculty. The state colleges get lower salaries, higher teaching loads, no significant research support, overcrowded campuses, and less of everything else. The community colleges, supported mainly by local funds, want more state aid.

Brokerage politics requires that pressure groups must work within a system of constantly shifting alliances with other pressure groups on particular issues. Higher education in California is not a united pressure group. The university does not need the state colleges. In fact, no one seems to need the state colleges, although they do gain allies on some issues. The price is sometimes high, however, for pressure groups have a habit of demanding a return. For example, Fresno State College once received a winemaking curriculum it did not particularly desire, and there are some required courses here and there throughout the system whose academic justification can only be explained as an expedient concession to power.

With the power positions of the component parts established

and generally accepted, the educational institutions proceed to use
their status to their best possible advantage—that is, either to maintain their position or to improve it. The university argues it must
maintain its prestige or its faculty will be pirated by the villainous
Ivy League institutions, constantly waiting to snatch its prestigious
faculty and their research grants. The state colleges say they must
have more money for salaries and research or they will be unable to
recruit and retain adequate faculty and therefore sink further into
the quagmire of mediocrity. They also apologize for second-rate
status and try to identify themselves as unique by emphasizing that
state colleges are teaching institutions and must attract good
teachers. Such an apologia is based upon the implied but fallacious
assumption that good teachers do not do research and that researchers
cannot teach. Community colleges, abetted by local government
pressure groups, seek a larger share of state funds. The relative
power of these groups at present is on the side of the university, but
the rapid growth of the state colleges and the large number of
graduates turned out by them annually is a potential and bother-
some challenge to the university. As yet there seem to be more university graduates in positions of influence, and its alumni are better
organized, but this may change rapidly in the future.

One ramification of the potential strength of the state colleges is reflected in the way campuses are located throughout the
state. The state college campuses are funded and approved by legislative act, and their ultimate location is often more of a testimony to
the strength of an individual legislator or group of legislators from
a certain area than an educational need. Some legislators have thus
"identified" with their local campus and protect it like a mother hen
when it is attacked. Someone once described state colleges as the
California version of post offices, since almost every legislator would
like one in his district. Sometimes the whole thing becomes ridicu-
lous, as it did several years ago when a powerful senator from a
sparsely populated area near the southern border of the state, who
happened to be chairman of the senate finance committee, tucked
away a few million dollars for a college in his area. The proposed
college was dubbed "Wetback U" among concerned staff people,
who could find no other source for students than people slipping
across the border from Mexico. The pressure was intense and only
diminished after the senator retired.

Scattering state colleges all over the state has been followed by establishing campuses of the University of California in the proximate areas or building up those that may have been there, as, for example, the expansion of the Davis agricultural campus to a full-blown branch of the university. Both systems have expanded at a rapid rate, and the expense is terrific. Educational logic, while given pious deference in justifying new locations and programs, is really a minor consideration in the competitive moves by the two systems.

It is an old cliche among budget analysts that most significant public policy is made with money. Grandiose declarations of public policy can wither through lack of funds, while other activities hardly mentioned in the statutes can flourish luxuriously if fertilized with enough dollars. The Master Plan for Higher Education makes certain that the legislature keeps a tight control of the state colleges' purse. Indeed, this was a major consideration when the law was enacted and grew out of long frustration with the University of California's fiscal autonomy. The university receives large sums of money from the state but also has sources of funds if state monies are not forthcoming. The control of expenditures rests with the Regents and they are thus able to authorize a new academic or building program even though the legislature says no. Understandably, legislators and governors do not like this situation very well.

The state colleges do not have such freedom. A minutely detailed line item budget, thoroughly sifted by a brace of budget analysts in the Department of Finance and the office of the legislative analyst, is presented to the legislature. The Department of Finance prepares the "Governor's Budget," which is the official document sent to the legislature, but the legislative analyst, who reports to a Joint Legislative Budget Committee, carefully turns his microscope on the budget in order to pick up any loose change he might find. Both documents (the executive budget and the legislative analyst's comments upon it) contain a great many policy declarations which may be sound but as often as not reflect the educational prejudices of the people reviewing the budget.

As a former budget analyst in two states, one of them California, I cannot overemphasize the extent of public policy made at this level. This control can take the form of hacking away at requested appropriations for specific programs or of raising all kinds of embarrassing questions about the programs in front of a legislative committee. To illustrate, state colleges depend partially on state support for outside speakers and dramatic productions. Recently a state college produced a highly controversial play entitled *The Beard,* and several state colleges have brought in controversial convocation speakers and paid them with state funds. As usual, political authorities have reacted to these events, since it is an unfortunate fact of political life that unpopular ideas expressed on campuses are good for some headlines and that many politicians, whether out of sincerity or opportunism, take advantage of these situations and make them public issues.

When such a flap occurs, a budget analyst can ride with the outrage, carve out a substantial amount of money itemized for convocation speakers or dramatic productions, and possibly gain support. If, on the other hand, he is sympathetic to academic freedom and the free exchange of ideas, he can defend the colleges and support their request. Many budget analysts are highly respected by legislators and are often looked upon as experts in their field. Very often they can use this respect to get their way, particularly if their prejudices are presented as objective. The more humble budget men are sometimes awed by their responsibility and potential power, but those who enjoy power are only too anxious to find out how much they have; thus educational policy can and often does depend on the attitudes, collective or individual, of the men preparing the budgets for executive and legislative approval.

In order to satisfy the ceremonies of being scientific or objective, fiscal experts have developed a variety of formulas which they apply to state college financial affairs. These formulas are often completely arbitrary and frequently come off the top of someone's head; when inquiry is made into their derivation and what criteria were used to develop them, it is often apparent that their only justification is habitual usage. But they are there, and budgetary ritual requires their use. The square feet per student in each classroom, the student-teacher ratios, square feet for faculty office space, unit teaching loads, percentage of total faculty in academic ranks, and staffing on the basis of full-time equivalent students are just a few of the formulas used to govern state college appropriations. Elaborate statistics are gathered and figures are pushed back and forth to arrive at dollar amounts for educational support.

Budgeting becomes a highly skilled game in which those seeking money attempt to outmaneuver those who control the budget. Skilled players have developed a variety of gambits. Padding is one of the more common and rather crude ploys, wherein bloated figures are presented with the hope that the inevitable cuts will leave enough for what actually needs to be done. The diversionary tactic also is used: a big new item is inserted to draw reaction and call attention away from the rest of the budget.

In fact, line item budgeting is a very wasteful method of using money, since the lack of flexibility in expenditure and the large amounts spent on the control devices of budget analysis and post-audits of items are very costly. Such a budgeting procedure also rests upon the demeaning assumption that institutional administrators lack the necessary expertness and integrity to manage their own expenditures for the programs for which they are responsible. But it is politically popular since legislators seem more comfortable debating the cost of a typewriter than alternative programs for a good education for students.

Historically, the budget moves of the state colleges have been disappointing. Several factors contribute to this, not the least of which is the lack of a united voice by trustees, administrators, faculty, and students. Another past weakness has been the state college's amateurish approach to lobbying activities. The reorganization of the state colleges under the Master Plan has provided a lobbyist, but he has had continuous problems in trying to get an agreed upon policy to present to the legislature. Also, academic people have a tendency to present a rational argument to public officials which is theoretically desirable and compatible with professional ethics. Unfortunately, however, this is not the best way to secure results when engaged in a power struggle. As one legislator put it to a delegation of faculty seeking salary increases, "If you guys would get organized and flex your muscles instead of coming down here to lecture us on the public interest, you could march in and take your raise. You've got lots of power but you don't seem to know where it is."

The long frustration of the state colleges with budgetary politics has led them to seek the promised land of fiscal autonomy. Hopefully, this would let them meet educational needs more effectively and with more flexibility. They want what the university already has because they feel it would help alleviate their second-class status of poor relative to their rich big brother. Also, the colleges could then be more dignified and less obsequious in their budget requests if they could build some reserve funds to finance new programs. No matter how much the state colleges talk poor and plead for fiscal autonomy, however, the governor and the legislature are not very impressed. Neither is the university. Even though a gesture or two has been made toward the state colleges, budgetary politics still finds them working their formulas while being hounded by budget analysts and auditors, with the result that their whole educational program has become extremely rigid. New ideas or the experimental use of faculty either inside or outside their twelve-unit teaching load must either be justified to the legislature, governor, and the bureaucracy or bootlegged, by using instructional funds for other purposes. Many college officials shy away from such devices since they fear the wrath of the state auditors. Generally, most faculty feel that all of the colleges are marching, lean and hungry, in an unimaginative lock-step to the cadence of budget men and under the scrutiny of cold-eyed auditors who will punish anyone who breaks ranks. The last question asked, of course, is whether students have learned anything during their undergraduate years.

Budgeting is very much a part of brokerage politics since it has a profound effect on the power position of the agencies seeking funds. In the educational competition in California, there are many reasons why the governor and legislature are not anxious to relinquish their control, but the primary consideration is the fact that to control the purse is to control the program. The university also knows this very well, and if the state colleges did gain meaningful fiscal autonomy the competition between the two systems, both for money and in educational programs, could become much more intense.

A system of brokerage has been developed within the state college bureaucracy to try to get all factions organized so they will be heard. The statewide academic senate represents faculty from all of the colleges, but its chronic complaint has been that it has no power and no one listens to it. A council of college presidents exists to make the views of the "branch managers" known to the head office, although there have been complaints that no one listens to it either.

Deans get together to share their views, and students are also heard from occasionally. The more cynical participants and observers of this whole scene regard the process as one of creating enough organization of separate factions so they check one another out. Actually, the motive for establishing these various advisory boards may very well have been to improve communication, but in actual practice communication seems poor.

Politicians often wonder, with much justification, just who is spokesman for the colleges. The trustees employ a lobbyist who is often in contradiction with the statewide academic senate. Confusion abounds, and the state college babble of voices is in definite contrast to the well organized and seldom contradicted pitch of the University of California, whose faculty is apolitical at the state level. This situation also considerably weakens the state colleges' legislative program, because they cannot pull themselves up to the negotiating table effectively if they are fighting among themselves for the only chair.

Unfortunately, the official voice of the state colleges is often the least representative of faculty viewpoints. Legislators and other political figures are themselves divided on whether the official position of the trustees and the chancellor is really the one to heed or whether the faculty should be given the most attention. Some lawmakers seriously want to know what the faculty feels is best for the system, while others want to know whether the best source of votes stems from trustee or faculty approval. The latter question would be most difficult to answer.

The California state colleges have grown from a haphazard collection of teachers colleges into a large multicampus system of general arts and science institutions. We offer our students one of the widest ranges of undergraduate programs in the nation, and we are increasingly developing graduate programs through the master's degree. Some state colleges are even beginning to develop joint doctoral programs to be offered in conjunction with the University of California. We are an educational supermarket, mass man's hope for inexpensive enlightenment and his passport to suburbia. But we are more than that, much more, which is why so many highly competent faculty devote their lives to the system. We are the answer to many hopes, dreams, and sacrifices of parents for a better world for their children. We get lots of bright, energetic, tough-minded, and unbelievably ignorant raw material to convert into bachelors of arts and sciences. The process involves a great test of talent for students and teachers alike, and the experience is often one of the most exciting either will ever have. Adequacy or mediocrity may be our planned place in the educational pecking order, but we do not have to be that way in the classroom if faculty and students demand that it not be so.

The future of higher education generally and the state colleges particularly is, as I have tried to make clear, facing a crucial political test. To meet this challenge is going to require some cool thinking and statesmanship which has not been particularly evident in California in the past, nor does it seem to be now. Perhaps if higher education were not so competitive between systems and regents and trustees better understood their functions, it would be possible to unite and effectively defend the whole higher education structure. But when vying for favor among political brokers is the practice, education in general can be torn apart rapidly if it has no united front or eloquent spokesmen.

This is the current crisis in California education politics. The entire educational apparatus has proven weak in resisting a calculated attack under the guise of economy in government or law and order on the campus. Had higher education developed a solid defense of educational purpose and put it ahead of expedient political compromises to gain funds or a new campus, it would have been in a much better position to defend itself. All of this is not the fault of the politicians but a failure of educators adequately to justify their function to the general public. The big task ahead is to prove to the people that education, with all its controversy and disturbances, is the best hope yet discovered for free men.

9

Statewide Academic Senate: The Sound and the Fury

Jerome Richfield

The academic senate of the California state colleges, established in 1963, has faced a series of crises which have dampened the hopes and challenged the faith of the faculties who saw it so bravely launched and who now fear that the current political waves will engulf it. At this time of social tension and polarization, with the strange pincers of inflation and recession squeezing educational budgets, and with hard hats, hard heads, hard work, and hard times pressing upon the entire educational establishment in California, it may seem quixotic to review the history of the academic senate. Yet perhaps not. Such a review may help all who cherish learning and value education to choose new paths and directions.

In the beginning the academic senate of the California state colleges was eager to develop a modicum of experience and a hint of stature. Unlike its sister institution, the University of California, in which faculty governance was already successfully operative, the state college system, gathered together from a clutch of semiautonomous colleges, had no tradition of collective action nor much of faculty governance. Under the relatively permissive if bureaucratic aegis of the Department of Education, subject to intrusions from the Department of Finance from which the constitution protected the university, the California state colleges had nevertheless grown and prospered. And all of California looked forward to greater growth and success under the new Board of Trustees and the Master Plan for Higher Education.

Yet in 1971 not only the California state colleges but the University of California and all education were under scrutiny, under pressure, and under attack. Perhaps the most virulent attacks were being made upon faculty governance. And, ironically, the highest administrative echelons sought to curtail faculty governance in order to demonstrate their own responsiveness and responsibility in times of unrest.

In the summer of 1970 the president of the University of California addressed a memorandum to the Regents in which he outlined a plan for improving administrative governance and faculty participation. He spoke about the changes which have placed "great burdens and strains" upon traditional modes of operation. His memorandum reflects some of the sentiment already voiced very much more bluntly by the chancellor of the state colleges who responded to public criticism of education by describing consultative procedures with faculty as a "kaffee-klatsch" form of governance that is too cumbersome to serve today's need for swift decision making.

Procedural changes and shifting attitudes that might result in some sudden trauma to members of the university faculty senate proved only to reinforce the academic senate's long-held conviction about its own negligible influence on state college administration. Whereas the president of the university claims that many of the decisions and plans which must be made cannot be well made except with the active participation of the faculty in the planning and decision making, the chancellor explains his repudiation of faculty decision making by recourse to something he calls the principle of accountability. Thus, while the university senate is surely having its power and influence curtailed and its relation to administration modified, the president of the university has still acknowledged that at the heart of the problem of administrative governance of the university is the relationship between the administration and the faculty, and the role played by each in determining what things are done and how they are done. By contrast, in the California state colleges the movement is to eliminate what precious little faculty participation has been allowed to develop and to make inroads into basic faculty prerogatives. Thus, the question is not what the role of the faculties and their senates shall be, but who can be fired for what he does and says and how the power to dismiss can be vested in the chancellor.

At the September 1970 meeting the Board of Trustees of the California state colleges voted to eliminate the only vestige of faculty decision making at the statewide level in the system. The newly created grievance and disciplinary procedures were changed on short notice to transform the decisions of the chancellor's review panel into mere advice to the chancellor. These changes struck so at the heart of any cooperation, of any shared responsibility, and of any process by which the profession could police itself that for the third or fourth time in just eight years most members of the academic senate of the California state colleges found themselves seriously considering dissolving the senate, or at least adjourning *sine die,* rather than stand as nothing more effective than a buffer between the administration and the more militant faculty organizations calling for some form of collective bargaining.

The movement toward collective bargaining as an alternative to the academic senate reached a peak in 1967. In that year the senate commissioned studies of collective bargaining and with other faculty organizations began the job of educating their colleagues about the issues and answers involved in the approach long advocated by unions. To deal with increased faculty discontent, the trustees passed a resolution that declared its support of the senate by affirming the concept of shared authority as the proper professional alternative to collective bargaining. The *AAUP Bulletin* (Winter 1967) proclaimed it a landmark resolution by the governing body of one of the largest systems of higher education in the

United States. The *Bulletin* gave the text of the resolution, which endorsed the AAUP's 1966 statement on government, and reprinted the commendatory telegram sent to the chairman of the trustee's faculty and staff affairs committee by the general secretary of the AAUP.

The telegram spelled out the understanding created by the trustee action: that it is not desirable to order faculty-administration relationships on the basis of employer-employee patterns. The telegram also pointed out that the importance and meaning of the principle of shared authority are set forth in the AAUP 1966 Statement on Government of Colleges and Universities referred to in the resolution adopted by the board. Faculty discussions of collective bargaining diminished very noticeably after this trustee action. Whatever encouragement faculty might have received from the board's endorsement of the AAUP principles was, however, short lived. In the three years since the action, the Reagan administration has had the opportunity to make a significant number of appointments to the Board of Trustees, and the orientation of the board has become steadily more autocratic. It has consistently rejected senate complaints about lack of consultation and the general failure of state college administration to permit any sharing of authority. One of the governor's more explicit supporters on the board has made the rather shrill observation that "faculty must give up its obsession with usurping the powers of administration."

While the principle of shared authority is clearly rejected by some trustees and very poorly understood by others, the fact that the board adopted it as trustee policy three years ago is not even known by many. What primarily disturbs members of the senate, however, is their growing belief that the academic senate was never seriously intended to participate effectively in the governance of the California state colleges.

The original formation and development of the senate in 1962 was careful, thoughtful, and serious, undertaken with elaborate concern for consultation. As we shall see later, this stands in marked contrast to the simplicity with which senate action was dismissed by the chancellor on the occasion of their first disagreement.

In April 1962, the chancellor brought together the chairmen of the various faculty councils to begin planning the development of a statewide faculty senate. He appointed the Phase I Committee, which consisted of a member of his own staff, three college presidents, and three faculty representatives to prepare recommendations as to the governing principles of the statewide senate and to suggest procedures for its function. The committee's report, submitted in July 1962, suggested that the senate could provide a wide base for the development of policies for the system, become a recognized faculty voice to advise the chancellor, and provide an avenue for participation for the faculties. The report ended with the view that the senate should begin with a limited role but should evolve in function and operation. The recommendations of the committee received the chancellor's endorsement, and he moved to implement them.

The chancellor named two presidents to a phase II Committee and the faculty representatives selected five of their members to complete the committee. Three members of the chancellor's staff were appointed to work with the committee. A questionnaire was developed to obtain the reactions of every faculty member to a number of policy issues. The members of the Phase II Committee individually visited campuses during October to discuss the questionnaire with local faculty.

From these visits and the results of the faculty replies to the questionnaire and amplifying documents which were also submitted, a draft of the statewide academic senate constitution was developed. In December 1962 a draft of a statement of principles in the delegation of responsibilities to the faculties and the proposed constitution of the statewide academic senate were discussed at a meeting of faculty council chairmen, presidents, and trustees at Fresno. In January 1963 the final draft of the constitution was sent to each campus for a secret ballot vote of all the faculty on its adoption. When the results were tabulated in February 1963 it was determined that 6,115 ballots had been distributed. A total of 3,312 or 54 per cent were returned. The yes vote was 2,939 or 88.7 per cent of those voting. The academic senate constitution was approved at the March 8, 1963, meeting of the Board of Trustees. The first meeting of the academic senate was held on May 14, 1963.

From the outset, the senate had the problem of establishing authority on two fronts, for both the Board of Trustees and the administrators and faculties of the several colleges indicated some wariness about the new organization. Since few, if any, of the trustees were very familiar with the academic scene and its history, some of them appeared to be impatient with the idea of organizing an "official voice of the faculties of the California state colleges." Yet some attempt was made to develop understanding; and the academic senate, it must be noted, was quite patient about a learning period during which roles could be defined. One attempt at clarification was the trustees' establishment of the Ad Hoc Committee on Development of Policies and Administrative Procedures, composed of trustees, senate representatives, some presidents, and members of the chancellor's staff. This committee reported to the academic senate and to the trustees. Faculty on the committee disagreed with the other members on many issues. The senate established its own special committee which prepared a very full response and rationale for its position and those of the faculty members of the original committee on development. That response, overwhelmingly approved by the senate after several months of meetings, revisions, and thoughtful consideration, was rejected out of hand by the trustees.

The administrations, senates, and faculty councils of the several colleges, on the other hand, were exceedingly jealous of whatever power and influence they had gained. Talk about local autonomy assumed quasi-religious tones at all levels of state college governance. Faculty who feared something could be lost to a statewide group that might grow in stature were often reinforced in their anxious concern by various local administrators, many of whom had enjoyed much greater autonomy before the creation of the system.

In the *Report of Phase I Committee to the Chancellor of the California State Colleges* (1962) a separate entry for autonomy was made in the section providing definitions of pertinent terms and concepts. After defining such terms as *faculty, policy, responsibility,* and *participation,* the report goes on to say that "the individual colleges should enjoy the maximum degree of local autonomy feasible within the range of systemwide requirements and standards. It follows that the body would not interfere with local autonomy and would affect the individual colleges only through the development of general policies applicable to all campuses."

Not long after this statement was approved by all parties the chancellor and two trustees visited a meeting of the academic senate to ask its support for the chancellor's decision to close an art show at one of the colleges. The senate's refusal to act in this matter was not much appreciated, except, of course, by the faculty and administration at the college in question. Ever since, the meaning of the chancellor's endorsement of the Phase I Committee principles has remained unclear, just as it is unclear what, if anything, is implied by the board's endorsement of the 1966 AAUP Statement on Government. Relations between the statewide senate and the local senates are uncertain, but the need for closer ties is evident.

Much of the discontent that has characterized the statewide senate has been attributed by some observers to the fact that members of this body have expected to exert as much influence on statewide governance as local senates generally do upon the administration of the individual colleges. The question of whether or not a local senate is an appropriate model for the statewide senate has been discussed extensively. There are considerable differences between dependence on faculty support by a chancellor and by a college president, in that a president has to work with his faculty day to day while the chancellor works in isolation. There is, if not always a trust, at least a modus vivendi established on a campus.

Given not only the systematic internal ignoring of faculty rights, wishes, and aspirations at the statewide level but also the overt attacks upon the faculty role in general, both from within and without, the leadership of the academic senate over the years has had to develop closer and more systematic relations with the independent faculty organizations throughout the state as well as with public employee and teacher associations. Provisions of the law which call for meeting and conferring with these organizations have sometimes served as a last resort in an attempt to achieve meaningful faculty participation. Staff assistance from the other professional groups has sometimes provided the only way to obtain and disseminate information. And the possibility of organizational sanctions or lawsuits has sometimes seemed more persuasive than reasoning and the presentation of evidence. On the whole, however, the senate has served to stand between the board and these faculty organizations, especially the American Federation of Teachers and the equally outspoken Association of California State College Professors (which merged in 1970). Few senators doubt that the budget for the senate, eliminated until the eleventh hour by the 1970 legislature, was restored chiefly on the basis of the senate's merits as a buffer. On these grounds, the trustees would sometimes make concessions to the senate, thus enabling it to claim that it has kept some bad policies and procedures from being worse. More positive achievements rest with the development of educational matters, such as the new general education program, which were not of particular concern to politicians and for which one senate committee functioned essentially as an extension of the chancellor's staff.

The academic senate faced difficult problems when it considered collective bargaining, a mode perhaps foreign to it, but the actions of the trustees and of the chancellor have helped to move the senate from a no-position stance to one which tends to favor collective bargaining. Actions such as the punitive denial of cost of living increases by the 1970 legislature and unilateral changes in grievance procedures may change attitudes and relationships.

The prime issue during the senate's first year was the question of how the state colleges should react to pressure from the Coordinating Council for the statewide adoption of year-round operation of the colleges. But continuing attention was given to development of procedures and of working relationships between the senate and the chancellor's office. At the November 1962 meeting of the Coordinating Council, university representatives asked for a delay in order to present the issue of year-round operation to their academic senate. The chancellor of the state colleges objected to such a delay and warned that if it were granted then he, too, would carry the matter to his senate. The issue was postponed, and the chancellor met with the Educational Policy Committee of the senate as well as with the senate in plenary session to plead for certain positive recommendations. But the senate was not convinced that year-round operation would achieve its goal of economy, a foresight which time seems to have justified amply. More time was needed to study the problems engendered by such a changeover. Many senators found it hard to believe that the financing necessary to initiate the system would ever be forthcoming. The senate did not provide the chancellor with the recommendations he sought; instead, after making its position clear, the senate referred the matter to its Educational Policy Committee for study.

Thus the senate and the chancellor failed to reach agreement on a major matter. This in itself was not so surprising as the fact that the chancellor did not transmit the senate's position to the trustees. The chancellor later explained that he did not feel compelled to present recommendations of the senate made without consultation with members of his staff. Secondly, he did not submit the senate's opposing views to the trustees because, as he stated it, he wanted things his own way. The second explanation speaks for itself. The first is curious since the senate had considerable consultation on the matter with the chancellor himself. The senate was severely frustrated by its experiences on the issue of year-round operation, and the first chairman wrote to the chancellor in the middle of the senate's first year to protest the chancellor's treatment of the senate.

As you know this problem was referred to the senate by yourself, and its two major committees met at some length to reexamine the problem. Thereafter, the senate met in an emergency session devoting a substantial part of the day to further consideration of the problem and the development of its report. The study was costly in terms of professorial time and involved a substantial amount of state funds. It would seem under these circumstances that the report developed by the senate would and should receive careful consideration by the Board of Trustees. I was surprised therefore to discover that year-round operation was not placed as an action item on the agenda of the educational policies committee of the trustees in its meeting on Thursday. I was further embarrassed to discover that the report of the senate had not been distributed to the educational policies committee when it met again on Friday in a special session held at my request for the sole purpose of considering year-round operation [Mathy, 1964].

It is clear that from the start members of the senate did not feel they were being taken as seriously as they took themselves, although the chancellor had proclaimed that "the assembling of the senate constituted a major step in the achievement of a long-held personal objective." The first chairman completed his letter of complaint to the chancellor with the observation that "the senate was placed in a stance unrelated to the dignity suggested by its title and that its recommendations were as a consequence unlikely to receive favorable consideration. In light of this unhappy experience I see very little usefulness in further expenditure of faculty time and state funds for the work of the senate unless new procedures for the presentation of its deliberations can be developed."

For the senate to move from this point to its subsequent condemnation of the chancellor took six years, but in other respects it was not a long trip. At its meeting in January 1968 the senate directed its executive committee to prepare a report which would constitute a review and summary of the relations between the academic senate CSC and the chancellor from 1962 to the present. By March the study was complete and the report written. By May resolutions were passed which expressed the senate's "lack of confidence" in the chancellor and requested that he resign.

In calling for his resignation, the senate condemned the chancellor's stewardship in four major areas of educational management. The reaction of the Board of Trustees was swift and disdainful. Moreover, the chancellor simply stated that since the senate did not hire him, it could not fire him. Since the public was told by the chairman of the board that the senate action was not representative of faculty opinion throughout the system, the senate conducted a referendum. Faculties of the eighteen colleges voted three to one in support of the senate. Still, nothing happened, except perhaps a perceptible increase in grumbling among faculty.

The document (Academic Senate of the California State Colleges, 1968) upon which such resolutions rested was itself a succinct history of the plight of the senate, a chronicle of the fate of its aspirations.

The executive committee of the academic senate is cognizant of the scope and extent of the many problems which have beset the chancellor and the Board of Trustees. The executive committee is also fully aware of the special problems of implementing a new Master Plan, of establishing working relationships with the governor, the legislature, the Department of Finance, and the Coordinating Council; and it is well advised on most matters of curriculum, finance, faculty and staff affairs, and other aspects of statewide academic and administrative concern.

There is no desire to belittle achievement. . . . Yet, overall—on balance—the condition of the California state colleges has worsened and is worsening: in support, in quality of staff, and in educational excellence. Much of this decline may be traced to failure of public officials and legislators to provide proper support . . . [But] the executive committee sees the greatest deficiencies in the performance of the chancellor in those areas where funding and support are largely irrelevant. The most significant shortcomings, in our opinion, lie in (1) lack of communication, (2) lack of consultation, (3) lack of delegation, and (4) lack of leadership.

The report went on to explain and document its complaints.

Since its inception [the senate has] awaited in vain the establishment of a settled, orderly working relationship with the chancellor and with the Board of Trustees through the chancellor—a relationship which recognizes its significance and its responsibilities. Repeatedly, the academic senate, by resolution in writing and by oral presentations by its officers, has respectfully urged establishment of open lines of communication, only to be ignored and indeed rebuffed.

After providing examples in support of the charge of lack of communication, the report continued.

It is axiomatic that no deliberative body such as the academic senate can be an effective organization unless it is communicated with and is consulted on *all* policy issues which are to be decided by the Board of Trustees, and unless *all* of its recommendations intended for the Board of Trustees are transmitted by the chancellor to the Board of Trustees in time for them to be considered before action is taken. That he prefers or proposes other recommendations or that he feels that the response of the Board of Trustees will be negative never justifies withholding academic senate recommendations. The academic senate has presented to the chancellor and to the trustees simple, automatic procedures for orderly communication processes. Most of these have been ignored; others have been more honored in the breach than in the observance. Ironically, such procedures, which cost nothing and yield so much, exist in only the most rudimentary form; and the academic senate is forced into eternal vigilance as well as continuous monitoring to make certain just where its proposals and communications are.

The constant preoccupation of the senate with its effectiveness has continued. At its first meeting of the 1970–1971 academic year, the senate created a special task force consisting of its past chairmen, with a charge to pool experience, insights, and past failures in order to recommend to the senate methods by which the senate could hope to become effective.

The nature and meaning of consultation has been a subject of discussion, debate, and resolution in the senate from the start; and the issue has remained unresolved. One aspect of the problem concerns the senate's relationship with other segments of the system with whom the chancellor or the board may consult, such as the Council of Presidents, the Association of Student Body Presidents, or some special task force or committee created to deal with a specific issue. The second involves disputes over the meaning, scope, and timing involved in consultation. The third chairman of the senate, retiring in the spring of 1966, made the following observations in his chairman's report (Academic Senate of the California State Colleges, 1966):

The relations of the senate with the chancellor's office continue to pose problems and difficulties. Senate recommendations seem often to disappear into the procedural labyrinth. To some considerable extent the resulting frustration for the senate is attributable to a general confusion about the role of the senate in relation to other channels of consultation in the system. The recommendation in the report of our special committee on the ad hoc report which urges that the senate be recognized as the final policy-recommending body in the system would, if adopted by the trustees, go far to clarify relations and obviate our current frustration. So, too, would our recommendation, adopted at the last meeting, that the senate be delegated legislative authority in appropriate areas. Certainly this objective must remain at the center of our concern. Short of these developments, the resolution on "Procedures and Relationships in the Disposition of Senate Actions," adopted at our March meeting would, if accepted by the chancellor, insure that senate resolutions are included in the trustees' agenda and would insure that senate actions go forward to the trustees expeditiously. These provisions would help clear the atmosphere. There remain still, however, questions of procedure in situations where the chancellor's office disagrees with senate recommendations. These questions have created misunderstanding and confusion.

More recently, the senate has tried to work more closely with the Council of Presidents. Some of the presidents, like some of the trustees, had disliked the ever-growing militancy with which the senate responded to its own disappointments and failures. Although the faculty and presidents had common interests and similar perceptions about most of the serious issues that come before the board, lack of mutual cooperation and trust permitted one group to be played off against the other. Some senators now recognize that faculty viewpoints are better preserved by making concessions to the presidents and then coming to the trustees with a joint position, for it was only on the politically loaded issue of imposing tuition that the *combined* voices of the senate and the presidents were not successful.

The senate responded to the growing restlessness of the students by extending a permanent invitation to have two representatives of the Association of Student Body Presidents join the senate tables and participate as they might wish in senate proceedings. This representation soon terminated, however, partly because the students quickly recognized faculty wheelspinning and partly because of internal problems in the student organization.

The senate and the chancellor have been steadfastly working with significantly different concepts of consultation. The theme has been frequently repeated in senate discussions both formal and informal, in resolutions, entreaties, and demands. The 1968 executive committee report on relations of the academic senate with the chancellor stated (Academic Senate of the California State Colleges, 1968):

Another integral part of the lack of proper consultation has been demonstrated in the protracted impasse between the chancellor and the academic senate on matters of high-ranking appointments in his office as well as to the presidencies of new colleges. The effort of the chancellor to establish a system of *pro forma* consultation rather than *real* is too well documented in the proceedings of the academic senate to require rehearsal here. The academic senate refused to agree to such a facade and pointed out that the chancellor could make appointments without consultation if he wished to protect his powers, but that the moral support of senate concurrence would demand *real* participation. To date the problem has not been definitely solved.

In spring 1970 the senate reminded the chancellor and the board that the California state colleges had formally endorsed the AAUP statement on government which provided that "joint effort of the most critical kind must be taken when an institution chooses a new president" and, further, that the president should have the mutual confidence of the faculty and the governing board. The unanimous senate resolution stated that any president appointed in a manner inconsistent with these principles should be notified by the chairman of the academic senate CSC that he would be serving without the explicit approval and confidence of the faculty. The senate also resolved that the state chairman should advise the chairmen of local campus academic senates and the chairmen of campus presidential selection committees regarding these resolutions and encourage them to make their participation in the selection of a president contingent upon the acceptance of the stated principles (*Minutes of the Academic Senate of the California State Colleges, 1970*).

In spite of the trustees' "endorsement" of the idea, the requirement of mutual confidence remained the stumbling block. The faculty position was that mutual confidence could be tested only by procedures providing for mutual veto of candidates. The chancellor maintained, however, that "any procedure which divides the responsibility in making such appointments or dilutes the responsibility puts me in an impossible position." The trustees, it was said, will not accept divided responsibility. Some senate hostility seems predictable when an administration promises shared authority with one voice and rejects divided responsibility with another. For whether or not such contradictions on basic matters are devious, they prove enormously frustrating to faculty who are serious about their work in the senate.

In June 1966 the office of the chancellor issued a ten-point memorandum entitled *The Consultative Process for Appointments to Executive Academic Positions on the Chancellor's Staff*. In it he made clear that the selection and appointment of an individual is fully the responsibility of the chancellor, but he also included certain provisions for involving the senate in "the consultative process." He agreed to make a formal announcement of a vacancy and to send a request to the chairman of the academic senate for names of candidates. In addition, he stated the following: "Upon the development of a list of candidates acceptable to me, I will forward to the chairman of the academic senate a list, along with the full information available to me on each candidate's educational and professional qualifications. I, or my designee, will meet in executive session with senate representatives, in order to hear their advice on each candidate. No appointments to executive academic positions on my staff will be made except from such lists."

By the time the executive vice-chancellor resigned and his replacement was appointed in the spring of 1969, none of the above provisions was observed. The senate chairman protested to the trustees that again the well-established policy of consultation with faculty has been violated. After stating that the rejection of faculty consultation on such appointments was for the academic world a radical idea which unhappily leads to other radical ideas, such as the substitution of confrontation politics for dialogue, the chairman asked, "Finally, if there is to be a repudiation of this established policy of consultation with faculty, should it not be openly declared and discussed and debated, rather than to let it stand as a silent violation of policy?"

The testy reaction of the board to this plea was expressed by a trustee who pointed out that the board itself had no policy of consultation with the senate and that if the chancellor had violated any policy, it was solely his own. At the next meeting of the senate, the chancellor proclaimed that past interpretations of concepts regarding the implementation of consultation for the appointment of members of the chancellor's staff are no longer acceptable.

But changes with respect to consultation were not confined to the appointment of the chancellor's staff. For after saying, "I think in the case of the appointment of a president, obviously if the purpose of consultation is to be fulfilled, the president has to be acceptable and supported by his faculty," the chancellor supported the appointment of S. I. Hayakawa to the presidency of San Francisco State College. The faculty selection committee reacted sharply and urged a vote of no confidence in anyone who would acccept the presidency of any state college without meaningful faculty participation in the selection process.

Members of the senate were somewhat bitter in recalling the

chancellor's earlier assurances about the importance of consultation, such as: "I think the consultation process in the state colleges is agreed to by all parties. Certainly by me; I started it. We need it because with it we are going to come to better answers and better solutions to our staffing than we would without it." Also, "I think the consultative process is a valuable one. I have defended it, supported it, and I will continue to defend it and support it."

Yet, by spring 1970 conditions had so deteriorated that the senate at Fresno State College requested the chancellor to "rescind the order divesting the presidential selection committee of any meaningful function" and asked to have the "normal and necessary faculty participation in the selection of our new president." What brought about these dramatic changes, changes which speak so clearly to the question of the future role of the senate?

The decade of the sixties saw the introduction of politics into the planning and administration of higher education in California as never before. The new centralized state college system was formed under statute, without the constitutional safeguards offered the university. A Board of Trustees was appointed to set policy for a very large "business" involving hundreds of millions of dollars worth of new buildings, great operating budgets, incredibly rapid expansion, and myriad educational problems completely unfamiliar to it. The board chose a chancellor; he chose a staff, and the great endeavor began. There was very little experience, on the board or on the staff, with problems of a great statewide educational system. There was not much statewide leadership among the college presidents or the faculties. And there was much to be done. Problems and tensions arose at once; yet there was at the outset a willingness by all parts to explore and to attempt definition and delineation of roles. But too soon positions were hardened, abetted by accidental and planned lack of communication. As political lines sharpened and took shape in the broader social and political sphere, they sharpened and took similar shape in the state colleges; and student unrest and violence have been seized upon by the trustees and the chancellor as rationale for seizure of virtually all power, for destruction of faculty governance at the statewide level, and for redefining their roles without due regard for the educational charge and purpose of the state colleges. By 1968, the Academic Senate of the

California State Colleges (1968) in a position paper, *Politics in Higher Education,* outlined the attack upon public higher education.

It is now clear that, in addition to financial strangulation, the California state colleges face a mounting assault upon the very conception of a free and intellectually open higher education in the state of California. This assault is rendered all the more dangerous in that it is basically *political* in nature, and many politicians themselves are entering into it, moved undoubtedly by the conviction that it is politically realistic to do so. Significantly, few voices among concerned legislators have been raised, either to defend the state colleges or to identify the attack for what it is—political.

The paper ended with the recommendation that, "in hiring professors for our system, those who do the hiring make perfectly clear what the situation is in the California state colleges and what it may become."

Since this senate action, the politicizing of educational administration has continued unabated. In 1970, the action of the Board of Trustees on grievance and disciplinary regulations seems, if not a fifth column coup, a remarkable utilization of outside threat as impetus for internal repression. The senate is firmly caught between the misplaced hostility toward faculty in higher education generated in the public by demogoguery and the overriding need felt by the chancellor and the board to appease the budgetary powers.

With each new threat posed either to academic freedom or to the professional status of the faculties, the chancellor has suggested that the senate take the initiative in conforming to political demands for new controls. Thus, the senate was asked to create a code of conduct for the faculties and to propose measures for the review of tenured faculty. It was expected to acquiesce in the denial of peer judgment to faculty on questions of professional ethics and to accommodate itself to the unrestricted authority delegated to the chancellor by the trustees to revise grievance and disciplinary procedures for both students and faculty whenever he sees fit.

The academic senate was helpless against this naked display

of power, but at least it was not speechless. The senate chairman
wrote to the chancellor in the spring of 1970.

As you know from several recent meetings with me, I am deeply
troubled by the pronounced surge of undisguised authoritarianism taking place in the administration of the California state colleges. I am
certain that such developments are far more destructive to the welfare
of educational institutions and the society they must serve than the
ills they are intended to cure. In observing from close quarters the
practices and pronouncements of your office, I am distressed by what
I have come to regard as a constant sacrifice of educational values to
political pressures and to expediency [Richfield, 1970].

After resigning from certain joint ad hoc committees on the ground
that he could no longer assume that their work would be judged
in terms of educational significance rather than political merit,
the chairman ended his letter. "Having made a considerable effort
to have the senate function effectively in our system as a significant
group of professional colleagues, I am especially disappointed at
your determination to have us all see ourselves as merely your educational employees. I would be surprised if your current posture
does not greatly radicalize a faculty which is not permitted to regard
itself in appropriate professional terms."

      A few months later, this was followed by the minority report
from the Academic Senate of the California State Colleges, Ad Hoc
Committee on Grievances and Disciplinary Procedures (1970),
which stated:

[The new] provisions demonstrate that the steady erosion of trustee
policy setting forth the principle of shared authority is now complete.
There cannot be a clearer or more demeaning repudiation of the professional status of faculty in the California state colleges than the proposed denial of the long established right of faculty to peer judgment
on charges of unprofessional conduct. In no other profession would the
idea be either entertained or tolerated that an individual executive
officer should have the power to stipulate the boundaries of acceptable
professional conduct. (We are not, it should be clearly stated, questioning now the competence of the present executive officer; we are questioning the competence of any executive officer to make such decisions.)

There is a significant difference between grievance and disciplinary procedures in this regard. It is not unreasonable to presume that the power of the executive officer in making any final determinations in grievance matters is supported by some appropriate qualification. But with respect to questions of professional ethics, the board is about to manufacture a moral authority for which even the most meager theoretical justification is lacking. There are no infallible authorities in education, and no educational theology to sustain any. The power of such an "authority" would be a quite naked one indeed. If such naked power is really to be asserted, then with this move the board will make its announcement of this fact for all to see—to the enormous detriment of the welfare of our colleges.

The faculties should not be asked to endure such a demoralizing demonstration from their trustees, especially on the heels of the punitive actions of the legislature and in the face of an inordinately difficult period ahead. The chancellor has insisted that the record of the California state colleges is really worthy of confidence. Let the Board of Trustees lead the way in this regard. Bolster the faculties. For what but sufficient professional pride can really be counted on to preserve the sound standards of academic freedom and integrity?

Finally, the senate's current situation was clearly stated by its chairman for the fall of the 1970–1971 academic year in his opening remarks at the first meeting of the senate (Academic Senate of the California State Colleges, 1970):

It must be obvious to even the most casual observer that the situation in which the senate now finds itself is one of crisis proportions. Our budgets have suffered drastic and punitive cuts that not only reduce real faculty salaries and benefits but also threaten the quality of our educational programs. While it is possible that these funds will be restored in the coming legislative session, I see little cause for optimism. . . .

Tenure appears to be the next lamb to be led to the slaughter. The chancellor says he supports the concept of tenure but he proposes to extend the probationary period and to restrict the according of tenure to associate and full professors. The governor and numerous legislators appear to be ready to do away with tenure altogether.

Finally, but foremost, is the undeniable fact that academic freedom is in more serious jeopardy now than at any time within my memory. On the one hand it is threatened internally by bands of disrupters who, in pursuit of political ends, have adopted means of achieving their objectives that interfere with the rights of others to teach and learn. On the other hand, academic freedom is threatened just as ominously by official proposals which for the purpose of controlling political partisanship and advocacy on the campuses restrict the right and indeed obligation of faculty and students to consider controversial issues in a proper academic context. It is not clear to me which of these opposing forces constitutes the greater danger, but it is clear to me that both threaten the integrity and survival of our institutions.

It should be clear that given the conditions that confront us, this cannot be a year when the senate proceeds on a business-as-usual basis.

The future will be decided more by the ebb and flow of political tides in the state and in the nation than by anything the senate might be able to do for itself. For the powers of the senate to serve the causes of education are now thoroughly circumscribed by a Board of Trustees far more sensitive to the pressures of public impatience with campus unrest than to the needs and values of the faculty which feels that, more than ever, it must succeed in providing a quality education in this period of unprecedented turbulence on campus.

10

⊓⊔⊓⊔⊓⊔⊓⊔⊓⊔⊓⊔⊓⊔⊓⊔⊓⊔⊓⊔⊓⊔⊓⊔⊓⊔

Faculty Organizations

James O. Haehn

⊓⊔⊓⊔⊓⊔⊓⊔⊓⊔⊓⊔⊓⊔⊓⊔⊓⊔⊓⊔⊓⊔⊓⊔⊓⊔

Four organizations presently compete with one another to represent faculty in the California state colleges. Although outside of the official structure these associations play an important part in the working of the system. They have gained many benefits on behalf of professors, and in addition they have often had a significant influence on decisions with much broader scope. The impact the organizations have had on policy making, in fact, has sometimes extended well beyond the boundaries of the state colleges to the entire realm of public higher education in the state.

Formally, state college faculty are represented by local faculty senates or councils and the statewide academic senate. These bodies are limited as to the issues with which they can deal and the tactics they can employ. As official groups the senates exist because of trustee policy, and their dependent position is underscored by the fact that they receive their financial support from the state. Also, under trustee policy the senates only advise the local presidents, in the case of the campuses, and the trustees in the instance of the state-

129

wide senate. As a result the senates can exercise leverage on policy only in circumscribed ways.

The faculty organizations are not bound by formal ties to the system. Further, they are dependent upon the voluntary membership of faculty for their support. The organizations can thus operate with a much wider range of alternatives while keeping closely attuned to the thinking and interests of the faculty. They also must translate their interpretations of faculty concerns into definite positions on issues and active programs to cope with them. Any faculty organization that failed to do this would soon find itself unable to attract new members or even retain those it already has.

In practice the differences between academic senates and faculty organizations are frequently difficult to maintain. Most leaders of faculty groups work closely with the senates. A proposal was made in 1970 to allow representatives of the four associations to hold nonvoting seats on the statewide senate, with full rights of participation in discussion and debate. Should the suggestion be adopted it may make the organizational representatives similar to senators, but their official presence might also make the senate increasingly like an outside association.

The drift of senates toward becoming independent faculty organizations has been evident on a number of occasions. In the course of the debates on collective bargaining which swept the state colleges, the statewide academic senate came very close to declaring itself as a candidate for the position of bargaining agent, in competition with the regular faculty groups. On one campus, Chico State, the local faculty senate did run for the position of bargaining agent and won.[1] The senates will probably not change themselves into faculty organizations. Yet, when the dependence of these bodies upon the legislature and trustees is called to attention as dramatically as it was during the 1970 session of the legislature such a step does become a little more likely.[2]

---

[1] The faculty senate at Chico State College not only sponsored an election to select a collective bargaining agent, it placed itself on the ballot. Once the senate declared itself as a candidate the campus chapters of the faculty organizations decided not to file and thus the senate was chosen to be the bargaining agent for the faculty.

[2] Funds for the statewide academic senate of the state colleges were

Numerous societies and groups are active among state college faculty, but most of these are concerned with academic disciplines or scholarly matters. It is important to not confuse such societies with the faculty groups being discussed here. Only in special instances have the professional societies made any effort to affect the working conditions of their members or to influence the policies of the institutions at which their members are employed. In contrast, faculty organizations concentrate on the immediate job and other institutionally related interests of professors. To a degree, then, the faculty organizations function as unions while the professional associations operate in a different area of faculty concern.

Professional societies sometimes have taken an interest in the jobs of their members. Within the California state colleges organizations representing nurses, chemists, social welfare specialists, and engineers have been especially active in this area. Still, these cases are exceptional and take place mainly in occupations where most of the practitioners are employed outside of an academic setting. In these professions the nonacademic members have had to cope with increasingly complex problems relating to their jobs and have turned to the professional societies for help. Where this has taken place the group's efforts are largely a byproduct of the work it does for its other members. Since few faculty are in such situations the majority of professors must rely upon the faculty organizations, or possibly the senates, to address problems growing out of their jobs.

Many people ask why there is a plurality of groups trying to represent state college instructors. The reasons are complicated and must take into account ideological, historical, and sociological factors. It is also necessary to recognize that formerly there were five active organizations; two of the groups merged in 1970, lowering the number of faculty associations to four. When examining the different groups it is essential to discuss the older organizations as well as those now active.

---

cut in half during the budgetary process of the 1970 legislature. The amount requested was finally restored during the closing days of the session, but for some time it appeared that it would not be. The reasons for the cut were quite clear—the displeasure of legislators with the senate's activities. The University of California academic senate was also threatened, except in that case the legislature almost deprived the group of all of its funds.

Prior to 1963 there was no statewide academic senate in the
California state colleges and consequently no means for faculty to
register their views before the trustees or the chancellor. The only
systemwide vehicles for bringing professors' concerns to the policymakers were the faculty organizations. Given this important role
and the fact that college professors have as much diversity of opinion
as any other group of people, different associations emerged to
represent different orientations and opinions. They originated to
serve different subgroups within the faculty population and their
policies have reflected such differences.

Despite ideological differences between organizations membership has never been mutually exclusive. Each group represents a
separate facet of the faculty role, and thus many professors belong
to more than one association, even though the positions of the groups
on particular issues may be contrary. Overlapping membership also
is due partially to the benefits each organization makes available to
those who join. Most provide insurance programs at favorable rates
and some have other side benefits, such as group travel plans. Consequently, some instructors are attracted to an association solely
because of these benefits. Three of the organizations, in fact, have
substantial numbers of "insurance members," a proportion of whom
belong to other associations for ideological reasons. The high level of
multiple memberships serves to prevent conflict among the organizations from becoming overly bitter or intense but it has hardly
erased competition.

As mentioned, the faculty organizations can be viewed as
based upon one dimension of the professor's role. The instructor
occupies a position with lines running from it in diverse directions.
For example, professors share common concerns and problems with
people at all levels in education. In more than an abstract sense
everyone from the nursery school teacher to the graduate professor is
engaged in the same basic process of teaching. Two faculty organizations were built on this aspect of the faculty role: the California
College and University Faculty Association (CCUFA) and the
American Federation of Teachers (AFT). Both are affiliated with
national associations open to teachers in all sectors of education.
CCUFA is linked to the National Education Association (NEA)
through the California Teachers Association (CTA). As is well

known, the NEA is the largest and most powerful teacher organization in the United States. By comparison state college locals of the AFT were coordinated by the College and University Council of the California Federation of Teachers (CFT), a state unit of the national AFT—the oldest and leading teacher union in the country.

If the college aspect of the instructor's role is emphasized, another dimension of the position comes into view. Higher education is clearly different from the secondary or elementary school levels, and thus a distinct bond exists among those in college and university teaching that sets them apart from others in education. The American Association of University Professors (AAUP) is the organization founded upon this line of faculty interest. The California state college chapters of the AAUP are bound together with chapters from the private colleges and the University of California into a college conference. The significant relationship in the case of the AAUP, however, is between the chapter and the national organization. The AAUP has been most effective at the national level, where it is unquestionably the major spokesman for university and college instructors.

Still another important dimension is the faculty member's role as an employee of the state. As such he shares many interests with all other state employees. The California State Employees Association (CSEA) is the organization active on this line of faculty concern. Composed of more than 120,000 members, the CSEA is an extremely strong group in California. State college faculty are only a small percentage of the total CSEA membership, but they have their own academic council which is represented on the CSEA Board of Directors.

State college faculty are not just professors in a general sense, they are distinguished by their position in the California state college system. The immediate problems of the state colleges are often unique, and policy decisions affecting professors are made within the context of the system. The organization which represented this facet of the professor's role was the Association of California State College Professors (ACSCP). The ACSCP was the oldest of the faculty groups and it had no national, state, or regional affiliations with other organizations. For many years it was the most active faculty organization in the state colleges.

The ACSCP ceased to function in 1970 when it merged with college locals of the AFT to form a new faculty association—the United Professors of California (UPC). The UPC has sought to become more than simply a union of two older faculty groups. Many of those involved in its establishment hoped that it would prove to be a rallying point for state college faculty, unifying the majority of professors within a single, strong association. The founders also saw the UPC as a device to bring together professors from the state colleges with faculty from the University of California. Although the UPC's success may not be judged now, since it did not begin activities until fall 1970, one can speculate that its efforts both to unify state college instructors and to bring together university and state college professors will encounter much difficulty. But before making predictions it is useful to examine briefly the background and major characteristics of each faculty association.

The AAUP was founded in 1915 by a small group of professors from certain select eastern universities. The organization was established to protect faculty from a wave of attacks upon academic freedom which were occurring at the time. From this beginning the AAUP has grown to become the largest and most prestigious of the associations representing university and college teachers in the United States. The defense of academic freedom has consistently been the central concern of the AAUP. This is not to say that the organization has totally ignored other problems in American higher education, but by holding to its original focus the AAUP has proved a highly effective instrument. It has developed careful procedures for investigating cases brought before it and a system of sanctions that can be mustered when necessary. Because it is willing to accept cases and is efficient when its procedures are employed, the AAUP has gained much respect among college faculty and administrators. Many professors, in fact, belong to the association solely because of its reputation as a defender of academic freedom.

The AAUP has given much less attention to questions of salaries, teaching loads, and general working conditions than some faculty would like. The organization does publish an annual listing of salaries paid in most American institutions of higher education together with a rating of these salaries in terms of a scale it has developed. Many schools use the AAUP figures in establishing their

own rates of faculty compensation, but until very recently the association has not carried its activities on economic questions much
beyond the publishing of these reports. Similarly, the AAUP seldom
takes an active position on other job-related issues. In one case the
AAUP was chosen as the collective bargaining agent for teachers in
a midwest community college, Belleville Community College in
Illinois, without the knowledge of the national leaders. Since then
it has become the bargaining agent for faculty at five four-year
colleges and was quite active in the effort to represent professors in
the State University of New York (SUNY).

In part the historical absence within the AAUP of programs
dealing with working conditions is due to a continued insistence
that it is not a trade union. AAUP members have been quite reluctant to engage in any activities which might bring the union label
upon the association, believing that to do so would reduce the effectiveness of the group and lessen the professionalism of its members.
Since 1965, however, the association has begun to alter its stance on
work-related concerns of faculty. At national AAUP conventions
heated debates have occurred on such questions, resulting in a slow
but clear shift in the organization's policies on collective bargaining,
faculty strikes, and the importance of economic matters.

For many years the AAUP operated primarily from its headquarters in Washington, D.C. In 1967 it opened its first regional
office, in San Francisco, and plans are underway to establish others
in various regions of the country. The purpose behind this is to provide better service to AAUP members in areas removed from the
Washington headquarters and to allow greater flexibility in adapt-
ing association policy to local and regional requirements.

The AAUP has long had members throughout the California
state colleges and it maintains active chapters on several campuses.
Altogether the association has about sixteen hundred members in
the state college system—just under 20 per cent of the full-time
faculty.[3] The commitment of these members to the AAUP is prob-

[3] AAUP membership as a proportion of state college faculty has remained fairly stable over time. In 1959 it had approximately 19 per cent of
the professors as members, in 1966 21 per cent, and in 1968 20 per cent. Of
all AAUP members in California, state college faculty represent 36 per cent
of the total.

ably not as great as to some of the other faculty groups. Many
professors join the AAUP because of its prestige; to them it represents a form of insurance against attacks by politicians and administrators. For others the benefits of the organization, such as the free
subscription to its bulletin or the low-cost insurance, are reasons for
membership. In short, the influence of the AAUP among faculty
in the state colleges has not been particularly great and has been
considerably less than what might have been expected from a group
of such high standing nationally.

　　The opening of the western office could have had an effect
upon AAUP influence in the colleges, but it did not. The staff of
the office has responsibilities extending over the entire western region
of the country and thus it is limited in the time and energy that can
be given to the state colleges. Further, although national AAUP
policies have been changing, the pace of change has not kept abreast
of the dominant issues in the California state colleges. To illustrate,
when the struggles over collective bargaining were taking place the
AAUP was the least conspicuous of the five faculty organizations. It
never initiated a publication aimed at state college faculty, as did
all of the other associations, nor did it adopt clear positions on the
issues confronting college professors. By remaining relatively aloof
from the day to day problems of the system the AAUP has not been
able to exercise much influence among the instructors. On the other
hand, the association has held a position of influence with the
trustees because of their high regard for the national AAUP.

　　It is unfortunate that the AAUP has such a low level of
involvement in the state colleges. The association has repeatedly
demonstrated its ability to help faculty in those areas where it has
chosen to act. Policy modifications may gradually strengthen the
group among college professors, but these changes may occur too
late to keep the AAUP in the picture as a visible faculty organization. On the other hand, the withdrawn posture of the AAUP may
work to its advantage in the long run. Untarnished by past defeats
and debates and operating with more flexible policies, the AAUP
could possibly arise as a leading organization representing faculty
interests. The key to success, of course, is timing. If the AAUP does
not come to life soon in implementing its new programs and in tak-

ing a more active stand on issues, the time might pass when these tactics would prove effective.

Yet, even if the AAUP suddenly rose to action it would have to overcome certain problems of image. For a long time the association has been seen as a conservative organization which mainly represents the prestigious schools and the senior faculty. Younger professors in particular show little enthusiasm for the association. To the degree that they do join, the attraction is likely to be the other-than-job-based benefits. In the college system the AAUP would have somehow to win the attention of these younger staff and convince them that the organization is concerned about the practical, daily concerns of faculty. Without the support of a substantial percentage of younger instructors the AAUP's chances of becoming an important faculty organization in the California state colleges are slim indeed.

The American Federation of Teachers (AFT) technically ceased to function in the state college system when locals of the union merged with the ACSCP in 1970. In reality, the new organization formed by the merger is largely a product of the AFT's programs, goals, and policies. Before 1965 there was little AFT activity among college faculty. Union locals existed on a few campuses, but as late as February 1965 total AFT membership in the system was estimated to be only three hundred. Until that year the national union centered most of its work among public school teachers and its college membership was incidental. The majority of American teachers are employed in the public schools and thus work among them was crucial for the success of the union. Also, the problems of public school teachers, economic and professional, were much more severe than those of professors. Finally, as a group, college faculty had never shown any strong interest in unionization and, in fact, had often expressed disdain for the very idea that unionism could be applicable to them. In short, prior to 1965 the tie between the union and college instructors was a very weak one.

In 1960 the AFT won its most important victory—the right to represent the public school teachers of New York City. On the heels of that gain the union began to expand its efforts across the country. As it launched more and more campaigns it began to attract junior college faculty and later professors from four-year institutions of higher education. In 1965 it initiated the first major organizational drive in four-year colleges, and the California state colleges were chosen as the site of the campaign.[4]

Aided by a grant from the industrial union department of the AFL-CIO and encouragement from long-time union members in the state colleges the AFT began its campaign with considerable enthusiasm. The initial reaction of the other faculty organizations was mixed and confused. As a result the AFT was able to win substantial faculty support in a short period of time. During its early stages the unionization drive focused upon certain campuses, and at those schools AFT leaders mounted pressure for local senate-sponsored elections on the bargaining question. At four colleges such elections were held during the spring 1966 and fall 1967 terms— San Francisco State, San Diego State, San Jose State, and San Fernando Valley State. The outcome was mixed. At two of the colleges (San Fernando and San Francisco) collective bargaining carried, while at the other two the issue lost. However, the total vote from all four campuses showed that more faculty voted for bargaining than against it. This positive evaluation of the results is precisely the assessment made by the proponents of bargaining.

Under growing pressure from the AFT and ACSCP (which had come to support bargaining after initially opposing it) and faced with the outcome of the four campus elections the statewide academic senate decided to address the question. An ad hoc committee on collective bargaining initiated a series of steps which eventually led to a statewide election under senate sponsorship. The election was conducted in March 1967 and dealt solely with the issue of collective bargaining for state college faculty. The majority of professors registered opposition to the concept of bargaining as applied to themselves, but the vote was so close that it left the issue essentially unresolved. At seven of the eighteen colleges bargaining won a majority of the vote and at two other colleges the vote was extremely close. ACSCP and AFT leaders interpreted the outcome as an endorsement of collective bargaining and were con-

[4] Following the start of the California drive the AFT began similar efforts in other states. Some of these later campaigns have proved much more successful for the union than the state college drive.

vinced that if the issue were raised once more it would carry. Academic senate leaders, in contrast, regarded the vote as a defeat for bargaining and proceeded to act as though the issue were closed. Pressure from the organizations did not prove sufficient to obtain a second poll and to this date no second election on the question has ever been held by the senate.

Within two years after the start of its drive the AFT had established locals on all state college campuses and had increased its membership to nearly 1,500 faculty. Support for the union, though, was not evenly distributed within the system. Strongholds of union backing soon emerged at San Jose State, San Francisco State, San Fernando Valley State, and Los Angeles State. The union gained members at the other schools as well, but at several campuses it achieved a membership plateau early in its drive which changed little. As the impetus of the 1965 campaign subsided, a second effort was begun late in 1967. By that time, however, faculty opinion on the union had begun to polarize. Also, AFT energies began to be diverted from the initial goals (collective bargaining and union recognition) to other issues. Some faculty enthusiasm was dampened as they felt the union was being drawn from job-related goals to social and political ends. This led to some disenchantment with the AFT's leaders and their styles of operation. Thus by 1969, two years after its second drive had been launched, the union's membership stood at about two thousand in the state colleges. These two thousand members represented almost the same percentage of faculty as did the fifteen hundred members two years earlier—20 per cent of the full-time staff.

When the AFT began its second drive its competition with the ACSCP had subsided considerably. Thus when the ACSCP announced the start of an effort to reduce the teaching load in the system the AFT rapidly joined with it. A special committee of representatives from the two groups was established, and the work of this group garnered campaign backing from many faculty. The drive grew in strength to the point that many professors signed a pledge to accept no more than nine units of teaching during the spring term of 1969. Based upon this support the joint committee secured an agreement from the trustees to meet on the matter in late 1968. The meeting was diverted by events taking shape at San

Francisco State, and the drive was never revived after the conflict
there was resolved.

The AFT's success among state college faculty was blunted
by its frequent reference to, and later use of, the strike. Faculty have
always been uneasy about unionism because of a belief that striking
is inappropriate and basically unprofessional. Since AFT leaders
often cited the possibility of a strike as they took positions on given
issues, the union and striking came to be seen as correlates. This
stance attracted the more militant professors but strengthened the
opposition of many others. All of this remained on the level of discussion until 1968 when the AFT called for a one-day strike of all
state colleges to support a professor who was not granted tenure at
San Francisco State. The actual walkout proved very disappointing
from the union's perspective. Nonetheless in December 1968 the
AFT led another faculty strike at San Francisco State. The strike
lasted for several weeks and the issues associated with it became so
involved that it would take an entire volume to adequately analyze
what took place. (In fact, several have been written on this subject.)
In any case, the San Francisco State strike reduced the overall level
of faculty support for the union. Some felt the use of the strike was
wrong while others believed the strike issues were not tenable.
Further, sympathy for the strikers waned as the areas of conflict
became more and more involved. This withering of support fur-
thered discussions of a merger between the AFT and ACSCP.

At the peak of its activity the AFT generated considerable
interest among faculty in collective bargaining. The union did more
than stimulate acceptance of collective bargaining, however. The
AFT forced the other faculty organizations to address the basic
problems facing the system and to take much more definite stands
on these questions. In other words, the union functioned as a catalyst
in the state college system, setting off a chain of reactions which
forced the other faculty groups and the faculty itself to face major
problems and develop approaches for coping with them.

If the new UPC is unable to satisfy the demands of the more
active professors it is possible that the AFT will be revived. The
UPC is a coalition and as such it will have to develop policies which
are compromises among the diverse groups making up the organization. Should this decrease the level of militancy which the old

AFT members feel is necessary they may quit the UPC and reestablish the union.

The Association of California State College Professors (ACSCP) was the oldest of the faculty organizations active in the California state colleges. The association was the product of efforts begun in 1925, although the founding of the organization did not occur until 1928. Originally called the Association of California State College Instructors, the ACSCP was the major faculty group and the leading spokesman for state college teachers until the AFT campaign was initiated in 1965. Through its history the ACSCP was instrumental in obtaining numerous benefits for professors and was therefore one of the largest of the faculty groups.

In addition to being large, the ACSCP attracted a diverse group of teachers. ACSCP leaders tended to represent the more liberal viewpoints on state college issues, but within the ranks of the ACSCP were significant proportions of people with moderate and conservative opinions. Tensions and clashes between these factions were common, and in some instances the organization was unable to adopt and hold definite positions on basic issues. By the mid-1960s these disputes had reached high levels of conflict and on occasion neutralized the ACSCP at critical points.

For the most part the ACSCP was a bread and butter association which resisted any bonds with unionism. Its leaders lobbied and made appeals to public opinion. For many years these approaches worked relatively well and the association enjoyed high esteem among state college professors. The organization took its obligations to faculty quite seriously and it contracted for excellent health insurance plans for its membership. Thus, many of those who joined ACSCP were "insurance members" and contributed only in marginal ways to the functioning of the organization. The conflicts described above involved differing factions among the more committed faculty. Although the ACSCP had nearly 40 per cent of the state college faculty as members, local chapters were often unable to muster more than a tiny fraction for meetings or elections, and these tended to be the more vocal and active teachers.

When the AFT campaign began in 1965 the ACSCP vacillated for a time, then jumped into the fray as the leading opponent to the union. Initially ACSCP policy was against collective bargaining, but by 1966 it had changed and competed with the union in encouraging support for bargaining. In the first campus election held on the question (at San Francisco State) the ACSCP was formally chosen over the AFT as the bargaining agent for faculty. The association was never able to secure recognition of its status from the trustees or chancellor, and by 1968 it had lost its position as the leading organization on this campus.

Between 1967 and 1969 the ACSCP suffered a decline in membership. As it moved closer to the AFT's positions on issues many of its earlier backers withdrew from the organization and others simply joined the union. By early 1969 the ACSCP had only 27 per cent of the faculty, compared to nearly 40 per cent only two years before. There can be little doubt that this drop in membership was a very important factor in making ACSCP leaders conducive to merging with the AFT.

Of the several faculty groups the ACSCP most directly and specifically represented state college interests. From its beginning the organization remained independent, although it did maintain some cooperative ties with the California State Employees Association. This independence proved a problem, for when struggles among faculty factions became increasingly intense, the ACSCP was the only group lacking a parent body to which it could turn for financial or other forms of help. Nonetheless, the association did hold a high level of faculty support, partly because it was well geared to the views of those who took the time to be active within the organization. The ACSCP was the first of the organizations to initiate a publication aimed solely at state college instructors. It was also the organization most likely to raise key problems before the policymakers and to ensure that professors were represented at legislative committee hearings and the like.

Many ACSCP members were uneasy about the merger with the AFT, fearing a takeover by the union, and shortly after the constitutional convention for the new organization some tried to gain support for a withdrawal of ACSCP chapters from the UPC. This opposition seems to have been stilled, and it is not probable that the ACSCP will be revived no matter what takes place in the UPC.

The California College and University Faculty Association (CCUFA) is one of the smaller faculty organizations and one which appeals to specific groups among state college faculty. It was founded in 1957 by the California Teachers Association and operates as a branch of that organization. CCUFA is open to faculty from all segments of higher education in California, but state college faculty make up the largest group within its ranks. In 1968, for example, CCUFA had approximately 1,900 members of whom nearly 1,400 were from the state colleges. The CTA is the principal teacher association in California. Its policies and programs are closely akin to those of the National Education Association, of which it is an affiliate. For a number of years CTA competed with the AFT, particularly in the major cities of the state, but in 1969 the common problems faced by both groups led to a merger of CTA and AFT chapters in the Los Angeles area.

In general, CCUFA reflects the more moderate perspectives of the CTA. It also reflects the education-oriented commitments of its parent group. As a result those who join CCUFA tend to come disproportionately from the education and related teacher training departments of the state colleges. In spite of concerted efforts CCUFA has never been able to make significant inroads in recruiting liberal arts faculty. This specialized base of CCUFA membership has affected the influence the organization has been able to exercise within the system. When its leaders speak before the trustees or legislature it is widely recognized that they represent a closely defined portion of the general state college faculty. The deeply held belief that the CTA is fundamentally a public school teacher organization also keeps some faculty from joining CCUFA. Despite its image problems with the faculty CCUFA has affected policy relative to the state colleges. Its usually rather conservative positions appeal to the legislators and trustees. Also, the power of the CTA carries over to enhance the influence of CCUFA.

Over time CCUFA has had approximately the same proportion of faculty membership. In 1964 the association had 873 state college members, close to 15 per cent of the full-time faculty in the system. In 1968 the organization had nearly 1,400 state college members, or 14 per cent of all full-time professors. There are no indications that this level of strength will change markedly in the future. Some of its faculty members belong for insurance reasons, but the majority are in the association because of its orientation.

Unless the organization makes some dramatic changes in its approach, which is not likely, it will have no greater appeal for most faculty than it has had in the past. On the other hand, there is no indication that CCUFA will suffer any sharp losses in membership in the future.

The California State Employees Association (CSEA) is the primary organization representing state employees in California. The association has over 120,000 members, drawn from all types and categories of state workers, and included among these are college faculty. The association was established in the early 1930's as part of an attempt by state workers to fight pay reductions caused by the depression. It has grown considerably from that beginning and no longer is it a purely defensive body, protecting state employees from political attack or administrative policy. Especially since 1965 CSEA has become increasingly militant, as evidenced by its removal of a no-strike provision in its constitution in 1969 and its endorsement of collective bargaining for all state workers.

State college faculty constitute only about 3 per cent of the total CSEA membership. Still, within the state colleges CSEA has long been the largest of the faculty organizations. For example, in 1966 the organization had more than 3,700 professors in its ranks—about 52 per cent of all state college instructors in that year. Its proportion of membership among faculty has declined since then, but the association still has more than 4,000 instructors as members.

State college faculty have been represented within CSEA since 1940 by a special subgroup. Originally this was called the State College Academic Committee, but in 1965 the title was changed to State College Academic Council. The council is chaired by a CSEA officer from outside the state college system and he also represents the council on the Board of Directors of the CSEA.

Of the faculty organizations CSEA has been traditionally the most conservative. Oddly enough this stance was not a product of policy emanating from the parent organization but a result of positions taken by the members of the academic council itself. Yet even within that council changes have been taking place, and in 1970 it became the last of the principal faculty groups to endorse

collective bargaining and to advocate establishing bargaining procedures.

Even more than some of the other groups, CSEA contains
a large share of insurance members. Thus in spite of its high proportion of faculty membership the organization has little backing
for the policy positions it adopts. Even so, in 1965 the academic
council did leap into the struggle with the AFT and emerged as
the major opponent to the changes the union and ACSCP were
trying to secure. The council has a publication for state college
faculty, *The Scope,* and employs a full-time coordinator to work
with the professors.

Legislators and officials in the executive branch of state
government have high respect for CSEA and tend to pay attention
to its proposals. Not only do most of the people who work for these
policymakers belong to the association, it also has substantial financial resources and a large staff of professionals to back up the stands
it takes. It maintains a political arm, a program called EPIC, which
is financed by CSEA members to deal with the more partisan aspects of representing state workers. Obviously the role of the academic council is bolstered as it functions on behalf of faculty by the
availability of these resources within its parent body.

Because professors are such a small minority within the
CSEA, they often feel that their interests are relegated to a minor
place in the organization's overall efforts. In part this is true, and
the reaction of many CSEA members to the recent waves of campus
disorders have made them less sympathetic to the problems of
faculty. Still, when the legislature denied faculty a salary increase in
1970, after granting a 5 per cent cost of living increase to all other
state employees, the CSEA was the only organization to take action
in support of the faculty. It immediately filed a suit against the
state, arguing the action was discriminatory and punitive. This suit
is still in the courts and will probably not be settled for several years.

The CSEA academic council has recently begun a self-evalu-
ation of its position among state college faculty. Should the group
shed its conservative image among professors and also demonstrate
that it can muster the resources of the CSEA on behalf of the
faculty, the association could emerge as a powerful spokesman for

state college instructors. If the council proceeds with present plans
to work more closely with other faculty organizations, its policies are
likely to change more rapidly and become more aligned with the
concerns of faculty. The association would then be much more
attractive to a larger proportion of the faculty in the system.

Since the United Professors of California (UPC) did not
come into being until the fall of 1970 it is too early to say much
about the organization. The merger of the AFT and ACSCP was
formally initiated in May 1970 when a constitutional convention
was held for the development of a new organization, but talks leading to the merger can be traced to 1968. To some faculty the UPC
is an effort to unite all state college and University of California
professors into a single organization.[5] No other association has
attempted to accomplish this in a concerted way. CCUFA, CSEA,
and AAUP are all open to college faculty regardless of the institutions at which they work but none has openly declared itself as an
organization dedicated to developing such a union.

Initially the UPC was titled the Union of Associated Professors (UAP). This name reflected the two associations which were
parties to the merger, and the change in title was made to express
the more ecumenical emphasis of the body. Yet, in program and
approach the UPC is quite close to the AFT. It strongly favors
collective bargaining and endorses a militant stance on the part of
faculty. The carryover from the AFT to the UPC has kept some
faculty from joining the new group, in that they view it as simply the
union in a new form. In contrast, the stress on unity has drawn
other professors to the UPC, professors who previously had belonged
to neither the ACSCP or AFT. The extent to which the UPC can
overcome the reticence of the former faculty and retain the interest
of the latter remains to be seen.

It is estimated that the UPC began its life with about 3,500
faculty members; approximately 800 are university faculty while
2,700 come from state colleges. One can surmise from these proportions that UPC programs will be centered on the state college system. The goal of uniting faculty from the two systems of public

[5] In the University of California system the UPC functions under
the title of the Faculty Union.

higher education is a noble one. Faculty in each are faced by a wide range of common problems, especially those related to state support of higher education. Yet the status and concerns of professors in the two sectors are rather different. Given limited resources, gains for members of one segment could well come at the expense of those in the other system. For example, if the state increases the level of research support for the state colleges it would probably reduce its assistance for university research. Problems such as this might cause serious schisms in the UPC or the reluctance of faculty, especially university faculty, to affiliate with the association.

The UPC faces other problems as well. The other faculty organizations have become concerned with their position relative to this new group. The CSEA began a large-scale membership drive at the same time the UPC was being established. Further, alliances among the other organizations seem to be developing to counter the influence of the UPC. Again, the long-run effects of these efforts are difficult to predict, but it is clear that the UPC will encounter difficult times as it seeks to establish itself.

Faculty organizations afford professors a means to express their opinions before the public and those who govern higher education. They also make available alternative channels for dealing with specific problems, such as grievances. The senates are not likely to provide these opportunities because of their official place in the structure, and therefore the organizations fill an important role in the functioning of a system such as the state colleges. It may be true that the plurality of faculty groups injures the faculty as they seek specific ends. Legislators and trustees have rejected proposals from the organizations on the grounds that they do not represent a majority of the instructors. It is also true, however, that the existence of different groups makes it possible for divergent viewpoints to find expression. What the colleges could use is the cooperation of all of these organizations on issues of common concern, and the statewide senate has made a step toward this goal by fostering interorganizational cooperation. Following that approach, unity could be obtained on especially significant issues while preserving the benefits of having different organizations. In the long run, if collective bargaining is accepted, faculty will probably have to select some group to serve as its bargaining agent. Assuming that agent is not the academic senate but one of the existing organizations, the plurality of groups may become a luxury too costly for state college faculty to pay.

There is at present a quiet among state college faculty, but this must not be interpreted as a sign of satisfaction among professors. The actions of the 1970 legislature and the governor in 1971 denying salary increases to faculty have kept alive discontent and restiveness. The lack of cohesion and clear direction on the part of the faculty organizations, and the relative absence of strong action by the statewide academic senate, have prevented such dissatisfaction from becoming mobilized. Leaders from all of the faculty groups have made statements and symbolic gestures to indicate the existence of faculty unhappiness, but none of this has been translated into actions involving the majority or even large numbers of professors.

As evident over the years, state college professors have displayed an unusual lack of willingness to become involved in miltant collective action. It does not seem probable that instructors will suddenly change in this regard, especially with the example of the San Francisco strike still in the minds of many. Perhaps the statewide senate or the CSEA will take the lead in advancing faculty interests within the college system in a quiet, moderate way. The dilemma for the professors is simply that the nonmiltant approaches of these two organizations have not proved effective in recent years, while the majority of faculty are not eager to support groups more prone to militancy—which might be more effective if widely supported.

Achieving collective bargaining, however, will hardly solve all faculty problems. Although bargaining may improve salaries and some aspects of working conditions it may aggravate other sources of faculty discontent, or leave them relatively untouched. The experience of the City University of New York, for example, has shown that faculty-administrative relations, a source of tension in the California state colleges, become more formal under collective bargaining. That is, the lines between instructors and administrators become more rigidly defined and flexibility in administration is more circumscribed. Student-faculty relations may also become more tense should bargaining be implemented. Faculty efforts to win lower teaching loads, greater research support, or improved sabbatical leave policies may well be interpreted by students as further attempts by professors to escape the classroom or to gain benefits at the expense of student needs.

Finally, a major factor in the unhappiness of state college faculty has been the relationship of the colleges to state government, and it is not likely that bargaining will markedly change that relationship. Political pressures and considerations will continue to influence the governor and legislators as they develop policy and budgets for state-supported higher education, and the existence of a formal contract or agreement with state college instructors will not alter these factors or their significance.

It is increasingly clear, though, that professors within the California state colleges, as well as faculty in institutions of higher education across the country, are turning to organized means of coping with their occupational problems. While collective bargaining will not produce a utopia relative to these sources of strain and tension it will bring about a greatly different environment for higher education, affecting students, faculty, administrators, and all others within academia. Whether this new environment will prove compatible with better education, professionalism, and academic traditions generally may well become a major test for the state colleges during the decade of the 1970s.

11

Minority Group Pressures
in a Statewide System

Kenneth S. Washington, Robert O. Bess

If the first half of the 1960s in the state college system was note-
worthy for the establishment of new campuses and the implementation of the Master Plan for Higher Education, the second half can
readily be seen as the period when "ethnicity" became a part of
the state college consciousness. Some have viewed this new focus
as nothing more than another symptom of confusion and disorienta-
tion within higher education while others see educational change of
a nature as basic and as significant as that which occurred in the
land grant era. Only the perspective of history will provide a true
assessment of the ethnic thrust in the California state colleges, or
indeed in all of higher education.

What has occurred in the state colleges cannot for the most
part be labeled unique or innovative. The behavior of minority students and minority community leaders and the initiation of pro-

grams or policies related to ethnic concerns represent, most often, responses to a greater movement, one which involves all facets of society.

When Stokely Carmichael spoke of "black power" in Jackson, Mississippi, in 1965 this conjured up for the man on the street visions of brute force, violence, and insurrection. Members of the academic community, on the other hand, generally took a more charitable view and saw in Carmichael's slogan a call for developing self-identity, self-respect, and self-determination. To many this effort paralleled that of the Chinese, Japanese, and Jewish subcultures in the United States. Responding to this interpretation, higher education attempted to make the tools of education more accessible to black and other minority youth.

At the same time that Carmichael, Malcolm X, and Charles Hamilton were teaching a new philosophy, American students were being awakened by their fellows returning from voter registration drives in the South and Peace Corps assignments abroad. A new idealism and heightened sense of social concern had replaced the characteristic student apathy of the fifties. Higher education began to assess its role in perpetuating racist characteristics in our society and to consider how it might now help to eliminate this blight which drains so much of the national energy.

Activities related to this ethnic focus cannot be separated into totally discrete categories, but discussions usually seem to focus on topics concerning educational opportunity programs, the student, and ethnic studies curricula. Out of the social framework mentioned above there emerged in 1967 a number of pilot efforts designed to raise the educational horizons of "minority poor" individuals. These activities varied in scope and technique, but all had a common objective—higher education for those who had been neglected. In most instances the manpower requirements associated with those efforts were met by regular college staff doing a little extra. At two colleges, Long Beach and San Diego, available resources, administrative leadership, and various local pressures joined to bring about structured formal programs with full-time staff leadership. At three other colleges, Fresno, San Francisco, and Los Angeles, a small number of minority students were admitted by "exception" without there being any formal support program.

In short order it became obvious that such activities were capable of interrupting the poverty cycle. Students in the pilot programs appeared to be persisting and performing as well as regular students. In light of this evidence, albeit limited, college personnel and members of the chancellor's staff joined, at first informally, to explore means of expanding and strengthening nascent programs. Several pieces of legislation were introduced during the 1968 session aimed at providing resources for educational opportunity. Bills which would have funded state college programs were not successful, but a bill establishing a special opportunity grant program and a resolution calling for the expansion of "exception" admissions were passed. These provided the impetus needed to move the state colleges from pilot to full-blown involvement.

Urging from numerous quarters, campus, community, and government, together with a call by state college Chancellor Glenn Dumke for a special effort to overcome educational inequities, appears to have triggered some sort of program on all but one of the state college campuses. In a few instances the term *program* overstates what actually took place—the admission by special action of a handful of minority students who also received some financial aid. However, in the main, enrollment of students and financial assistance were accompanied by significant efforts at providing supportive services such as counseling, tutoring, and peer group advising.

Unfilled faculty positions were used to hire program directors, special counselors, and clerical staff. Supplies and equipment were borrowed from other college areas. The original objectives of the Federal College Work-Study Program, implemented nationally in 1965, came closer to full realization when funds previously used to pay student readers, clerical assistants, and maintenance workers were diverted to employ tutors and student advisors for educational opportunity programs (EOP). Perhaps for the first time, the primary use of these funds involved a dual purpose—aid for the recipient, enabling him to stay in college, and assistance to those working to increase his chances of success. Recruiting activity in ghettos and barrios previously isolated from higher education was carried on by students, concerned faculty, and administrators as well as the few program specialists hired early enough to participate in the process of 1968 student intake.

The result of this surge of activity was that between 1,800 and 2,000 students enrolled in the California state colleges who would probably not have attended anywhere under former conditions. While no complete and comprehensive statistics are available for all of these programs, thoughtful estimates show an ethnic background distribution of 59 per cent black, 34 Chicano or Mexican-American, 2 Asian, and 5 others. While no official statement has ever been made which would identify EOP as being minority oriented, these figures, when compared with the all-student ethnic distribution for the same year, eliminate any doubt about the relationship between EOP and the ethnic thrust. Percentages for all students based upon the fall 1968 Civil Rights Act Compliance Report to the U.S. Department of Health, Education, and Welfare show 2.9 black, 2.9 Spanish surname, 0.7 American Indian, 3.4 Asian, and 90.1 other. A slightly more current indication of the orientation of educational opportunity programs and related activities can be seen in the shift of the ethnic mix of financial aid recipients. Between 1967–1968 and 1969–1970, the percentage of recipients of federal financial aids increased from 18 to 39.

An unfortunate byproduct of the obvious relationship between EOP and minority educational aspirations has been the exclusion of nonminority enrollees in one or two instances. This, however, has been ameliorated by adjustments in thinking on the part of both college staff and community leadership. Colleges have made it clear that needy whites will be welcomed, and program critics have come to understand that given the current set of circumstances a preponderance of minority enrollees is natural and perhaps even desirable.

Continuing our historical sketch, the next critical incident occurred in the 1969 legislative session. The Board of Trustees had requested nearly $2.5 million for EOP in their budget. The governor failed to concur and the case was laid before the legislature. Few issues have received so much attention during budget hearings. Dozens of witnesses were heard in formal session. Almost every member of the legislature was visited by one or more students, members of the community, and college staff. The result was favorable action, although at a slightly reduced level, coming at the very end of budget deliberations. The absence of a gubernatorial veto was a surprise to many since the final state college budget has rarely included substantial amounts for programs not originally proposed by the governor. This in itself suggests the degree of support behind the program. Perhaps the greatest credit belongs to the EOP students who appeared before the legislature to plead their own case. The young man with a prison record who now is on a dean's list provided quite a convincing exhibit.

Following on the heels of the Budget Act came the Harmer Bill (Senate bill 1072), legislation to provide statutory continuity for state college EOP. Unfortunately, as is often the case, the bill as finally passed provided too much law and the beginning of bureaucratic regulations which could dull the freshness of the EOP approach.

As programs moved into a second year of operation, the first as a recognized state college function, their strengths and their weaknesses became more evident. Questions about ethnic divisions, involvement of EOP students in campus disorders, appropriate uses of funds, and similar issues were continually raised. Against this backdrop proposals were made to place most responsibility for educational assistance for the minority poor on the community colleges and to severely curtail state college student intake for EOP. Most suggestions were for halving new student enrollment, and this became the basic position of the administration before the legislature. During the 1970 legislative session, special hearings were held once again, but substantially less time was devoted to the topic. The legislature was not ready to reduce its support for what appeared to be one of the more successful educational experiments of recent times. The final budget included funds for a program comparable to that of the previous year and limited grant assistance for continuing students.

In the fall of 1970, some 3,500 new students were enrolled in nineteen programs ranging in size from a dozen participants to five hundred. It appears that 80 per cent or more of those enrolled the previous year were continuing and less than 25 per cent were on academic probation. Even when one assumes that some of this striking success was caused by halo effect, the results are still impressive, for these were students who had been defined by traditional measures as failures.

The effect of ethnic thrust is reciprocal. Certainly, one must be deeply interested in the impact higher education has on deprived minority groups. But equally important is the effect that new human concerns, culturally different groups on campus, and a link-up with a new community may have upon higher education, particularly the California state colleges which have been described as being people's colleges. To better assess the potential influence of these programs on people and the people on higher education, it is instructive to examine a number of factors.

EOP minority students differ substantially from those few minority students found on most state college campuses prior to 1967. Those in the earlier group were largely from middle-class oriented families whose goals and aspirations were likely to coincide with the traditional collegiate-vocational values. Their adjustment to college life was occasionally marred by incidents of racial conflict and inability to satisfy the academic demands of the institutions. But by and large these students and their colleges agreed on the essential purposes and the desired end product of the four-year college experience. That is, the college was preparing them to join an industrial-professional society, raise their standard of living, and enjoy the good life.

The first EOP students were admitted during a period of rising racial and ethnic pride. They were children of the ghettos and barrios. They brought new life styles and values with them. Rather than present themselves for molding and initiation into a culture which they perceived as largely responsible for their basic plight, they felt obliged to seek modified educational experiences and to equip themselves in a manner which would best serve the ends of their own cultures. Here now were students who tended to reject the more traditional forms of social reward and, instead, were searching for an educational experience which would be directly relevant to the quality of their lives on campus and in the communities from which they had come.

The meeting of cultures on the college campus causes several forms of conflict. Confrontation rhetoric taught many members of the academic community that there was a language form commonly used by several million persons which they were unable to comprehend. A great many also became painfully aware that a significant portion of California's population was Spanish-speaking and that, likewise, they were unable to partake of that part of American culture because of social, economic, and political barriers which had effectively separated the Mexican-American from the rest of society.

Perhaps the deepest wound to academic tradition was EOP's impact on established admissions practices. Educational specialists have known for many years that grades and test scores leave much to be desired as predictors of collegiate success. While they are related to success in terms of college grades, there is a great deal of error. More important, their relation to drop-out is minor. However, this issue did not receive much serious discussion until concern arose over their tendency to systematically exclude the poor, the black, the brown, and the red from selective institutions of higher education such as the state colleges. Granted, the framers of the Master Plan recommended that allowances be made for exceptions to general admission rules. However, the limited utilization of this provision prior to 1968, and then chiefly in connection with athletic recruitment, suggests a failure to come to grips with reality. The performance level of students who fall far short of meeting regular admission requirements has forced another look at approaches which over the years have achieved a certain undeserved sanctity.

The first step has been to double the proportion of students who may be admitted by special action. This move by the state college Board of Trustees followed recommending action by the Coordinating Council for Higher Education and the introduction of a resolution in the legislature. More recently, the Coordinating Council has indicated that admissions practices should be thoroughly reevaluated and that a coordinated program of experimental approaches be initiated. These actions grew directly from a sensitivity fostered by the new presence of minority students on campus and the quality of their academic promise. Consider, for example, the following somewhat cautious statement from the staff report to the council on admissions policies for the 1970s: "There has been a recent upsurge in the desire to attend college among students from minority and low-income environments. There is some evidence that traditional admission criteria and procedures do not adequately identify those students from minority and low-income situations who have the capacity and motivation to benefit from college. New criteria and procedures appear to be needed for this group of students, and perhaps for other students with particular sets of characteristics" (Coordinating Council, 1970, p. 14).

The attitude of the new minority student concerning his place on the campus has likewise required substantial adjustment on the part of both fellow students and college staff. During the late fifties and early sixties minority initiates were readily available when fraternities were ready to fight "the nation" on the race issue. Now the black or brown student is far less likely to accept efforts to integrate him. Just as he is not likely to be interested in the traditional social activities, neither has he generally been willing to ally himself with so-called "new left" campus radicals, even when the latter expressed a desire to further the objectives of minority students. One author had an opportunity to observe this rejection first hand during a particularly "heavy" demonstration in the spring of 1969. A leader of a Students for a Democratic Society (SDS) group entered a tutorial center occupied at that time by some twenty-five black students. His exhortations that they join in a planned march on the administration building were answered by a very strong suggestion that he "run along and play his white folks' games." Several weeks later at another campus a group of white students burst into a faculty senate meeting to present demands related to minority enrollment and curriculum. On the following day minority student leadership (black and brown) held a press conference in which they disavowed the group and indicated that they could manage without the help of such groups.

While intercollegiate athletics is not big time on most state college campuses, the character of the new minority student is evident here as well. More and more, the minority student athlete is demanding assurances that he will have an opportunity to earn a degree and ready himself for a meaningful future. He is far less likely today to accept the idea of playing out his eligibility before fading away quietly. Even though state college athletics have been relatively low key, difficulties at one institution, San Jose, were sufficient to provide the initial phase of the 1968 Black Athlete's Revolt, led by Dr. Harry Edwards.

Perhaps the one characteristic of the new generation of minority students which has most troubled administrators, trustees, legislators, and others is their strong urge to organize and politicize their less active fellows both on campus and within the surrounding communities. In order to understand this sort of drive, one must step out of the typical middle-class set of life experiences common to most of those who occupy positions of responsibility and authority on campus and in government. Black students now attending college are the sons and daughters of men and women who often were subjected to the indignities of total segregation in the South and in many instances total exclusion from many California communities. Mexican students in college have heard from their parents of incidents such as the Sleepy Lagoon case in 1942 in which nine Mexican-Americans aged seventeen to twenty-one were all convicted of the murder of one individual and spent two years in San Quentin before the conviction was reversed. The "Zoot Suit" riots of 1943 left indelible scars (literally and figuratively) on a generation of Mexican-American as well as black residents of Los Angeles. The indignities heaped upon American Indians (or native Americans) require no examples.

More than their relatively docile predecessors, the current generation of minority youth have attempted to bring about change, both inside and outside the system. The foothold they have achieved has become the basis for bold assertiveness and a determination to press for greater gains. They are intent that their fellows be part of the solution rather than part of the problem. Large numbers of minority students now enrolled at California state colleges believe deeply that the effort they expended and the risks they took (often substantial) are the reasons why the doors have opened wider for others. It hardly matters whether this belief is true or not (we believe that it is). What is important is that it is felt deeply. As one student said, "If I had to shed blood to ride the train, I'll be damned if I'm going to let 'bourgeois Bessie' ride for free!"

A manifestation of this felt need for unity and strength through organization is the emergence of what are essentially exclusively minority organizations on college and university campuses. Black Student Unions (BSU) and United Mexican-American Students (UMAS) were formed at first to provide a home away from home as well as an arm for furthering minority student interests. Their headquarters or center provided a place where the student could lapse into his traditional styles of speech and behavior without fear of ridicule. Once these groups became more secure they turned outward both politically (demands) and culturally (influence patterns of speech, dress, music, and so on). Today it is most difficult to label such organizations as political or cultural. Members do not see any real difference between these two elements. The chief concern of certain nonminority members of the college community and the community at large—that such organizations represent reverse racism by their de facto exclusiveness—is beyond the comprehension of minority students. If this is so bad, they ask, then why was a similar cry not raised for a hundred years before. They attempt to explain, often to deaf ears, that there is a difference between separation chosen and segregation imposed.

In spite of marked enrollment increases among minority students during the past few years, they still represent roughly half the proportion in the college population that they do in the college age group. There are indications that the college-going pool of minority students (those whose academic backgrounds are comparable to most college students) is nearing exhaustion. The gap between minority and majority socio-economic status is a major factor in widespread social unrest. It is in the best interest of all segments of society to eliminate such unrest. Higher education is the single most important avenue to improved economic status. Taken together, the previous four statements point unquestionably toward continuation of special efforts to enroll minority students who are not part of the regular college-going pool. The authors do not hesitate to predict that a significant portion of future enrollees will come from ethnic groups heretofore grossly underrepresented in higher education. While there may be efforts to curtail special programs in the face of limited resources, it is not likely that the tide will be turned.

The outstanding question, then, is not whether ethnic minorities will make up a major portion of college enrollment but whether higher education will undergo significant change as a result of their presence. An examination of the ethnic studies movement provides important clues to the answer.

Awareness that traditional collegiate courses and textbooks have almost totally neglected the contribution of minority ethnic groups to the development of western civilization is of long standing. Early efforts to remedy this shortcoming all seem to have fallen short of the mark. Perhaps instructors and textbook writers lacked expertise, or perhaps motivation was lacking in the absence of minority students. The dominant theory today is neither of these. Rather, it is asserted that so long as the efforts of educators and those few minority students who were enrolled in predominantly white institutions were focused upon accommodation through absorption of minority interests in the majority culture they were doomed to failure.

At any rate, the arrival on state college campuses of substantial numbers of minority students, many of them representing the new look of ethnic pride and self-assertiveness, brought with it vigorous demands for curricular change. In a few instances these demands were accompanied by disruptive incidents, but generally they involved firm and persistent negotiation with faculty committees and academic administrators.

Initial college efforts to accommodate minority interests involved some intensification of minority hiring and the addition to existing courses of supplementary materials. Departments of English, sociology, and political science were most responsive. In general, this method has not been acceptable to the minority student. Numerous reasons are given and it is difficult to separate fact from rhetoric. However, a number of words and phrases seem common to most discussions about the shortcomings of this approach. One hears "patronizing," "unreliable," "fails to relate to the needs of our people," and "tokenism."

From these beginnings grew a concerted effort to identify materials and structured courses dealing specifically with minority concerns, but within established patterns of departmental and course organization. Concurrently, new demands were made by student leaders and a small number of faculty spokesmen not only for separate courses but for separate departments with their own degree programs. This new pressure appeared on college and university campuses across the nation at approximately the same time as it was occurring in the state colleges, but few locations experienced this force as intensely and persistently as did San Francisco State College. Directly or indirectly the struggle here resulted in the "resignation" of two presidents within a six-month period and the firing of the college's first ethnic studies coordinator before the program could actually be initiated.

Action led to reaction which in turn led to further action by opposing forces until on November 6, 1968, a student strike was called. Shortly thereafter, students were joined by faculty under the banner of the American Federation of Teachers. This strike lasted for nearly four months and left scars of mistrust which are very much in evidence today. An examination of certain of the root issues of the San Francisco strike will serve to describe significant elements in the continuing controversy over the role and place of ethnic studies in the California state colleges.

First was (and is) the issue of just what constitutes ethnic studies. At the outset there was no definition available to guide all parties. Students had their ideas but were unable to articulate them, at least not in the language of the system. Academic decision-makers tended to think solely in terms of the history, art, music, and so on of various ethnic groups. Some people in this group tended to focus upon each of these aspects in relation to the minority in American life while others felt that the earlier "pre-American" aspects of minority culture were sufficient to the need.

Minority students and a handful of faculty spokesmen saw an ethnic studies curriculum as one which involved not only history, art, and music, ancient to contemporary, but psychology, sociology, anthropology, political science, philosophy, literature, and economics as well. In effect, the goal was to recast a substantial number of disciplines in a manner which would make them meaningful. They wished to create a curriculum which would serve the respective minority groups as it has the majority culture—by legitimizing and glorifying their existence, by leading toward an understanding of the forces which mold their lives and which would equip them to improve their circumstances.

An assessment of all these factors leads one to conclude that the concept of a comprehensive and separate ethnic studies program arose from combined feelings of resentment, impatience, and mistrust. When one considers the years of purposeful delay which followed the 1954 Supreme Court decision on school integration, it is not difficult to understand minority students' unwillingness to accept the slow pace of institutional adaptation. Explanations that this was the way academia works simply fell on deaf ears.

Coupled with mistrust learned through years of conditioning was an emergent view that only a black man could understand the needs of other blacks, that only a Chicano could teach about "La Raza." If this basic premise was accepted, it followed that only members of the minority group could evaluate the quality of ethnic studies courses and the faculty teaching them. This contention lies at the root of the demand for autonomy which was a central issue in the San Francisco strike. The idea that students should choose and evaluate their teachers did not fit prevailing notions about college and university governance. Even attempts at compromise by faculty in various ethnic studies programs or departments have generally failed, conflicting as they do with traditions and policies calling for evaluation by tenured colleagues.

Another aspect of the controversy illustrated so graphically at San Francisco relates to the nature of courses in the ethnic studies curriculum. In addition to revolutionizing content, ethnic studies practitioners more often than not espoused an activist, community-related approach to methodology. When this methodology involves areas of significant concern to authority, conflict is virtually inevitable. Since dealing with insignificant matters would hardly be consistent with the minority student demand for relevance it is not surprising that such conflict has occurred.

The most recent and at the same time most illustrative incident involves Fresno State College. At Fresno, several potent elements came together: large numbers of minority students, largely as a byproduct of EOP recruiting, a fairly large and somewhat hastily organized program of ethnic studies, and a major community issue—the grape boycott. To the faculty of La Raza (Mexican-American) studies, field work associated with Cesar Chavez's United Farm Workers Organization and its strike against table-grape growers was quite natural. To the college administration, city fathers, and a number of other interests, permitting any official involvement between the college and the strike was totally inappropriate. The different perspectives on this issue are graphically illustrated in the commentary of one Chicano student who stated that he, the son of a worker, failed to see the difference between his being involved in the strike as a curricular adjunct and the son of a ranchowner doing field work with a local growers' cooperative.

Because so much heat, and in some instances relatively little light, accompanied the beginnings of ethnic studies, a number of initial questions remain unresolved in the minds of many. Just what is the content of ethnic studies? Is this a means of assuring academic success for minority students? Is ethnic studies another name for revolutionary activity? When one surveys the current scene, it is difficult to conceive how some of these questions can ever be answered satisfactorily. For example, one state college was charged with awarding grades that were unreasonably high in ethnic studies. The institution responded by demonstrating that there was no difference between the ethnic studies grade distribution and the all-college grade distribution. Some then said this was probably due to minority instructors giving low grades to students who disagreed with them.

There are no easy answers to questions related to appropriate degree of autonomy, course content, evaluation of faculty in new areas of instruction, and most especially the relationship between the search for knowledge in the classroom and the confrontation of social issues in the community. And these issues are not limited to the area of ethnic studies; they are often being raised about the entire social institution of higher education.

In spite of the questions which remain unresolved, it is a fact that thirteen state colleges offer majors in one or more areas of ethnic studies. It is a fact that at least ten state colleges offer a substantial amount of course work under the auspices of administrative units separate from traditional departments. It is a fact that in 1969–1970, more than 5,300 separate enrollments occurred in courses prefixed with such words as: Black, La Raza, Native American, and Asian. Thus, ethnic studies is at present very much a part of the academic landscape. Yet we hesitate to predict what the future may hold. One black faculty member has suggested that ethnic studies is more perspective than content. If he is correct, substantial enlargement of the number and range of offerings may not be necessary to achieve minority objectives—they could come by a form of osmosis. If he is incorrect and there is a continuing drive for expansion of ethnic studies because of their perceived intrinsic value, then a number of other possibilities present themselves.

Unwillingness to allocate resources during a lead period is certainly probable. Reallocation of existing resources to satisfy student demand is likely to meet with the resistance which normally accompanies proposals to cut back established programs. In the context of ethnic controversy such reluctance could lead to further strife. On the other hand, if there is a drop in ethnic studies enrollment there is likely to be the same sort of resistance to cutbacks. In short, we are too near in time to the issue. We must wait to know whether ethnic-orientated curricular change will become as much a part of the state college scene as has the minority student.

A final element in our examination of the impact of ethnic concerns on the California state colleges relates to employment patterns. An increase in the proportion of faculty identified as representing ethnic minorities is the natural outcome of expansion of ethnic studies curricular offerings and the attendant demand for minority instructors to teach them. A more generalized effort to employ faculty with backgrounds more nearly representative of the population appears to be making slow progress. In 1965, 3.5 per cent of all faculty were from minority ethnic groups. By 1969, this percentage had increased to 6.1 per cent. Minimal progress is generally attributed to unavailability of qualified persons and the extensive competition for those who are in the marketplace. The gap between the goal (California's minority population is 34 per cent) and achievement has forced a reasessment of qualifications which could have major implications for recruitment of all future faculty, minority or not.

Some recent trends in minority employment are encouraging. Among all types of employees, the lowest proportional growth appears in the clerical, trades, custodial group—the lowest paid and least underrepresented categories. Greatest increases have occurred among such groups as: over $10,000 annual salary, supervisory, and faculty. Hopefully, it will soon be possible to add to this list the category "administration."

12

Students in Governance

John D. Bacheller

Student government began many years before the establishment of the state college system in 1960. By then, several state colleges had well-organized, well-financed, on-going student governments. Their development was aided significantly by a section of the California Education Code which permitted state college students to impose a tax upon themselves to support student government and its activities. This mandatory student body fee, which can be no more than twenty dollars per student per academic year, is in force at all but two of the state colleges at this time. One of these two opened its doors for the first time in September 1970 and will probably have had a fee election by the time these words are set in print. At the other, Sonoma State College, students chose to exercise the option contained in the Education Code and voted to eliminate the fee in the spring of 1970. Of the remaining seventeen state colleges, all but one are charging the maximum twenty dollars per student.

Given this relatively stable base of funding, student governments were able to enter into the development and support of programs on a far broader scale than has been customary in public higher education. There are restrictions on the use of state monies for intercollegiate athletics and certain other instructionally related activities, such as drama, music, and debate. Thus for a number of years a major source of financial support for several academic areas has been student government; its voice in decisions relating to such matters is fairly proportional to the funds allocated. As a consequence, student government—particularly at the larger and more well-established colleges—has traditionally been involved in many activities other than those of the sandbox variety which characterize many other student governments.

The general quality of student leadership, coupled with this opportunity to become involved in more significant campus matters and a stable base of funding, resulted in the responsive and responsible student governments that characterized the state colleges by the mid-1960s. As has been pointed out elsewhere, a high percentage of state college students come as upperclassmen after completing their first two years at a community college. Many of these students are working and have a heavy personal investment in their education. The net result is a student body which is older and more mature than that on most campuses. As might be expected under such circumstances, formal student leaders tend to reflect this maturity. Student body presidents are often over twenty-five, or graduate students, or veterans, or married, or a combination of two or more of these.

The typical state college student government operated with little outside control prior to the late 1960s. The larger student governments had hired professional business managers to supervise their day to day operations, and college presidents tended to permit these individuals to exercise the supervisory authority that was legitimately their own, perhaps forgetting that in the final analysis, regardless of how professional they might be, these business managers were employees of student government.

In the latter third of the sixties, several new developments contributed to significant changes in student government as it has been known in the state colleges. These factors were: the emergence of a group of ultra-liberal to radical students who attempted to use student government as a base for furthering their aims; the growth of militant minority organizations, such as the Third World Liberation Front; a growing awareness among a majority of students of the weaknesses and injustices of our society; a greater involvement on the part of student government with off-campus, community-oriented programs; and the election of a governor who promised to clean the radicals out of Berkeley and the rest of public higher education in California.

The example of student government at San Francisco State College, while admittedly an extreme, will show how these factors combined. Briefly, over a period of years a group of ultra-liberal and radicalized students worked their way into positions of leadership until they had literally gained control of student government and its treasury. This government was especially attuned to the demands of militant minority organizations to do its fair share to right the wrongs of our society. A majority of the student body either did not care or was in sympathy with many of these demands.

Many of the programs established, such as storefront tutorial centers in minority neighborhoods, had positive value. At the same time, several radical students, with no constructive plans, were living off the income they received from student government. Despite the relative affluence of state college student governments, they do have a financial breaking point. It became impossible to continue financing traditional programs and still meet the demand for new community-oriented programs. When the student government tried to eliminate its long-standing subsidy of varsity athletics, the Establishment suddenly became alive to what was happening. The resultant discord was resolved some time later, and then only by court action, initiated by the attorney general of California, that placed the funds of student government in receivership.

The situation at San Francisco State College was exceptional. Yet it cannot be dismissed that simply, since occurrences there and at a few other state colleges have been used repeatedly by legislators and trustees to justify greater controls over student government. As a consequence, the following actions directly related to student government and its expenditure of funds have been taken within the past two years. Early in 1969 the Board of Trustees of the California state colleges for the first time placed limits on activities for which income from the mandatory student body fee could be expended. Under present provisions of the California Administrative Code, such money may only be utilized to fund programs that fall within categories approved by the board. At the same time the board clarified and strengthened the role of the college president in reviewing and approving the student government budget. He could now veto specific items within the proposed budget, whereas prior to this time he had to either accept or reject the budget as a whole. During its 1970 session, the California legislature enacted the Harmer Bill, which made the chief fiscal officer of the college custodian of all monies collected for student government through the mandatory fee. Such funds will, upon request from student government, be disbursed by the college business office, but only after insuring that expenditures would be in keeping with the approved budget.

At its November 1970 meeting the board passed a resolution which will require legislative action to become functional. Such legislative action if taken—and there is no reason to believe it will not be—would allow the establishment of a special fund at those campuses chosen by the board. This fund would be used to support intercollegiate athletics and other instructionally related activities which had been aided by student government in the past. The size of the fee involved would vary from campus to campus, with the maximum being fifteen dollars per student per academic year. Whether or not such an approach to funding these activities would be put into effect at any given campus is a decision that would be made primarily by the college president. If the fee were established, the amount collected for the mandatory student body fee would automatically be reduced by a similar amount.

Most student body presidents recognize the legitimate concern of both legislators and members of the Board of Trustees regarding the expenditure of funds that are authorized through state law. They also realize that these same individuals are concerned about stable funding for the instructionally related programs that student government has helped in the past. At the same time, the presidents look at the responsible manner in which their governments have carried out their obligations and they resent being cast in the same light as the less responsible; so it is not difficult to understand their developing rift with the formal leaders of the state col-

lege system. While admitting that they are uncertain as to whether
they are becoming clairvoyant or paranoid, many of these student
leaders see even greater controls being placed on them in the future.

Prior to the spring of 1969, student bodies were relatively
free to set appropriate standards for their student body presidents.
Some state colleges had developed complex requirements meant to
insure the ultimate selection of highly qualified individuals to positions of formal leadership. Other institutions' requirements could be
met by virtually all students enrolled during the term of election. In
a similar fashion, some schools had election codes that covered any
contingency that might arise, short of earthquakes, while others
barely covered the process of casting and counting the ballots themselves. As one might have predicted, serious difficulties arose. In
addition to the annual problems caused by hotly contested elections
plus admittedly inadequate election procedures, a major incident
developed in the spring of 1969 at Sonoma State College. A black,
thirty-four-year-old ex-felon won a close second election after he had
successfully contested the results of a losing first effort. A number
of individuals questioned the propriety of having anyone with such
a background serving in that capacity. The trustees in July 1969
called for an ad hoc committee to study and make recommendations
regarding qualifications for student body officers and conduct of
student elections. The committee's report, which was presented in
late September and finally adopted by the board early in 1970,
made several general recommendations of a positive nature that did
little, if anything, to interfere with campus autonomy in these areas.
The net effect, however, was to further widen the rift between student leaders and the decision-makers at a systemwide level.

As a consquence of all these occurrences the relationship
between local student governments and those who make policy for
the system has degenerated over the past two to three years. While
most student governments are still strong and able to support a
wide variety of programs, an aura of suspicion and mistrust has
developed. The spectre of student government deliberately disestab-
lishing itself at Sonoma State (primarily on a platform of "we can
no longer do what we want, only what the trustees want") is in the
minds of most student leaders.

Student government also exists on a statewide level, although in a rather loosely knit form. An organization of student body presidents, appropriately enough called the California State Colleges' Student Presidents Association, was formed at about the same time the state college system came into being. In the summer of 1963 the Board of Trustees adopted a resolution which, in effect, recognized CSCSPA as the voice of the students and invited its president to sit in routinely at all board meetings. This practice has continued to the present time.

By the mid-1960s CSCSPA was fairly well organized. It held three or four large meetings per year, passing resolutions on a variety of topics of concern to students within the system. While not possessing any real power or authority, the association was in the unique position of having the attention of the trustees, a form of power in itself. A relationship was also established with the statewide academic senate. Eventually CSCSPA developed an academic affairs assembly to deal with items of a more academic nature, leaving its presidents council free to work with the trustees on more political matters.

In spite of its relative success, CSCSPA was not a strong organization. As mentioned previously, its power lay in its ability to communicate with the trustees, a privilege totally dependent upon the good will of the board itself. The typical state college student had little if any knowledge of the organization. Funding was an almost constant problem; since the association offered little in the way of services, it was difficult to charge the level of dues necessary to provide adequate support. Smaller state colleges in particular saw insufficient benefits from membership to justify even moderate expenditures on behalf of the organization. Therefore, to keep all state colleges as active members and thereby annually revalidate the claim of representing all of the colleges, CSCSPA charged only token membership fees.

Perhaps the greatest weakness of the association lay in what at first glance was its greatest strength—the core of the organization was composed of student body presidents. As a group these individuals were intelligent, articulate, and concerned. At the same time they had great difficulty in placing the good of their own campus second to the good of the system. If the state colleges had been homogeneous in nature this might not have presented a problem, but one of the most striking characteristics of the state college system is the diversity of its institutional members.

The 1968–1969 academic year was a year of crisis for CSCSPA. By January of 1969 the academic affairs assembly was practically nonfunctional. The presidents were devoting most attention to political matters and were unwilling to give adequate time to more academic items. With an increased emphasis on politics, the internal diversity of the presidents council became apparent to even the casual observer. The group could not reach consensus on issues of major concern and by the end of the academic year the organization's survival was in considerable doubt.

The following year found only the faintest heartbeat in CSCSPA. An executive coordinator represented the organization at board meetings, but the major conferences characteristic of previous years were no longer to be seen. The trustees began to question whether CSCSPA could any longer legitimately purport to represent the students of the system. Clearly, another year of such disorganization could only result in the total dissolution of CSCSPA.

In the spring 1970 student government elections, however, an interesting phenomenon took place that had an immediate impact upon CSCSPA. At an overwhelming majority of the state colleges, students of a moderate philosophic stance were elected as new student body presidents. For the first time in a number of years, much of the diversity among student leaders was gone. This new development, coupled with the recognition that 1970–1971 would be a make-or-break year for CSCSPA, led to a series of meetings during the summer of 1970 in an effort to reconstitute the organization. While some internal diversity remains, the formal leadership of CSCSPA now seems to have recognized the need for public unity, and the association appears headed down a path that will allow it to continue to represent the system's students to the Board of Trustees.

In addition to the role student government itself plays in the governance of individual state colleges, on virtually all campuses individual students participate in a wide array of administrative and faculty committees that, in total, constitute a significant portion of institutional governance. In many instances these students are members of the formal student government; in others they are appointed through this structure. At the beginning of the 1970–1971 academic year, a total of 770 students were serving as voting members on 118 administrative and 153 faculty committees of an all-college nature. (These figures do not include the sizable number of students serving on departmental committees.) Membership ranges from seats on the college president's council and the local academic senate to seats on curriculum, faculty personnel policies, and graduate studies committees.

While each year has shown a steady increase in such involvement, one faculty committee remains without student representation—the tenure, retention, and promotion committee. Several local academic senates have debated the value of student representation on this committee, but as of this writing none has acted to include students as members. Since many students see this particular committee as the key to effective and competent teaching, the absence of student representation leads some students to question the meaningfulness of their involvement in general.

Although it is relatively easy to document the quantitative aspects of student involvement in institutional governance, evaluating the effectiveness of such participation is quite difficult. As might be expected, there is considerable variance, but a few generalizations are worth noting. The greater the perceived relevance of the committee to students' needs and interests, the better the performance of the student representative(s). Evaluations of student committee members have tended to compare student performance in such roles with that of most administrators or faculty performing similar committee roles. Committees with moderate to heavy work loads and frequent, regular meetings tend to have more effective student participation than do those with light work loads and/or infrequent meetings. Thus, the most effective student representation is more often connected with major administrative or faculty committees. Among such committees are the president's council, the local academic senate, and faculty curriculum committees.

Those state colleges with a relatively long history of student involvement in institutional governance have generally developed selection and training procedures that seem to increase significantly the effectiveness of student participants. The development of such procedures on campuses which have only recently begun to involve students in the local committee structure is necessary if students are to adequately fulfill the responsibilities inherent in such membership. In a number of instances, in spite of an obvious institutional commitment to student involvement in governance, student government has yet to develop the machinery that will draw out those individuals with the greatest potential for providing responsible representation.

The involvement of students at the academic departmental level is relatively new but is expanding at a rapid rate. For the average student, whose educational-vocational goal is centered in his academic major, participation in department-level decision making seems more relevant than involvement in most all-college committees, since at this level most major decisions affecting the student and his education are at least initiated, if not decided. Thus it is clear that students do play a vital role in institutional governance. Although the breadth and depth of such involvement show considerable variance from college to college, there is a widespread commitment to meaningful participation by students in the decision-making process.

The role of students in the governance of the state college system itself has been far more limited than in the governance of individual institutions. The most obvious form of such involvement has been the interaction of the Student Presidents Association and the Board of Trustees. In addition, there have been two other types of participation worthy of note: work with the statewide academic senate and involvement in study groups appointed by the board or chancellor to examine particular issues and make recommendations.

As noted earlier, CSCSPA has had a form of official board recognition since 1963. While the organization does not have full discussion and debate privileges at board meetings, it may, with only minimal restrictions, present a student view on any matter to come before the board. These restrictions have typically been a limitation on the number of speakers to talk to any one issue and an insistence that board members have an opportunity to interact among themselves before opening a topic for more generalized discussion. Although the membership of CSCSPA would be in general agreement that they have been given reasonable discussion privileges at board meetings, there is considerable disagreement about both effectiveness and approach. CSCSPA presentations to the board prior to the fall of 1968 were generally moderate in tone. In the period 1968–1970 a much more militant approach was taken, followed by a return to a constructively critical, presentation-of-alternatives approach. No matter which route they choose, it appears that the opinions and arguments of student leaders have increasingly less impact upon most of the board. Many CSCSPA members attribute this to the increasing conservativism of the board, a majority of whose membership was appointed by Reagan.

Whether or not these opinions are accurate is difficult to state. However, the voting record of the board does reflect a shift to the political right and a high percentage of those policy positions opposed by student leaders have been adopted by the board during the past few years. Regardless of victories or defeats, however, the present membership of CSCSPA intends to continue to provide the board with as much student input as possible and to suggest alternative methods of resolving problems that would emphasize local campus judgment.

For several years CSCSPA maintained a close liaison with the statewide academic senate. At one point during the 1968–1969 academic year, the student affairs committee of the senate was prepared to support a proposal that would have given five voting seats to students. The internal difficulties that developed within CSCSPA, however, led to a shelving of this proposal. While the senate, like CSCSPA, has only the power of persuasion in its relationship with the Board of Trustees, a united front on the part of both organizations, whenever practicable, was felt to have many advantages. Such an approach may still have considerable merit, but the difficulties each group has experienced with the board have helped to keep them from joining together more often. CSCSPA will have to pay more attention to its own internal reorganization before it can enter into any meaningful relationship with a group such as the statewide academic senate.

Over a period of time a large number of task forces and other study groups are appointed to examine topics of systemwide concern. Some of these groups are directly authorized by the Board of Trustees while others come into being as a result of action by the chancellor. Virtually all of them have at least limited student

representation. Recommendations of these groups carry great weight
with the board and the chancellor. Effective student participation
in such task forces could have great impact upon the governance
of the system. Within the relatively quiet confines of a conference
room students can present a point of view and argue for its acceptance in a manner that lends itself to success far more readily than
do presentations made to the board in an emotionally charged
atmosphere. More often than not, recommendations of such groups
have been accepted by the chancellor and the board. Unfortunately,
students have tended not to put their best efforts into these study
groups and they have therefore ineffectively utilized this means to
influence decision-making.

On balance, students have played a less significant role in
systemwide governance than they have at the local campus level.
The members of the CSCSPA have yet to display as a group the
abilities they have often demonstrated as individuals on their own
campuses. While there are a number of understandable reasons for
this, the end result is little significant input in policy-making for
the system.

In a discussion on the role of students in policy making
within a state system of higher education, it would normally seem
rather strange to talk of student relations with the state government.
However, these are far from normal times for the California state
colleges. The governor and members of the legislature have become
actively involved in the policy-making process of the state colleges.
The governor sits as president of the Board of Trustees, as well as
makes appointments to the board. The legislature has seen fit to
enact legislation that directly affects the day to day operation of the
state colleges. Given these facts, it is not unusual to find student
leaders actively involved with both the governor and the legislature.
In return, both the legislative and executive branches of state
government have opened new channels of communication for student leaders within the past two years.

During the 1970 session of the legislature, the joint legislative
committee on higher education established a student advisory council which included four student leaders from the state colleges.
Apparently the council was intended to improve communications
between lawmakers and students. While it may have achieved that

purpose, little else of a positive nature was accomplished by a group that, from the beginning, had little idea of its purpose. In addition to those individuals who served with the council, students have on a number of occasions testified on behalf of, or in opposition to, pending legislation relating to the state colleges. Probably the most effective work done by CSCSPA during the 1969–1970 academic year was accomplished in legislative hearing rooms.

Beginning in the fall of 1969 the governor held fairly regular meetings with student leaders from the various segments of higher education. Many of the state college student leaders who participated in these joint meetings felt that the governor had initiated them solely as a public relations device, and little occurred to change their minds. In spite of this negative attitude, student body presidents took advantage of the opportunity whenever it arose. In the fall of 1970 the format of such meetings changed somewhat; the governor met more often with students from a single segment rather than with a more general group. The new student leaders, while still suspicious of the governor's basic motivations, had a more positive attitude toward him. Although it would be difficult to pinpoint any specific gains that have resulted from this interaction, student leaders continue to feel that it affords them an opportunity to communicate directly with the state's chief executive.

As one attempts to assess the future of student government and the role students will play in decision making in the state colleges, one cannot help but think in political terms. The reelection of the state's governor assures him of the opportunity to have completely appointed the Board of Trustees by the time his second term in office expires. There is no reason to expect that his future board appointments will differ philosophically from those he has made over the past four years.

If these assumptions are accepted, it appears likely that significant changes will occur in student government within the next decade. Many of the actions taken by the board the past two to three years have limited the freedom of student governments to act as they wished. Whether or not this is a desirable limitation is a value judgment to be made by each individual. Students at Sonoma State College in the spring of 1970 viewed the limitations placed on them as being too restrictive—thus they eliminated student government. Students at other state colleges may take similar action, particularly if the trend to place restrictions on the authority of student government continues.

At the same time, we cannot ignore the trend to greater student involvement in the governance of individual institutions. This trend will no doubt continue, with the greatest growth at the academic department level. We may even find some institution willing to break down the traditional, but artificial, barriers between faculty government and student government. The development of a unicameral governance structure is possible.

It seems unlikely that CSCSPA will be able radically to improve its position. The lack of an adequate base fund, the inability of many student leaders to see beyond the boundaries of their own campuses, and an increasingly conservative Board of Trustees will probably result in continued impotence. The greatest prospects for CSCSPA to become a significant force lie in a union with either the statewide academic senate or a similar student organization from the other segments of California higher education. A single, unified organization of faculty and student leaders offers the potential political muscle needed if faculty and students are to retain any major voice in policy making for the system.

The prospects for the future, then, appear quite mixed. As individuals, students may have even greater involvement in governance than heretofore. On the other hand, formal student government structures may well have to undergo considerable change if they are to survive. But then, students have adaptive qualities beyond the comprehension of most older and more rigid members of the educational establishment.

13

⎍⎍⎍⎍⎍⎍⎍⎍⎍⎍⎍⎍⎍⎍⎍⎍

Changes in Governance
at a College

J. Malcolm Walker

⎍⎍⎍⎍⎍⎍⎍⎍⎍⎍⎍⎍⎍⎍⎍⎍

Although governance in the California state colleges was quite stable until the late 1940s, substantial and rather frequent changes occurred after that time. As the oldest and one of the largest of the colleges, San Jose State College (SJSC) has experienced the full range of governance systems and has sustained several periods of change. San Jose therefore presents an apt case study through which to identify types of governance experienced by the California colleges and to explain shifts to successive systems.[1] Until the late

[1] The case study of SJSC is based upon: (1) a wide variety of documentary material covering four decades, including correspondence of key college personnel, minutes and reports of major decision-making bodies and investigating groups, records of college policies and procedures, and surveys of opinions and practices; (2) the *Campus Digest* and the *Spartan Daily*, SJSC's student newspaper; (3) statistical data on enrollment, employment, number of committees and departments, terminal degrees, and others; (4) interviews with some seventy college personnel.

1940s, power at SJSC was tightly held by a small group of administrators and exercised in a system with a low degree of bureaucracy. Governance was bureaucratized during the 1950s, while administrators retained control. Faculty then sought power and achieved it in 1964. Three years later attempts were made to incorporate students into governance by developing a tripartite bureaucratic system. During the same period an organic—tripartite but nonbureaucratic —system was implemented in parts of the college. Periods of transition were characterized by: dissatisfaction with the existing system; the "pull" of a new system; and a mix of behaviors by excluded groups, top college leadership, and groups outside the college.

SJSC was a normal school and then a teachers college until the 1940s. Educational programs, limited in scope and depth, taught students elementary and secondary school subjects and how to teach them. Vocational programs were gradually introduced in commerce, home economics, journalism, industrial arts, and similar fields. Because college programs were similar and few, little systematic coordination was required. The structure of governance was simple and may be characterized as personal-arbitrary. As late as 1946 there were only four hierarchical levels: president, college dean, department chairman, and faculty. Committees were little used. Decision making was centralized. The president, T. W. MacQuarrie (1927–1952), advised by the two college deans and the business manager, participated in decision making on all important matters. MacQuarrie would reach down into departments to change curriculum and to reassign or dismiss faculty members of whom he disapproved. He allocated funds for travel and for reduced teaching loads and kept close watch over the contributions of individual faculty members to communtiy chest campaigns. A moral man of the opinion that faculty should set a good example for students, MacQuarrie forbade smoking on campus.

When faculty reminisce about those days, they tend to ascribe to MacQuarrie everything that happened in the college. He is described as "paternalistic," a "dictator," an "autocrat," a "dominating, authoritarian person." Decision making was often arbitrary, and faculty members made few decisions outside the classroom, Administrators occupied most decision-making positions—including 65 per cent of college committee positions in 1947—and controlled the appointment of faculty members who occupied the others. The faculty had no independent representative units which could give even advice to administrators. In departments, the department head made decisions, alone or in consultation with individual faculty members. Faculty meetings were social affairs; most departments had no standing committees; and only the head's opinion counted with the president. Heads served indefinitely so long as they retained the president's favor. MacQuarrie rejected all pleas for faculty participation, claiming that he already had advisors (the administrators); the college was his to run; he did not need advice from "little soviets." Only the president had significant sources of power: the law and hierarchical delegation from the State Department of Education. The faculty had little power of expertise and, until the 1940s, no tenure law or other bureaucratic safeguards. The Department of Education opposed faculty participation in governance. Faculty associations in the college were passive.

Despite the strains in the system—deriving from the wide power disparity and the accumulation of cases of arbitrary action—the faculty could not effectively challenge the president. Further, so long as the institutional characteristics of the college did not substantially change, the system of governance was quite efficient. In a small college with a narrow range of programs, policies could be developed by a few men at the top who could easily reach down into the college to issue orders and monitor performance. When departments were small and the subject matter within each quite uniform, department heads could make effective decisions. A complex structure was unnecessary.

In the decade following 1945, SJSC became a quasi-university.[2] The mission of the teachers college was retained, but the primary goal was now an educated citizenry. Teacher-training programs lost ground as a greater diversity of academic subjects developed in a more rigorous manner. The sciences and liberal arts expanded. Master's degrees were offered, first in education (1946)

[2] The other old colleges developed in a similar fashion. Los Angeles, Sacramento, and Long Beach state colleges, founded in the decade of the 1940s, adopted the quasi-university rather than the teachers college model. See *The California State Colleges*. Sacramento: California State Department of Education, 1955.

and then in a variety of fields in the arts and sciences (1955). By
1956 a majority of students were in graduate or upper division programs. A greater variety of administrators, support staff, and faculty
entered the college, the latter increasingly from fields other than
teacher education. The faculty became heterogeneous, with a variety
of subject-matter backgrounds, degree levels, and previous experience. As the college became "academically respectable," many
Ph.D.'s were recruited from the better graduate schools. The college grew quickly: from 6,000 students in 1951 to 12,000 in 1961;
from 81 faculty members in 1945 to 329 in 1954, and over 700
by 1960; expenditures rose from $741,407 in 1945–1946 to more
than $10,000,000 in 1959–1960.

Greater complexity of programs, heterogeneity of personnel,
and size led to the bureaucratization of governance. As the number
and variety of problems expanded, processes of decision making
became more complex, and pressures developed for more systematic
patterns of governance—in the words of administrators during the
1950s, for "well-coordinated structure," "well-defined lines of authority and responsibility," "authority commensurate with responsibility." Decentralization was necessary and it required a more
elaborate structure.

Pressures toward bureaucratization of the internal governance of the other state colleges were also building as the rapidly
growing schools faced similar problems of inadequate structure and
shortage of administrative personnel. Following suggestions from
the presidents, the State Department of Finance conducted the first
study of the internal governance of the colleges in 1950. This so-
called Chandler Report introduced managerial "principles of administration" into the colleges. According to the report, governance
in each college should be based on these "sound principles": a
hierarchy with precise lines of authority; each person responsible
ultimately to the president; subunits made up of related activities;
a limited number of subdivisions to permit narrow spans of control;
and staff services to facilitate management and coordination. Subsequent reports adopted by the Department of Education authorized
additional staffing and increasingly complex structures. Implementation of these recommendations made it possible for SJSC to acquire
larger administrative and support staffs and to adopt more elaborate

structures. Between 1945 and 1965 the number of administrative positions tripled and support staff rose from 55 to almost 900. Faculty declined as a proportion of total employment, from 64 per cent in 1949 to 47 per cent in 1964. Informal, personalized relations were no longer feasible. Top administrators became remote, available only through formalized channels and procedures. Decisions could no longer be made by simply seeing someone down the hall. As rules and procedures proliferated, they were codified and written down. Job descriptions were written, relationships specified, and elaborate criteria for decision making developed. The first *Staff Reference Manual* was issued in 1948 and successive issues were increasingly elaborate.

When MacQuarrie resigned in 1952 some faculty leaders attempted to obtain a faculty council from the new president to prevent the revival of presidential autocracy and permit the faculty to influence the rule-making processes in the emerging bureaucracy. The proposal had great faculty support and was endorsed by 231 of the 254 who voted on the issue (of 364 eligible). The Chandler Report had recommended that each college have such a council—without, however, indicating what its power should be—and the new president endorsed the concept. After negotiations with the new president, a weak council was secured. It could not develop policy, being designed only to help the administration promote faculty understanding of administrative proposals and to be a means for the administration to determine the views of the faculty.

The council's powers were never clearly defined. The faculty was never satisfied that the powers were great enough and felt that the council was not consulted enough. Its jurisdiction was carefully restricted by the administration. It was never more than one among many advisory bodies to the main, administrator-dominated organs of governance. The administration never recognized the council as speaking for the entire faculty and the council did not control the college committee system. It existed, in the words of a former chairman, "apart from the real administration of the college." Similar faculty councils were developed in most of the colleges during this period as well.

At the college level decisions were made by the president and the president's council, the chief administrative and policy-making body of the college, including the president, four deans, and the business manager. Administrators made decisions at lower levels, alone or together with subordinate administrators. Faculty opinions were sought and considered but usually in unsystematic and informal ways. Department heads had full authority in departments and were clearly defined as administrators rather than as faculty colleagues. Administrators dominated the college committee system. They were represented in proportionately much greater numbers than that of the faculty: in 1958, while there were only some 40 administrators compared with more than 600 faculty members, administrators held 254 committee positions and the faculty 226. Key administrators served on all important committees, and faculty members were in the minority on such committees. Faculty representatives were appointed by administrators.

Although managerialism persisted until 1964, it was under continuous attack by the faculty during the preceding decade. The college continued to grow rapidly. Teacher education was clearly subordinated to the mission of producing liberally educated students prepared for effective citizenship. Academic programs became more rigorous and faculty research expanded rapidly. Apart from the lack of a university name and independent doctoral programs, SJSC became a full university.

New faculty members were committed to upgrading the academic quality of educational programs. They were very conscious of themselves as professionals and of the notion that professionals should govern themselves. They argued that faculty power in decision making was necessary on these bases: that faculty possess specialized expertise necessary for effective educational decisions; that participation would motivate faculty members to perform more effectively; that high-quality faculty would be recruited into institutions where they could participate; and that faculty power would reduce the influence of "educationalist" administrators who were perceived as inhibiting the shift to high quality, specialized academic programs. Faculty power was justified as appropriate to the type of institution that SJSC was becoming—faculty should share governance powers in a quality academic institution. The influence of patterns of governance at the University of California was especially strong; its academic senate was a model which SJSC might emulate.

The faculty became increasingly dissatisfied with the power disparity on campus. The faculty council attempted, without much success, to expand its jurisdiction. Reports of faculty meetings and papers developed by faculty included criticism of "the authoritarian structure," "inflexible administrators," "the big stick," "unilateral action." When the faculty voted on proposals developed by the Master Plan Survey Team in 1959, large majorities endorsed academic programs for SJSC duplicating those of the University of California and favored research opportunities for state college faculty.

Since similar pressures were developing in other state colleges, the SJSC faculty became involved in the statewide movement to remove the colleges from the Department of Education. It was anticipated that a separate state college system would facilitate acquisition of greater resources for the colleges, reduce the influence of educationalists, and permit faculty to share in the governance of each college and of the statewide system. As the Master Plan study got under way, the college presidents recommended "effective faculty participation" in policy making in the colleges. But without clear statewide directives, progress in each college depended on the president and faculty leaders. Both maneuvered for position. Progress was slow. While the president advised "restraint" and cautioned against unrest, the faculty council proposed a plan that would exclude full-time administrators from the campus policy-making council and put policy-implementing groups under control of that council. Faculty felt that the presence of administrators would inhibit free expression of views. But administrators could not accept exclusion from a policy-making council. There were disputes, also, over whether the president should have to accept council proposals.

During the slow transition (1959–1963) strains in the managerial system became acute. Divisions on campus were accentuated, and conflict increased. Faculty activists took advocatory positions in articulating the strains in the managerial system, stating alternatives, creating polarization, and stimulating change. They seized upon issues—nonretention of faculty activists, denial of admission to a student expelled from a southern college for civil rights activities—and used them for generalized attacks on the administration. Revolts occurred in some departments and divisions. Successive crises could not be settled on the basis of right or wrong, since the processes of decision making were themselves being questioned.

After legislative adoption of the Master Plan, under pressure from the statewide faculty associations and following a legislative resolution endorsing faculty participation in governance, the new Board of Trustees and chancellor in 1962 issued criteria for the establishment of policy-making councils and for other procedures for joint faculty-administrator governance in the colleges. Both would sit on the council, and the college committee system would be subordinated to it. The effectiveness of the new system depended on how well the president and aspiring faculty could work together to overcome hostilities and develop trust while implementing the new system. A new president, Robert D. Clark (1964–1969), identified himself with educational progress in the college and endorsed faculty participation. He established close relationships with faculty leaders and used his formal authority to implement the new system, which I shall call a collegial bureaucratic system.

In such a system administrators, and in particular the president, seek the approval of the faculty before action and rarely act in the face of disapproval. The faculty also formulates proposals for action by the responsible administrator. The faculty may also execute decisions and formal structures are established to incorporate such faculty participation. One such is the department acting as a whole. This becomes the core unit of collegial relationships, and departmental decisions, based on peer judgments, are given great weight throughout the college. The department head no longer rules the department; he is now called a chairman and considered a faculty colleague, subject to review by departmental faculties. Deans are subjected to similar reviews. Faculty committee systems are established in schools and departments and the major college-level unit is the academic council. Comprised of both administrators and faculty, it considers and develops policies for final approval by the president. The college committee system is subordinated to the council. Faculty hold a majority of committee positions—64 per cent in 1968—and at least 50 per cent of the membership of each committee. Administrators and faculty together control appointments to committees.

In such a system law and administrative delegation are inadequate bases for administrators' power. They must show an ability to reconcile varied interests on campus, lead in improving educational programs, and implement policy effectively. The majority of the faculty, many of whom had cooperated with Clark and with Hobart W. Burns (academic vice-president, 1966–1969; acting president, 1969–1970) in implementing the new system, expressed strong satisfaction with their performance.

Faculty participation, then, came to pervade the entire organization; faculty were involved to some extent at all levels and on all significant issues and had greatest power in those areas—such as instruction, curriculum, research, faculty personnel decisions—in which the relevance of faculty expertise is most clear. The system remained bureaucratic, with faculty sharing power through bureaucratic structures. Indeed, this system was more bureaucratic than the preceding managerial system. Faculty powers and functions were specified in detail. Mechanisms were established to protect them: grievance procedures, elaborate disciplinary procedures, committees of all kinds.

In fall 1967, pressure developed for generalized student participation in decision making. This, of course, was a nationwide phenomenon. The arguments used at SJSC to justify such participation were the same as those used elsewhere and need not be repeated here. From 1967 through 1970 student leaders ranging from leftist to conservative presented these arguments, volunteered to serve in governance, mobilized other students, and maintained continuous pressure for incorporation of students into academic governance. Pressure was organized through student government offices and supported by a significant number of students. Student demonstrations—supporting black and Chicano demands, protesting Dow Chemical recruiting and ROTC, and so on—brought crises, which strengthened the hand of "responsible" students. Once top administrators and some faculty leaders had accepted the legitimacy of student participation in governance, they were ready to join with "responsible" student leaders in attempts to deal with crises. Such students, in part to protect their left flank, vigorously promoted student interests. This vigorous action required pressure on administrators but also cooperation with them. Coalitions of top administrators, faculty leaders, and student leaders emerged. Clark and Burns were sympathetic to student dissent and both committed themselves to student participation in governance. In turn, student leaders had confidence in both men and frequently praised their efforts.

Three academic council seats were given to students in April 1968. The number was increased to eight in 1969 and to twelve in 1971. Student membership in college committees was expanded significantly: in 1967–1968 students held 11 per cent of committee positions; three years later they held 29 per cent. Students serve on all standing policy committees, which are the key college committees. Students have participated in other ways at the college level, through frequent meetings with the president, membership in a tripartite liaison committee to develop proposals to deal with emergent crises, through work in the college mission and goals committee and in the college presidential selection committee in 1970. Student leaders were claiming in 1970 that governance had become "more and more democratic," that student participation had "reached a peak of involvement," and that students had "the power . . . to determine our own education." But, in fact, tripartism has been only partially implemented and its future is in doubt.

Implementation has been impeded by the wide dispersion of power in the collegial bureaucracy. It has been difficult to develop student participation in the more than sixty departments. Department have had considerable independence, and the faculties have been protective of their powers. Despite academic council policy declarations, prodding by top administrators, and a general faculty sympathy for student participation, only a minority of departments —six of twenty-six surveyed in 1970—have gone far in implementing tripartism. However, many of the others have incorporated minority student representation on committees or have established student advisory groups. Similar developments have occurred in the schools. Student leaders have been unable to organize sustained student pressure in most departments. Indeed, it has been difficult to locate enough students to fill the college committee positions available to them, and several committees surveyed in 1969 indicated only sporadic attendance by student members. Apparently student apathy has inhibited further development of the tripartite system. Little progress was made in 1970–1971. Present student government leaders have not been as aggressive as those preceding them. John H. Bunzel, the new college president, has indicated a lack of sympathy for tripartism; in particular, he has opposed student participation in faculty personnel decisions and student voting in departmental affairs.

Another system, which I label organic, has been established in a part of the college. This system sharply reduces the degree of bureaucracy and redistributes power in more radical ways than does the tripartite system, by recasting roles and implementing new types of relationships. New College was established at SJSC in 1968 as a subunit of the college at the initiative of the president and academic vice president, supported by some faculty members—all believing that an innovative, organic subunit should be established on an experimental basis in order to counter the impersonality of the large college. In New College power is distributed in egalitarian ways among individuals—administrators, faculty, students—and among learning groups. Decisions are made through "town meetings" on the basis of one man, one vote. Structure is simplified to permit direct participation in learning and governance by all participants. Interdisciplinary learning groups are formed, and departmentalization is avoided. Relationships are personal and informal. No orders are given, and codified rules are few. Professionalism is discouraged: all participants are seen as scholars learning together. Power derives from expertise, defined in experiential as well as rational terms. Rewards go to those who provide such expertise.

Except for some minor efforts to create postbureaucratic structures, the organic system thus far has been confined to New College for several reasons. There is criticism that the curriculum is vague and lacks rigor. Such a system undermines the specialized disciplinary orientation favored by most faculty and the departmental pattern which supports much of faculty power. Many faculty members would find it difficult to adapt to egalitarian relationships with students. New College students are suspected of undue radicalism and unconventional life styles. An organic unit such as New College reflects mainly the experience of small liberal arts colleges. Creation of organic units at SJSC and at other large state colleges depends on decisions made at a collegial bureaucratic level. Neither administrators nor faculty are likely to want to dismantle power relationships and governance mechanisms laboriously constructed over the years. Nor will outside authorities permit such radical transformation.

Growing pressures on the colleges for efficiency seem to imply a rebirth of managerialism within the colleges. In 1970 the chancellor called for an end to systems of governance in which decision making is widely dispersed and in which administrators, chosen by consensus, govern by persuasion ("The Chancellor Comments," 1970). He argued that such a "kaffee-klatsch method of academic governance" appropriate to an "older and calmer day" is obsolete. Administrators, with authority "commensurate with . . . responsibility," must be freed to make speedy decisions. Big colleges require "a new managerial type of administrator." Administrative initiative will expand despite faculty opposition based in part on remembrance of things past. Preservation of the collegial bureaucratic framework under such conditions will require great care and imagination because of the possibility of collective bargaining.

Governance has changed almost continuously for more than a decade. Continued instability can be expected, as a complex set of pressures now impinge upon the colleges. No one has yet succeeded in developing a governance system which integrates all the conflicting pressures in a coherent way. We await such a genius.

14

凵冚冚冚冚冚冚冚冚冚冚冚冚冚冚冚冚冚凵

Mandate for Change

Willard B. Spalding

凵冚冚冚冚冚冚冚冚冚冚冚冚冚冚冚冚凵

As the 1970s begin, the California state colleges are at a cross-road. They can evolve new levels of quality and function or slide back to a system of second-rate institutions. However current issues are resolved, the colleges will not remain static. Strong political, societal, educational, and organizational forces are currently in evidence in the system and on the campuses. They conflict on each issue which must be resolved if progress is to occur. Not all resolutions will be positive or lead to progress. Yet even in those areas where progressive resolutions seem least likely in the immediate future, qualitative and functional changes for the better may ultimately occur. In spite of current problems and issues, the long-range prospect for the state colleges is one of new levels of excellence.

Higher education presently provides opportunities for states-men, politicians, and a few demagogues to influence votes by pronouncements about student disorders, faculty performance, employment policies, faculty work load, or any other activity which seems useful in campaigning for an elective office. Politicization of

many issues formerly resolved professionally has become nearly
universal in California. The political relevance of higher education
is reflected in the hundreds of bills about higher education which
were introduced in the 1969 and 1970 sessions of the California
legislature. At times the legislature seemed to be acting as a superboard for the governance of all public higher education. Such political concern will no doubt persist as long as the activities which stimulate it. The California state colleges could use political forces to
move forward, or they can be victimized by them. Full recognition
of the political milieu by all constituencies is essential.

Six issues or conflicts are uniquely central to the state colleges: diversity versus uniformity among the state colleges; the
region versus the state as the service area of each college; the status
of each college as a state university or a state college; the faculty
versus the administration in governance; the office of college president versus the office of the chancellor; centralized control or institutional freedom in the development of each state college. All are
interwoven; resolution of any one of them will have implications
for solving the others. Nevertheless, separate analyses provide insights about such interrelationships and thereby produce better
understanding of problems affecting development of the California
state colleges.

The colleges appear to operate on the implicit assumption
that what is good for one college is good for all. This is especially
true whenever a major policy issue is under consideration. For
example, if any state college is to be named as a state university, all
but one of the colleges wish to have the same title. If any college is
to offer master's degrees, all wish to offer them. If Asian studies, or
black studies, or some other area studies are offered by one—with
accompanying foreign languages—all wish to have them. Should
each state college succeed in getting what it wants, each will closely
resemble all others; uniformity will prevail over diversity.

Individuality is essential in a state as large as California, not
only to meet needs among its various populations and regions but
also to provide opportunities for comparison which insure continuing
progress. For example, the specific educational needs and desires of
Watts residents differ from those of Beverly Hills. Calexico and
Tahoe present different problems; so do Redding and Salinas. By

encouraging institutional individuality, the colleges can develop increasing public support as they move to new levels of quality and function.

Educational programs deserve special attention in the development of individuality. Humboldt State College has for some time been developing distinctive programs related to the forest and the sea. California State Polytechnic College at San Luis Obispo operates the largest undergraduate school of architecture in the United States and the largest school of engineering in the West. San Diego State College is actively developing joint doctoral programs and is also extending its service area by providing college-going opportunities to people in the Imperial Valley more than one hundred miles from the main campus. These programs are excellent examples of institutional individuality. They result from local leadership, consistent with a statewide policy of encouraging individual distinction.

With nineteen state colleges in operation and three more authorized, opportunities for diversity are substantial. Both San Francisco and Los Angeles offer unique programs for preparing teachers for special education. San Jose has highly specialized programs in police science, journalism, and industrial arts. While other specialties exist at each of the colleges, more planned diversity is essential. One college could become known for an unusually excellent program in mathematics, dramatic arts, or ecology, and so on. Resources needed to achieve unusual distinction in a specific academic area should be made available to a college which was developing an academic program to this end. Currently, too many academicians deplore, in theory, the formula approach to allocating resources but support it in practice as a way to get a "fair share" of the money. The knowledge that added resources could become available in selected areas could give each institution incentive to develop greater individuality. If each college had just one program which was nationally recognized, the entire system would be toned up.

Diversity among students needs to be emphasized as well. At present, basic admission standards are the same for all state colleges; individuality exists only in respect to a 4 per cent exception to these standards. The impact which could result from selecting students for special qualities thus varies little from institution to institution, with the possible exception of the two polytechnic colleges. Each college could be encouraged to develop its own criteria for selecting students, within a quota which will insure no overall increase in enrollment. For example, half of a freshman class could be admitted through systemwide criteria, half through a college's own criteria. The 50 per cent admitted on uniform criteria would be enough to take account of hardships and of diversion from and to other colleges. The remaining 50 per cent would provide an adequate base for increasing institutional individuality. Institutional criteria for admission could take unusual programs into account. A college with a unique program in music could select unusually talented students. One offering an enriched program in marine science could select students who had demonstrated an interest and who show promise in this area.

The second major issue concerns the service area of each institution. There is a history of regionalism in the state colleges, which have increased in number as a result of local demands. The 1960 Master Plan originated in the problems of a legislature faced by multiple demands for new state colleges. Regionalism was fostered by college presidents during the many years that they were part of the Department of Education. Each president, in effect, lobbied his budget and his capital outlay program through the Department of Finance, the legislature, and the governor, with strong regional support.

With the advent of the Board of Trustees, the concept of system began to be applied. In the process of developing a statewide organization, the idea of regional colleges fell into disrepute. Each college is now seen as having a primary statewide function and a secondary regional function. However, residents of the area surrounding a state college, especially one in a nonmetropolitan location, continue to perceive the regional function as primary. When a local applicant is redirected to a remote college, protests are sure to follow. When an expensive academic program is eliminated because statewide needs can be served best elsewhere, local citizens served by the program call for its reinstatement. Local community college students expect to transfer to the nearby state college. Local advisory boards often perceive themselves as having a governing role and expect their advice to be followed.

Some state colleges, notably those at Humboldt, Chico, San Jose, San Luis Obispo, and San Francisco, have historically enrolled a large portion of their students from areas of California remote from their campuses. Others, especially those in metropolitan Los Angeles, have enrolled many students from nearby communities. However, both statewide and regional demands are felt at all state colleges. The conflicts between these two sets of demands become most prominent in three areas: students, articulation with community colleges, and academic programs.

Many parents believe that it would be best for their children to attend college away from home. They feel that by living on campus their children could break family ties as part of the transition to adulthood; receive a broader education from a new environment and a new peer group; enter a socially elite class through a sorority or fraternity; or have rewarding campus experiences like those of the parents. They also see a chance to get relief and quiet at home. For these and other reasons, many students seek to enroll in state colleges which are remote from their homes.

However, the majority of students reside in counties near the state college which they attend. There are a variety of reasons for choosing a nearby college: less cost to the family if a student lives at home; the availability of work to supplement family support or to provide complete support; desire of parents or students to keep the family together; students' desire to attend college with friends. Other factors are also important in the choice. State college students are typically 25 to 26; a large number are married and many have transferred from community colleges.

In an ideal situation, any state college would accommodate all applicants, whatever their residence. But most colleges will have to decide which remote applicants will be excluded to admit local ones and vice versa. The argument that students from remote areas of California, like nonresidents and foreign students, contribute a needed leaven to the student mix, producing a ferment which can be an element of quality, is widely accepted in higher education. To a degree, it is supported by some of Robert Pace's research on institutional press.

On the other hand, the argument that a local resident who has planned to attend a nearby state college since beginning high school and who has shaped his high school program to fit the demands of a particular major should be admitted before students from remote areas finds strong support in the community where the college is located. Thus, admissions problems may assume many of the characteristics of ancient town and gown controversies in which the college seemed to be against the community.

Applicants who have successfully completed two years at a nearby community college force especially difficult decisions. These students fall into two categories: those who were originally eligible for admission to a state college and those who have become eligible through successful completion of appropriate courses at a community college. Denial of admission to a transfer student in the first group is perceived as unjust. If such denials become numerous and frequent, most eligible students may seek admission upon graduation from high school, with two undesirable effects. The number and proportion of able students in the community colleges would be reduced, to the detriment of the colleges' instructional programs. It would also become more difficult to decide between local and remote students for those fewer transfer admissions spaces remaining; many of those attending community colleges would claim priority for admission as transfer students based upon hardship, with considerable justification.

To refuse admission to the second group would be contrary to the traditional open-door policy of California. The state colleges are among the most highly selective public institutions in the United States. It is not generally understood that present state college admission standards are more selective than those of the University of Iowa, the University of Wisconsin, Michigan, Minnesota, or a number of other major institutions. High selectivity among high school graduates can be maintained only if college-bound students have another door by which to enter higher education. Once the opportunity to transfer is limited, the concept of the open door will be lost. Political pressures for less selectivity in admissions at the freshman level would inevitably follow.

A second major aspect of articulation lies in the area of educational planning. Here the problem of the region versus the state is again obvious. Officials and faculty at most state colleges develop informal relations with their counterparts in community colleges as they discuss mutual problems relating to transfer of credits and the development of programs which fit together with the fewest possible difficulties for transfer students. Statewide plans for articulation are developed under the auspices of the Articulation Conference, a voluntary organization composed of representatives of secondary schools, community colleges, independent colleges and universities, the University of California, and the state colleges. Through ad hoc committees appointed to examine major academic fields, policy proposals come to the administrative committee of the conference. When approved, a policy becomes an unofficial guideline for articulating educational programs. Guidelines thus developed arise because of statewide issues considered by a representative statewide committee. They provide little leeway for regional adaptations by a state college and nearby community colleges.

At least half the members of a committee examining articulation in an academic field come from a combination of state college and University of California faculty. Thus, they are likely to favor the interests of their institutions at the expense of the community colleges, which are often perceived to be servants of higher institutions. Domination of community colleges seems to be about as severe as was domination of secondary schools fifty years ago; but resistance is becoming stronger, change is imminent. Until change occurs, allegiances of faculty members on articulation committees to their disciplines and to the university and the state colleges are likely to produce proposals which enhance statewide guidelines rather than regional adaptations.

Academic programs, too, reflect both state and local needs. Each state college is required by trustee policy to offer a core of programs in the liberal arts and sciences. But beyond this foundation, programs may be added for a variety of reasons: faculty desire to attract students or to recruit prestigious faculty or to meet manpower needs; aggrandizement of particular individuals on the faculty; administrative desire to develop a multipurpose institution or to reach faculty goals or to serve special interest groups; external demands of organized professions or of other occupations; suggestions from advisory committees; or a desire for educational distinction.

All this is to be expected. Growth in size should be coupled

with growth in number of programs offered and in complexity of
the college. But programs which serve unique needs of the region
surrounding a college or which use the unique regional environment
should receive special encouragement. Fresno has developed a program concerned with the ecology of the Central Valley. Calexico
offers training for teachers of children to whom English is a second
language. State colleges in the Los Angeles area offer programs
related to the local aerospace industry. San Francisco presents programs in the creative arts. However, a firm statewide policy of
encouraging the administration and faculty of each college to develop academic programs which reflect regional needs or resources
could lead to greater recognition of the region, especially if it were
accompanied by allocation of resources primarily for this purpose.

The third major issue faced by the state college system is
concerned with institutional status. A university may be defined as
an institution of higher learning made up of an undergraduate
division which confers bachelor's degrees and a graduate division
which comprises a graduate school and professional schools each
of which may confer master's degrees and doctorates. With the
exception of San Diego State College, where three joint doctoral
programs are in operation, no California state college meets this
definition of a university. However, if the definition were modified
by eliminating the doctorate, ten of the state colleges could be classified as universities since all of their schools are accredited. The
problem of nomenclature provides an added example of the strength
of the drive for uniformity among the state colleges.

The 1969 session of the legislature considered a bill to change
the name from the California State Colleges to The California State
University. A 1970 bill proposed The California State University
and Colleges. An educational basis for separating existing colleges
into two classes is found in the wide range of size and complexity
among existing institutions. Some, notably Los Angeles, San Diego,
San Jose, and San Francisco, contain enough professional schools to
deserve the title of university. Others, like Stanislaus, San Bernardino, Dominguez Hills, and Sonoma, are clearly small liberal arts
colleges at present. Nevertheless, faculty organizations, persuaded by
egalitarian arguments, opposed the proposed nomenclature; in its
latest version, the bill has been amended to call all institutions state

universities. But beyond the issue of definitions and names, the basic question is, "What academic and professional services could state universities provide which are not provided fully by other institutions?" Three possible types of service are: additional professional schools, applied research, and doctoral programs.

The University of California is the only public institution in the state which prepares students for licenses in dentistry, law, medicine, and veterinary medicine. In developing each of the existing schools and in planning additional ones, the university appropriately devotes substantial attention to basic research facilities. Each professional school thus becomes a major research center which also produces dentists, doctors, lawyers, or veterinarians. Because of substantial research emphasis in their preparation, many graduates seek professional careers where their research skills can be used.

California will continue to need professionals to conduct research. But California also needs professionals who are more interested in practice which serves people directly than in research which advances knowledge and thus serves society generally. Publicly supported schools of medicine, dentistry, law, or veterinary medicine with strong primary emphasis upon practice should be developed. For example, a school of medicine at Chico State College, using hospital facilities in all counties from Sutter County to the boundary with Oregon, could prepare doctors for rural areas. Such a school could upgrade existing medical care, provide needed clinical services, and otherwise contribute to the area. The cost of a far-reaching program would probably be less than the cost of establishing and operating a great research center.

A dental school at Fresno State College could have similar relations with San Joaquin Valley and bordering mountain communities. The California Polytechnic College at Pomona, with its Arabian horses and proximity to the small animal population of metropolitan Los Angeles, would be an excellent location for a school of veterinary medicine. In fact, there have been strong pressures to establish such a school. Sacramento State College, using facilities of federal, state, city, and county courts, would be an appropriate location for a graduate school of public administration.

The University of California is designated by statute as the primary academic research agency of the state; faculty research in the colleges is authorized "to the extent that it is consistent with the primary function of the state colleges and the facilities provided for that function." Should some colleges become state universities, and should professional schools designed to prepare practitioners be developed in them, the limitations upon faculty research, while expressed in the same language, would change. As stated in the Donahoe Higher Education Act, "The primary function of the state colleges is the provision of instruction for undergraduate students and graduate students, through the master's degree, in the liberal arts and sciences, in applied fields and the professions, including the teaching profession." To this could be added, "A state university may have the additional functions of offering advanced graduate work leading to the doctorate in selected fields and of preparing practitioners in architecture, dentistry, law, medicine, teaching, and veterinary medicine." Research consistent with these added functions would, and should, differ sharply in its emphasis from research in the University of California. State university efforts should be directed primarily toward learning how best to apply what is already known. Basic theories of the application of new knowledge are lacking in most fields; discovering these theories could result from specific studies of how to use new concepts.

California industry can use significant numbers of applied scientists. Public schools would be better if more teachers knew how to interpret and use new discoveries in the humanities. Public service demand for skilled users of basic concepts in the human sciences will remain great. The state university could occupy a uniquely important place in public higher education as it stressed research in the application of knowledge as a basic element in its preparation of skilled practitioners.

Doctoral programs would follow the same lines of inquiry. Advanced graduate students would learn how to use in practice what was becoming known at the frontiers of knowledge. A state university should grant doctoral degrees. But the selection of a department to offer a doctoral program should be unusually careful. The California state colleges, as a relatively new system, have had brief experience in rigorous application of criteria which measure excellence. Approval of new programs has been influenced more often in the past by strong arguments about equality among colleges, by strong local pressures, or by the internal politics of the state college system than by evidence of unusual quality.

State college status has long been affected by competition with the University of California. Many college faculty and administrators feel strongly that the colleges are treated as second-class institutions while the university receives first-class treatment. Although some faculty strive proudly for excellence in performing allocated functions, many others envy the class loads, salaries, sabbatical leaves, travel funds, and research support of university faculty. While some administrators provide leadership toward quality in present responsibilities as a long step toward gaining additional responsibilities, others view presently allocated functions, standardized regulations, formula budgeting, and so on as barriers to improved quality.

The university, on the other hand, opposes legislative proposals to change any or all state colleges to state universities. It perceives a change in nomenclature as an opening wedge to changes in function requiring such massive support that university support would be jeopardized. Neither set of feelings will see much modification in the immediate future. Resolution of the issues seems more likely to result from political pressures than from considered educational judgment. Since both the university and the state colleges have friends and enemies in the legislature, the outcome remains uncertain.

The struggle for governance power between administration and faculty is the subject of the fourth major issue. Full-time faculty in the California state colleges have increased from some 3,500 in 1960–1961 to about 14,000 in 1969–1970. In the latter year 49.5 per cent of the faculty had served for fewer than five years in contrast with 35.9 per cent in 1960–1961. This massive infusion of new members has significant implications. Most new faculty show relatively little identification with either the college or the system as a whole, especially when this feeling is compared with their attachment to a scholarly discipline. Thus more and more faculty are concerned about personal professional goals rather than the progressive development of their college or of the statewide system. For this reason, funds for travel to scholarly meetings, sabbatical leaves for scholarly work, funds to support faculty re-

search, and instructional loads which allow time for faculty research
are increasingly desired by faculty.

A recent poll of state college faculty revealed that a majority
of the respondents favored collective bargaining, but no organization
was favored by a majority as the agency to bargain. If the poll
reflects considered faculty judgment, as opposed to casual replies,
collective bargaining may be seen by college faculty as the best way
to secure desired benefits and perquisites. In order for this percep-
tion to result in action, a collective bargaining agent must be selected
and the trustees of the state colleges must agree to bargain. Neither
eventuality seems likely to occur without considerable controversy,
which may become heated beyond the point of public tolerance.
Additional statutes would also be required.

The public accepts generally the idea that employees have
the right to organize in order to better their lot. But the right of
public employees to strike is not generally accepted. Further,
academia is currently in disrepute in California, due to unfortunate
actions by a small minority. A faculty strike would have almost
no public support. Should a strike occur, the same tiny minority who
have demonstrated violently against national policies could be expected to again display violent behavior, further alienating the
public.

Competition among organizations seeking to become the
sole collective bargaining agent could exacerbate the situation
markedly. They have been damning each other in vigorous and
occasionally purple prose. However, the 1970 legislature's decision
to deny cost of living increases to faculty has produced an alliance
of the four faculty organizations with membership in the state colleges. This marriage of convenience is not likely to endure. As
allegiance to a particular organization strengthens (a common
phenomenon during interorganizational conflict), attacks and coun-
terattacks seem sure to become more intense; diatribe will increasingly supplant argument. The organization finally chosen as bargaining agent may never be fully accepted by members of losing
organizations. Continuing strife seems inevitable.

Currently the trustees show little interest in faculty bargaining. In general, their actions reflect a view of faculty as employees
who should be told what to do rather than as professionals render-

ing a service. Given a faculty majority favoring collective bargaining and a conservative board opposed to collective bargaining, conflict over the issue seems certain. There is little evidence to indicate that either faculty or trustees would abandon their positions quickly.

Collective bargaining, although currently in the spotlight, is only one aspect of the governance struggle. Historically, faculty existed before administrators; the first administrators were former faculty members who, asked to perform routine tasks as services to the group, found these tasks dominating their academic roles. Today, administrators elected annually by faculty are found in some European universities where administration is a service, not a control. In the United States, colleges and universities are organized on a corporation model, with outside governing boards and highly paid administrative officers. But the tradition of faculty governance persists. Conflict between the corporate structure and faculty tradition is always possible in American institutions of higher education.

The California state colleges make up perhaps the largest system of public higher education in the United States. The trustees, the chancellor, and the chancellor's staff are necessarily remote from the faculty of each college. Thus the inherent conflict between faculty and administration extends to the governing superstructure, which is often perceived as indifferent or hostile to faculty participation in the governance of the system. The statewide faculty senate's vote censuring the chancellor, supported by a subsequent faculty poll, indicates the depth of faculty hostility.

What roles should faculty and administration have in governance? Authority and responsibility must be united in all decision-makers. Authority without responsibility is tyranny; responsibility without authority is scapegoatism. Many state college administrators believe that authority is vested in their position, and there is substantial support for this point of view. However, authority is effective only when expected results follow a decision. From this perspective, it is argued that authority rests with the recipient of an order—he grants authority to the order when he follows it. From either point of view, the authority of an administrator is revealed in the extent to which his decisions are implemented.

Many state college administrators believe that they are responsible to the chancellor, for it was his recommendation to the board which caused their appointments. They also feel a responsibility to their profession, higher education, and to their scholarly discipline. Thus they perceive themselves as being judged in three ways, by their superiors, by their professional peers, and by scholars in their field. The latter judgment is particularly critical for a president who wishes to preserve his retreat rights.

The extent to which college administrators believe themselves to be responsible to faculties is far from clear. If they are appointed after consultation with a faculty committee, they may feel responsible during the first years of service, but these attitudes often vanish with the passing years. On the other hand, college administrators may believe that they should become responsible to faculty if they are to perform successfully.

For each state college administrator, authority of some type is linked with some type of responsibility. When authority is derived mainly from faculty acceptance of decisions and when responsibility to faculty is at least as great as responsibility to superiors, decision making, while never easy, is less difficult. Probably the most important academic officer is the department chairman. In the state colleges he is perceived to be responsible to the faculty—not the president. There are few compensations the president may award him for any institutional loyalty he may display.

Authority and responsibility are rarely found together when faculty participate in the governance of a state college or of the state college system. Faculty decision-makers are sometimes tyrants, sometimes scapegoats. Tyrannical behavior is likely to prevail, for there are almost no procedures by which a faculty, a faculty committee, or a statewide senate can be held responsible for its decisions. A basic problem is the absence of clearly defined but limited faculty roles and responsibilities in statewide governance. Because of this lack, faculty seem to desire involvement in every decision, acting as if each statewide administrator should have at least two faculty members looking over his shoulder. Since faculty participation in all decisions is impossible, and since decisions in which faculty should participate are not clearly defined, dissatisfaction with both the statewide faculty senate and the chancellor's office is common among instructors. Their approval of local college senates is relatively high. Faculty satisfaction with local college administration, while not enthusiastic, is greater than with statewide administration.

The fifth central issue facing the state college system concerns the relative roles of the president and chancellor. Since the state colleges came under the control of the Board of Trustees, there have been forty-seven individuals holding the office of president or acting president. On July 1, 1970, four presidencies were held by temporary appointees, pending selection of a permanent president. Only three persons who were presidents in 1960 held that office on July 1, 1970. During these years only seven presidents retired.

State college presidents enjoy few of the perquisites of office found elsewhere. Only five presidents can live in houses provided for them by the state, or by gift, for the betterment of the college. They do not have unmarked cars for official and personal use. Expense accounts for official entertaining are small and must be accounted for in minute detail. Salaries are relatively low when compared with those paid presidents of comparable institutions in other states. Undoubtedly some of the high turnover is caused by these conditions.

However, some of the turnover may arise because new state college presidents expect to provide more leadership than is possible under present conditions. Like most large organizations, the California state colleges have a procedure whereby an unfavorable decision by a group or administrator at one level can be appealed to a decision-making group or person at a higher level. Thus, few important college decisions about students or faculty become final when a president makes his decision. Appeal to the chancellor's office is built into the process. Eventually everyone knows that the president does not have final power.

The president's role is limited by other factors too. The chancellor's office has developed a fiscal management plan which includes certain procedural guidelines for its operations. His office: accepts responsibility and accountability for the fiscal management of the colleges; develops policy and procedural guidelines for the control of fiscal operations; provides effective leadership in assisting the colleges to solve problems; develops procedures to assure prompt and accurate reporting; and enforces trustee and statewide fiscal policies. To implement these guidelines, the chancellor's office issues frequent planning memoranda which regulate decisions relating to capital outlay and support budgets. They also regulate the academic planning process, although the nature of academic life is such that many substantive issues within degree programs are still decided at departmental and college levels. In recent years decisions on many aspects of student life, such as student conduct and discipline and even student health service (for example, the birth control issue), have become increasingly centralized.

The chancellor of the California state colleges heads a system which enrolled considerably more than 200,000 students in 1970 on nineteen campuses. The 1969–1970 support budget totalled more than a quarter of a billion dollars. The system employed 14,000 faculty members and some 11,000 others including administrators and support staff. Although no additional positions were requested for 1970–1971, the chancellor's staff includes some 180 professionals and 120 other employees.

The trustees of the California state colleges, to whom the chancellor is responsible, are concerned about the efficient management of the system and of the colleges. Recently, for example, there was discussion of the desirability of changing the requirements for a college president so that men with experience in business management could be selected. The chancellor is expected by the trustees to be a strong manager who makes critical decisions needed to improve and maintain the system. When demonstrations and violence occurred at some state colleges, the trustees called for firm action by the chancellor and demanded quick punishment for offenders. The chancellor's responses have been not only firm but, as perceived by some faculty who led demonstrations or who instigated strikes, vindictive, since they (the faculty) have not been reemployed. Apart from the expectancies of the trustees, the size and complexity of the state college system work against the use of wide consultation by the chancellor's office prior to making a decision. As was pointed out earlier, the use of surrogates for faculty (the senate) has not been productive.

The chancellor meets monthly with the Chancellor's Council of State College Presidents. The meetings are characterized by announcements of tentative decisions by the chancellor's office followed by full discussion among the presidents. Although formal votes are seldom taken the final decisions often reflect presidential views. When the chancellor announces decisions which are not debatable, the discussion turns to ways to implement them. The chancellor's office sends instructions to presidents in memoranda on academic planning, budget planning, and facilities planning, as well as in executive orders. The first decade of the California state colleges has seen a steady increase in the number and types of decisions reserved to the chancellor's office through these memoranda.

The final basic issue relates to state control of the colleges. The California state college system, like all other elements of state government, is subject to frequent review by the Department of Finance. Under the terms of Section 13322 of the California Statutes, the department may revise, alter, or amend any fiscal year budget if in its opinion revision, alteration, or amendment is required in the best interests of the state. The department's staff is divided into units, each one of which oversees a specific function. The unit overseeing higher education analyzes budgets and expenditures of the Coordinating Council for Higher Education, the University of California, the community colleges, the State Scholarship Commission, and the California state colleges. Since each fiscal decision has educational consequences, controls exercised by the Department of Finance have profound influences upon educational programs in the state colleges and elsewhere.

Over the past several years, the Department of Finance has reduced significantly its fiscal controls over the state colleges. However, it still retains authority to approve transfer of funds among the major budgetary functions. It approves uses of excess salary savings out of the salary savings reserve, and it has authority to approve submissions to the federal government for loans, grants, or other financial assistance to students. The legislative analyst, in his report to the 1970 session of the legislature, approved retention of these functions by the Department of Finance.

The office of the legislative analyst serves the Joint Legislative Budget Committee. The staff of this office is also organized in functional units somewhat like those of the Department of Finance. The legislature frequently follows the advice of the legislative analyst as it acts to appropriate funds for the state colleges. Thus advice from this office has significant impact upon educational programs in the state colleges.

The Coordinating Council for Higher Education is charged with advising the governor, the legislature, state officials, and the governing boards of the public segments of higher education about the general level of support sought, changes in functions of the segments, and plans for the orderly growth of public higher education. Its staff reviews plans and programs of the state colleges and develops advice about present and future activities.

In each agency, few staff members who develop positions on higher education have worked in a college or university; even fewer have had significant administrative experience in an institution of higher education. The decisions of these staffs are thus likely to be based upon incomplete information about possible educational implications of decisions and upon individual biases or preconceptions about higher education. The state colleges must devote inordinate amounts of time to the task of informing, educating, and convincing a threefold variety of state bureaucrats. The extent to which these bureaucracies operate to improve the effectiveness and efficiency of public higher education deserves careful study. A superficial examination indicates that the overall effects are to increase conformity, reduce innovation, and impede progress.

State government control of the colleges has existed since the beginning. The major new element in their governance was provided by the Master Plan for Higher Education, hailed as a great achievement in 1960. The legislature, using the plan as a guide, established the Board of Trustees of the California state colleges, thus separating these institutions from the Board of Education and making them an independent segment of public higher education. But the Master Plan included effective controls upon the operation of the state colleges, largely because it was more a treaty among the public and private segments of higher education than a plan for their development. As a result of long periods of negotiation, the state colleges were distinguished from the University of California in three areas: function, admissions criteria, and institutional size.

The primary function of the state college system is instruction in the liberal arts and sciences and in professions and applied fields through the master's degree. The university has all of these functions plus exclusive functions in dentistry, law, medicine, veterinary medicine, and graduate architecture. (In 1970 master's degrees in architecture were authorized for the state colleges.) The state colleges may conduct research to the extent that it is consistent with their primary function and the facilities provided for that function.

The state colleges select students for freshman admission from the top one-third of all graduates of California high schools. The university selects from the top one-eighth. Both segments admit an additional 4 per cent as exceptions to their criteria.

The Master Plan recommended the following full-time enrollment ranges for the state colleges: in metropolitan areas a minimum of 5,000 students, an optimum number of 10,000, and a maximum of 20,000 students. Colleges outside urban areas should have a minimum of 3,000, an optimum 8,000, and a maximum of 12,000 full-time students. For University of California campuses, regardless of location, the relevant figures were 5,000, 12,000, and 27,500. The Master Plan's strictures upon function and institutional size, when coupled with an admissions policy which admits more students to the state colleges than to the university, leads to both an increasing need for more colleges and to increasing faculty dissatisfaction with the services which they are permitted to offer.

California would be served more effectively and efficiently, with greater prudence in the expenditure of state funds, if the state colleges were free to spend their budgeted funds in whatever ways seemed best to them, with accountability to be determined through annual postexpenditure audits. Under this procedure, educational needs would be given priority and conformity to line items in budgets would be forgotten.

A few years ago, some state colleges were willing to accept nearly a million dollars less for equipment if they could spend what they did receive according to their best judgments. But representatives of the Department of Finance were unwilling to accept the proposal. It is probably unreasonable to expect a bureaucracy to concede that on-campus decisions about expenditures are better than those made in Sacramento. Yet the state's true interests lie in getting the most and best education for the least money. These interests are best served by directing governmental attention to the overall figure for the system as a whole in lieu of bureaucratic attention to line items in the budget for each college.

Educational growth, once fiscal flexibility was assured, could follow the same general pattern. The Coordinating Council for Higher Education could establish broad guidelines along which each state college and the system as a whole could develop. Rather than approving programs in advance, it could ascertain annually the extent to which developments showed promise of meeting guidelines. The authority of the council's guidelines should replace restrictions of function resulting from the Master Plan. Provisions for doctoral programs and research should be included. These guidelines, developed with the participation of all segments of higher education, would not be fixed in law. They would be subject to constant scrutiny by all interested parties. They could provide needed freedom for educational development in the colleges.

Reviewing the six issues here presented, a common critical theme can be seen: the need for individuality among the state colleges. Also evident is the problem of developing appropriate governance roles for faculty, presidents, and the chancellor. Both the theme and the problem exist in a massive system of higher education, an organization which has few precedents and few peers and which has not been studied intensively. The large statewide system of public higher education is a recent phenomenon and not much is known about how it actually operates; little theory exists to guide its development. As a consequence, the colleges need freedom for invention and innovation as they meet the problems of their second decade. Creative innovation, a difficult task, is made more difficult by recent active protests on campus and public reactions to them. Pressure to return things to "normal" often prevents or retards innovations leading to a higher level of normality.

A pessimistic view of the future reveals a continuing struggle among faculty organizations seeking to become sole agents for collective bargaining. The conflict could be characterized by increased invective and diatribe directed not only by one organization against others but also by all organizations against administrators, especially the chancellor and his office. Demonstrations, occasional violence, and a systemwide faculty strike could occur, with consequent repressive actions supported by public opinion. Individual board members may intrude more deeply into operational aspects of each institution which is out of line with the personal philosophy of the trustees.

With such a tumultuous problem demanding everyone's attention, little could be done to develop policies which would produce diversity among the state colleges in academic programs, especially those related to the region where a college is located. The legislature would not be inclined to authorize new functions for those state colleges which should become state universities; even a change in name with no added functions might not be possible. New procedures for selecting students, with increased opportunity for each state college to select those most suitable for its programs, might not be initiated. The development of more appropriate roles in decision making for the chancellor, the presidents, and the faculty would be delayed. In short, the California state colleges would remain at about their present level of quality or possibly drop below it.

Even if faculty and faculty organizations do not becloud central issues which need to be resolved, the state colleges will not move toward the highest levels of quality envisioned in this chapter until plans and policies are developed to this end. A long-range plan for progressive improvement is needed. Such a plan could be developed with advisory participation by representatives of all interested members of the state college system. And once developed, the plan should be revised periodically.

An optimistic view of the future of the state colleges reveals a massive system of higher education in which central controls and decisions are devoted solely to broad policy issues affecting the system as a whole. Policy will provide uniformity where essential, diversity and individuality where essential. Each college, under the leadership of its president and faculty, will seek unique characteristics while trying to raise its general level of quality. Each institution will serve both the state and its nearby region, with the demands of each receiving appropriate attention. Some state colleges will become state universities with rigorously selected departments offering doctoral programs which stress the application of knowledge. Some state universities will include schools of dentistry, or law, or medicine, or veterinary medicine. All state universities will have adequate funds for faculty research in how to use what is known; from this work will come sorely needed theories about the application of knowledge in each scholarly discipline or profession.

This future can come to pass only if creative innovation can develop adequate roles in decision making for faculty, the office of the president, and the office of the chancellor. These roles must be defined so that all three groups will be strengthened as they work together and separately to achieve individuality within uniformity, salients of progress along a front that moves forward continuously.

15

‎⌐⌐⌐⌐⌐⌐⌐⌐⌐⌐⌐⌐⌐⌐⌐⌐⌐⌐⌐

Toward a Future

Donald R. Gerth, James O. Haehn

‎⌐⌐⌐⌐⌐⌐⌐⌐⌐⌐⌐⌐⌐⌐⌐⌐⌐⌐⌐

The California state colleges are one of the world's great higher education systems in size, in spirit, and as an experiment. This volume has covered a mountain of data, yet significant areas of the life of the system have not been thoroughly explored; central among these is academic planning, which we will touch on only briefly in this conclusion. In drawing together the topics covered in this volume, we have made certain choices. We will discuss the governance and administration of the system, academic planning, purposes and functions, several problem areas, and the organizational climate of the California state colleges.

Basic to these concluding observations is a central assumption: the continuation of the California state college system. In recent years, for a variety of reasons—general public dissatisfaction with higher education, finances, a concern for more orderly governance and planning—alternative modes of structure and governance have been suggested for public higher education in California. Calls

212

for substantial revision of the Master Plan continue to be heard. Among these are plans for the merger of the three segments of public higher education and the creation of regional governance; a single structure of governance for all three segments or two of the three (the university and state colleges); and proposals to move some campuses from one system or segment of public higher education to another (for example, shifting state colleges with the most developed graduate programs to the university system). We will assume the continuation of the system while addressing some of the issues in other forms of governance. We believe there is a genius to a system of multipurpose public colleges with a major orientation to excellence in teaching. The state colleges are university-like in their organizational complexity and have developed on many campuses significant thrusts toward research of an applied and nonexpensive nature; they are not lesser University of California campuses, despite allegations to the contrary. They are teaching colleges.

Many are critical of the California Master Plan. We believe that criticisms which conclude that the Master Plan should be scrapped are premature. When was the Master Plan tested? The decade of the sixties was the most turbulent in the history of American higher education. Colleges and universities were major targets in the political arena. There is emerging a new direction for American higher education. In the 1970s will come the test of the California Master Plan.

The Master Plan and its resulting legislation was a peace treaty, ratifying in significant ways the status quo yet leaving open a small crack in the door of functional change for the state colleges. Similarly, the Master Plan legislation provisions for the governance and thus the administration of the state colleges were a compromise, for the constitutional autonomy sought by the colleges was not enacted, while the system was created by statute. The system's first ten years of life were characterized by compromise in governance. Essentially, the system was established without clear lines of authority, and the lines are still somewhat obscure. The roles of the trustees and chancellor, the statewide and campus senates, the presidents, the central and campus administrative staffs, and student governing bodies all have lacked clarity and precision. This may be a strength as well as a weakness, for some measure of flexibility is a result. But so is a substantial measure of frustration, particularly with the always present financial controls of state agencies.

The Board of Trustees has a statutory mandate to govern the system, and yet this mandate is conditioned by the fiscal management of state government. The board has given the chancellor and the presidents a mandate, yet this is in practice limited by the occasional moves of the board, or for that matter the state agencies, into areas of administrative responsibility. Clearly the board, administrative officers, and faculties bridle at state agency control. Yet the system would be well served if this admittedly unsatisfactory structure of governance were accepted, provided that roles were defined clearly and all participants made a genuine effort to limit activity to defined roles. This would work both ways, up and down the system.

Early in the 1960s administration at the system level was carried on by the chancellor with the active involvement of some trustees and a relatively small staff. Midway in the 1960s the chancellor's staff began to enlarge substantially, crossed the 100-person mark, then the 200-person mark, and in 1971 approached 300 persons. As the chancellor and his associates faced the gigantic task of organizing the system early in the 1960s frequent reference was made to the large staff of the president of the University of California. How could such a substantial organizational task be accomplished by 60, 80, or 100 individuals? As the chancellor's staff grows ever larger, each campus administrative officer has a counterpart, or sometimes several counterparts. Administrative organization on the campuses is approximately standardized, for the line item budgets yield particular administrators on the basis of campus size, and guidelines for administrative staffing have been enacted by the board and accepted by the Department of Finance. One untried strategy would be to deliberately encourage the campuses to develop dissimilar organizations and discourage the counterpart relationships among campuses and with the chancellor's staff. Such an effort might reenforce program diversity.

One significant characteristic of system administration is the substantial turnover in administrative posts on the campuses. Prior to the Master Plan, administrators below the level of presidents secured tenure in their posts, and the continuity was great. This was, of course, during a different era in American higher education. In the 1960s, as new individuals were appointed to campus administrative posts, average tenure in office shortened drastically. In 1971, on the nineteen campuses only three presidents, four vice-presidents for academic affairs, and six deans of students had been in the office more than five years. To induce change the board and chancellor encouraged appointments of individuals from out of state to presidencies. This strategy in some measure succeeded, but it also induced instability, particularly as new presidents found it difficult to accept the constraints of a state system.

Shortly after the system began, as described in chapter two, the concept of academic planning took hold. At first campus resistance to academic planning as a process was great, for it was perceived as another intrusion in the autonomy of the campuses. In 1971, academic planning was an accepted way of life; indeed, the development of the process has been one of the more substantial successes of the system. This is not to say that the campuses have always agreed with the chancellor's staff and his dean of academic planning; but an orderly process has been achieved. Perhaps it is too orderly, for when any one campus secures a new program, other campuses immediately want to develop a similar program. To contribute to the orderliness, standard nomenclature for degrees has been developed and implemented almost wholly. The stated objectives of the board and chancellor have been to develop differences in academic programs and uniqueness among the campuses, but the logic of the financial constraints on the system and to an extent the systemwide process of academic planning has encouraged a high measure of uniformity. Moreover, the single most significant thrust toward uniformity and against diversity is from the faculties themselves, for typically each state college has sought to gain for its academic program most of what any state college has. When individual colleges have sought to create unique programs within the framework of the Master Plan, and such instances are few, approval and support generally has been forthcoming from the chancellor and Board of Trustees. The power of tradition is strong in higher education; significant breaks at least will require strong faculty interest and support and at best would come from faculties.

The thrust of academic planning has been to encourage

rational program development and decision making on the campuses, to work within the functions defined for the state colleges in the Master Plan, to maximize the use of resources within the system, and to provide for each campus and the system an array of programs that will serve the distinctive characteristics of a campus student body and faculty as well as the needs of the state's population. The functions assigned to the state colleges by the Master Plan—the peace treaty—continue to be reflected in the academic plans, and these are central to the system.

In 1961, state college admissions standards admitted approximately 45 per cent of high school graduates. The Master Plan called for a reduction to 33⅓ per cent; this was accomplished. The Master Plan provided for access to public higher education for all among the three segments. The state college stance, never quite made explicit, has been that no single campus had an obligation to accommodate all eligible applicants but that the system would find room for all. In the late 1960s, the system began to back away from this stance under pressure of scarce resources and waves of applicants. One byproduct of this pressure was the creation in 1970 of a common admissions program with northern and southern regional processing centers. The system in 1971 decided to take all eligible applicants for whom there was room but not necessarily all eligible applicants. This position was a departure from California's historic policy, reaffirmed by the Master Plan, of access for all to some higher education.

The California state colleges in their first ten years coexisted with two governors, Brown and Reagan. In any public enterprise, financial resources are scarce; there is always more to do than the resources seemingly permit. During Brown's administration, in the relatively affluent early and mid-sixties, the colleges fared reasonably well; funds were available to sustain the customary levels of support for existing programs as these expanded to meet greater enrollments. Some new operations were funded.

The first major crisis of Reagan's administration in 1967 was financial; all budgets were reviewed to determine possible lower levels of support. Nevertheless, in an atmosphere of continuing fiscal crisis and pressure, the colleges still received basic support for programs until 1970. In June 1970, in response to a clear public out-cry, the legislature failed to grant state college and university faculty members a 5 per cent cost of living salary adjustment given to all other state employees. This was merely a notice of things yet to come; when the governor submitted his budget to the legislature in 1971 for fiscal year 1971–1972, there were substantial and selec-tive reductions in the level of support. The most important aspect of the governor's 1971–1972 budget cuts was their selective nature. The greatest portion of money in the state college budget was for faculty salaries. The staffing ratios for instruction were changed in the budget submission. Clearly, the assumptions of the state college system about necessary levels of financial support were more open to question than at any time since the end of World War II.

In the decade from 1960 to 1970 the California state col-leges experienced enormous growth and the most substantial erosion of public confidence in education in the history of the nation; governing groups at all levels were questioning society's investment in education. These ten years may have been the period of consoli-dation when the system came together—the first five years of the seventies will make clear whether that period is ended. A harsh description of the first decade, sometimes made elsewhere in this volume, suggests authoritarian confusion. A less harsh and perhaps more realistic assessment shows a search for roles and efforts to define the ingredients for building, albeit in an environment of great tension. Perhaps the most remarkable feat of all was the develop-ment of nineteen campuses with about 14,000 faculty and 226,000 students. In a sense, one can ask: What is a good year on a campus? For most, it is a year when a college functions reasonably smoothly and faculty and students can work together readily. Most of the California state colleges have a good year most years.

Can a system of nineteen separate colleges have an organiza-tional climate or style, given all of the factors impinging from ex-terior and interior sources? We believe such a style is inevitable, even in a higher education system as large and complex as the California state colleges. Some critics have alleged that the state college system has no life of its own, that only the campuses have a life. This description is too simple. The system is not and cannot be merely a holding corporation, for an effort to be that kind of organization would set a style of its own, with inner and outer parameters of operation.

The important question, then, is what the organizational climate of the system is and will be. We believe this climate should begin to shift from consolidation to programmatic goals. In January 1971, the chancellor issued a statement entitled *Some Proposals for Change in the California State Colleges*. This statement, which was consistent with many national reports on higher education being issued by such groups as the Carnegie Commission, took into account many critical challenges made by the radical left as well as the militant right. It also suggests significant reordering of programs. The principles of the statement, if implemented, would cause substantial shifts in the expenditure of public funds, creating some savings and some additional expenditures.

If the system is to move from consolidation to programmatic goals, some decisions and choices are open to the planners. To create some stability in the style of the system, roles should be defined carefully. It is less important that this happen on paper than in the daily lives of the participants. Probably an effort to define roles has to start at the top and filter down through the careful and measured acts of the leaders. Confidence of the faculties, students, and public in higher education is not so eroded that such an effort would fail. A climate characterized by a certain calmness, stability, and tone of excellence might well begin to develop.

The next major-priority issue would be the character of the system and the relation of the nineteen campuses to each other and to the system. Are the nineteen campuses to be roughly comparable to each other? Many actions—such as the provision of guidelines for organization and staffing and the academic planning process itself—and the continuing posture of the state government with respect to line item budgets and fiscal controls have reinforced an attitude common in the system: that the campuses are nineteen copies in different places, that presidents are really more like assistant chancellors, that the system imposes on each campus a character which allows little moving room. In fact, much of this is myth, but it is accepted myth, which is then as real as fact. From the standpoint of state government, perhaps this view is desirable. If so, it should be made explicit. But a case can be made for maximizing the educationally sound differences among the campuses.

Perhaps the faculty, students, advisory board, and administrative leaders of each college should be asked to examine the character, programs, and long-range goals which would be unique to it. Some colleges would respond in the traditional national mold of liberal arts-oriented state colleges or universities, but many would not. To meld the character of the several campuses with the system framework and the goals and functions of the state college segment of public higher education is a responsibility of the chancellor and Board of Trustees. Such a course of action would be not only educationally but fiscally sound, in that it would result in maximum use of resources. Perhaps substantial engineering programs are really needed on only five campuses, though other campuses might offer engineering programs related to natural resources, the health sciences, or business. The point of such a strategy—a strategy moving the state college system beyond consolidation toward programmatic goals—would be to encourage all the component parts to maximize excellence, within a framework of public higher education closely tied to the life of the state and its people, and within the limited resources that may always be provided but never be as abundant as desired.

The implications of this volume for educators and political leaders in other states are relatively clear. California is perhaps unusual in its pattern of growth and in having a political climate which is often characterized by extremes. Allowing for these factors, the creation of a system or multiple systems of higher education within a state is a major task in educational organization. The most critical variable seems to be role definition. Obviously this problem has not been ignored in the California experience, yet it has so far defied solution; this failure is understandable not only because the system is still moving through a consolidation period but also because of the changing and as yet unclear role of higher education in American society.

There is a tone of optimism in these concluding observations, a tone which belies many of the observations and critical comments in previous chapters. Higher education, education in general, has always been an instrument of basic social policy and has led to much of our national development. Our national goals themselves are now being reassessed and reset. Higher education is a part of this process, and the California state colleges, perhaps invisible but on examination a giant among the nation's great educational experiments, may now move with the time to become an integral part of the life and development of the nation's largest state.

Bibliography

"Academic Governance." *The Chancellor Comments,* April 3, 1970, pp. 4–5.

Academic Senate of the California State Colleges. *Report of the Chairman.* Los Angeles, 1966.

Academic Senate of the California State Colleges. *Issues and Answers on Collective Bargaining.* Los Angeles, 1967.

Academic Senate of the California State Colleges. *Position Paper: Politics in Higher Education.* Los Angeles, 1968a.

Academic Senate of the California State Colleges. *Report of the Executive Committee on Relations of the Academic Senate with the Chancellor.* Los Angeles, 1968b.

Academic Senate of the California State Colleges. *Minutes.* Los Angeles, 1970.

Academic Senate of the California State Colleges, Ad Hoc Committee on Grievances and Disciplinary Procedures. *Minority Report.* Los Angeles, 1970.

Academic Senator, The. A periodical published by the Academic Senate of the California State Colleges.

Academic Statesman, The. A periodical published by the College Council of the California Federation of Teachers.

Academy for Educational Development, *Governance of Public Higher Education in California,* Report 68–15. Sacramento: Coordinating Council for Higher Education, 1968.

AFT Union Report. A periodical published by the College Council of the California Federation of Teachers.

ALLAN, R. "Staffing Practices and Problems of Business Units in the California State College System." *Academy of Management Journal,* 1968, *11,* 75–89.

American Alumni Council, Council for Financial Aid to Education, and National Association of Independent Schools. *Voluntary Support of Education 1967–68.* A co-sponsored survey. New York, 1969.

ASTIN, A. W. *Who Goes Where to College?* Chicago: Science Research Associates, 1965.

AXELROD, J. "The Coordination of Higher Education in California." *University College Quarterly,* May 1964.

BARLOW, W., AND SHAPIRO, P. *An End to Silence: The San Francisco State Student Movement in the Sixties.* New York: Pegasus, 1970.

BENEZET, L. T., AND ASSOCIATES. *Faculty Research in the California State Colleges.* Publication 68–17. Sacramento: Coordinating Council for Higher Education, 1968.

BONGARTZ, R. "No More Sombreros: The Chicano Rebellion." *The Nation,* 1969, *208,* 271–275.

BOYLE, K. *The Long Walk at San Francisco State.* New York: Grove, 1970.

BRANN, J. "San Jose: The Bullhorn Message." *The Nation,* 1967, *205,* 465–468.

BRATFISH, V., AND OTHERS. *A Report on the Status of Women at the California State College at Fullerton.* Fullerton, Calif.: Fullerton State College, 1970.

BROWN, E. G. "Public Higher Education in California." In L. Wilson (Ed.), *Emerging Patterns in American Higher Education.* Washington, D.C.: American Council on Education, 1965, pp. 104–109.

BROWN, E. G. "College by Plan." *American Education,* 1965, *1,* 9–12.

BUCHALTER, S. S., AND HAAK, H. H. "The California State Colleges: Adoption of a Systemwide Grievance Procedure." *Bulletin of the American Association of University Professors,* 1968, *54,* 365–371.

BUNZEL, J. H. "The War of the Flea at San Francisco State." *The New York Times Magazine,* November 9, 1969, pp. 28–30 and 133–140.

BUNZEL, J. H. "Black Studies at San Francisco State." *The Public Interest*, 1968, *13*, 22–38.

BUNZEL, J. H. "Student Participation: No." *The Humanist*, September/October 1970, *30*, 32ff.

BUNZEL, J. H., DUERR, E. C., AND HALPERIN, I. "Three Inside Views of San Francisco State College." *Educational Record*, 1969, *50*, 121–131.

BUNZEL, J. H., AND LITWAK, L. "Battle For a College." *Look*, May 27, 1969, pp. 61–72.

BURKMAN, J. A. *An Analytical Study of the California State Colleges.* Sacramento: State Department of Education, 1937.

CAHN, M. M. "The 1968–1969 San Francisco State College Crisis: A Minority Report." *Phi Delta Kappan*, September, 1969, 21–25.

California Constitution, Article IX, Section 9.

California Professor, The. A periodical published by the California College and University Faculty Association, California Teachers Association.

California Legislature, Assembly Concurrent Resolution No. 88, 1959.

"California State College at Long Beach: A Case Study of Academic Due Process." *Bulletin of the American Association of University Professors*, 1968, *54*, 64–77.

California State Colleges, Office of the Chancellor. *Report of the Ad Hoc Committee on Development of Policies and Administrative Procedures.* Los Angeles, 1965.

California State Colleges, Office of the Chancellor. *A Brief Historical Review of Procedures, Programs, and Progress of the California State Colleges Under the Board of Trustees.* Los Angeles, 1966.

California State Colleges, Division of Instructional Research, Office of the Chancellor. *Supporting Documentation for Changing the Name "College" to "University."* Los Angeles, 1968.

California State Colleges, Division of Instructional Research, Office of the Chancellor. *Enrollment Trends and Growth Rates in the California State Colleges.* Los Angeles, 1968.

California State Colleges, Division of Instructional Research, Office of the Chancellor. *Admissions Study Digest: A Summary of the California State College 1963 Admissions Study—Phase I.* Los Angeles, 1969.

California State Colleges, Division of Instructional Research, Office of the Chancellor. *Those Who Made It: Selected Characteristics of the June, 1967, California State College Baccalaureate Graduates.* Los Angeles, 1969.

California State Colleges, Division of Institutional Research, Office of the Chancellor. *Five Years Later: A Follow-Up to the California State College 1963 Admissions Study—Phase II.* Los Angeles, 1970.

California State Colleges Review. A periodical published by the Office of the Chancellor of the California State Colleges.

"California's Needs in Higher Education." *California Monthly,* 1956, *66,* 18–34.

Carnegie Foundation for the Advancement of Teaching. *State Higher Education in California.* Sacramento: State Printing Office, 1932.

CHAMBERS, M. M. *Higher Education in the Fifty States.* Danville, Ill.: Interstate, 1970, pp. 48–68.

Chancellor Comments, The. A periodical published by the Office of the Chancellor of the California State Colleges.

CHANDLER, E., AND FAZEL, P. *Organization of the California State Colleges.* Report AN 227–1. Sacramento: State Department of Finance, 1950.

CHRISMAN, R. "Observations on Race and Class at San Francisco State." In J. McEvoy and A. Miller (Eds.), *Black Power and Student Rebellion.* Belmont, Calif.: Wadsworth, 1969, pp. 222–232.

CLOUD, R. W. *Education in California: Leaders, Organizations, and Accomplishments of the First Hundred Years.* Stanford, Calif.: Stanford University Press, 1952.

COFFIN, J. H. *The Role of the State Colleges in Higher Education in California.* Sacramento: State Department of Education, 1939.

"Conference for Discussion of Carnegie Report." *California Schools,* 1932, *3,* 375–376.

COONS, A. G. *Crises in California Higher Education.* Los Angeles: Ward Ritchie, 1968.

Coordinating Council for Higher Education. *Faculty Recruitment in California Higher Education.* Report 1017. Sacramento, 1965.

Coordinating Council for Higher Education. *The Master Plan Five Years Later.* Report 1024. Sacramento, 1966.

Coordinating Council for Higher Education. *Feasibility and Desirability of Eliminating Lower Division Programs at Selected Campuses of the University of California and the California State Colleges.* Report 67–1. Sacramento, 1967.

Coordinating Council for Higher Education. *Federal Funds and California Higher Education.* Sacramento, 1968a.

Coordinating Council for Higher Education. *Study of Income for Public Higher Education.* Sacramento, 1968b.

Coordinating Council for Higher Education. *A Study of the Implications of Changing the Name of the California State Colleges to the California State University.* Report 68–6. Sacramento, 1968c.

Coordinating Council for Higher Education. *Meeting the Enrollment Demand for Public Higher Education in California Through 1977: The Need for Additional Colleges and University Campuses.* Report 69–1. Sacramento, 1969.

Coordinating Council for Higher Education. *The Undergraduate Student and His Higher Education: Policies of California Colleges and Universities in the Next Decade.* Report 1034. Sacramento, 1969.

Coordinating Council for Higher Education. *Academic Tenure in California Public Higher Education.* Report 69–5. Sacramento, 1969.

Coordinating Council for Higher Education. Agenda for meeting on April 6, 1970, Item 3.

Crocker-Anglo National Bank. *California's Knowledge Industry.* San Francisco: Crocker-Anglo National Bank, 1969.

DANIELS, A., KAHN-HUT, R. AND ASSOCIATES. *Academics on the Line: The Faculty Strike at San Francisco State College.* San Francisco: Jossey-Bass, 1970.

DEEGAN, W. L., MC CONNELL, T. R., MORTIMER, K. P., AND STULL, H. *Joint Participation in Decision-Making: A Study of Faculty Government and Faculty-Administrative Consultation at Fresno State.* Berkeley: Center for Research and Development in Higher Education, 1970.

DEGNAN, J. "California's Militant Professors." *Changing Education,* 1967, *1,* 35–39.

Department of Education. *A Summary and Classification of the Recommendations of the Carnegie Foundation Report on State Higher Education in California.* Sacramento: State of California, 1932.

Department of Education. *A Study of the Needs of California in Higher Education.* Sacramento: State of California, 1948.

Department of Education. *A Restudy of the Needs of Higher Education in California.* Sacramento: State of California, 1955.

Department of Education. *A Master Plan for Higher Education in California.* Sacramento: State of California, 1960.

Department of Finance. *Organization of the California State Colleges.* Survey 227–1. Sacramento, 1950.

DOUGLASS, A. A. "Report of the Survey of the Needs of California in Higher Education." *California Schools,* 1948, *19,* 81–89.

DUMKE, G. S. "Higher Education in California." *California Historical Society Quarterly,* 1963, *42,* 99–111.

DUMKE, G. S. "Campus Violence: Crackdown Coming—An Interview." *U. S. News and World Report,* 1968, *65,* 48–53.

DUNHAM, E. A. *Colleges of the Forgotten Americans.* New York: McGraw-Hill, 1969.

EARLL, L., "A History of the State Normal School at Chico, 1887–1910." *The Normal School Record,* Spring 1910, 1–11.

EELLS, W. C. "State Higher Education in California." *J. C. Journal,* 1932, *3,* 30–46.

FERRIER, W. W. *Ninety Years of Education in California, 1846–1936.* Berkeley: Sather Gate Bookshop, 1937.

Field Research Corp. Release 674. San Francisco, June 18, 1970.

FINBERG, H. *Crisis at San Francisco State College.* San Francisco: Journalism Department, San Francisco State College, 1969.

FINCHER, J. "Unmaking of a President." *Life,* 1968, *64,* 45–52.

FLOURNOY, H. I. Speech at University of Southern California, April 15, 1969.

FREEDMAN, M. B. "San Francisco State: Urban Campus Prototype." In G. K. Smith (Ed.), *Agony and Response: Current Issues in Higher Education 1969.* San Francisco: Jossey-Bass, 1969, pp. 82–90.

GERTH, D. R. "The Government of Public Higher Education in California." Unpublished doctoral dissertation, University of Chicago, 1963.

GILBERT, B. F. *Pioneers for One Hundred Years: San Jose State College, 1857–1957.* San Jose: San Jose State College, 1957.

GITLIN, T. "On the Line at San Francisco State." In J. McEvoy and A. Miller (Eds.), *Black Power and Student Rebellion.* Belmont, Calif.: Wadsworth, 1969, pp. 298–306.

GLENNY, L. A. *Autonomy of Public Colleges.* New York: McGraw-Hill, 1959.

GOLDMAN, R. M. "Confrontations at San Francisco State." *Dissent,* 1969, *16,* 167–179.

GREATHEAD, E. *The Story of an Inspiring Past: Historical Sketch of San Jose State Teachers College, 1862–1928,* San Jose: San Jose State Teachers College, 1928.

GRIMM, W. *Collective Bargaining in the State College System.* Sacramento: California State Employees Association, 1966.

GURLL, F. D. "The Development of a Master Plan for Higher Education in California." *College and University,* 1966, *41,* 269–280.

HAAK, H. H. *Collective Bargaining and Academic Government: The Case of the California State Colleges.* San Diego: Public Affairs Research Institute, San Diego State College, 1968.

HAAK, H. H., AND GRAVES, L. *Collective Negotiations and the Academic Senate.* Los Angeles: Academic Senate of the California State Colleges, 1970.

HAEHN, J. O. *A Survey of Problems in Faculty Recruiting in the California State Colleges.* Los Angeles: Academic Senate of the California State Colleges, 1968.

HAEHN, J. O. "A Study of Trade Unionism Among State College Professors." Unpublished doctoral dissertation, University of California, Berkeley, 1969.

HAEHN, J. O. *A Survey of Faculty and Administrator Attitudes on Collective Bargaining.* Los Angeles: Academic Senate of the California State Colleges, 1970.

HALPERIN, I. "San Francisco State College Diary." *Educational Record,* 1969, *50,* 121–125.

HANSEN, W. L., AND WEISBROD, B. A. "The Distribution of Costs and Direct Benefits of Public Higher Education: The Case of California." *The Journal of Human Resources,* 1969, *4,* 176–191.

HANSEN, W. L., AND WEISBROD, B. A. *Benefits, Costs, and Finance of Public Higher Education.* Chicago: Markham, 1969.

HARCLEROAD, F. F., SAGEN, H. B., AND MOLEN, C. T., JR. *A Study of the Historical Background, Current Status, and Future Plans of the Developing State Colleges and Universities.* Washington, D.C.: American Association of State Colleges and Universities, 1969.

HARRIS, S. "San Fernando's Black Revolt." *Commonweal,* 1969, *89,* 549–552.

HENDERSON, A. D. "State Planning and Coordination of Public and Private Higher Education." *Educational Record,* 1966, *47,* 503–509.

HILL, W. W., AND FRENCH, W. L. "Perceptions of Power of Department Chairmen by Professors." *Administrative Science Quarterly,* 1967, *11,* 548–574.

HOLY, T. C. "Coordination of Public Higher Education in California." *Journal of Higher Education,* 1955, *26,* 141–148.

HOLY, T. C. "California's Master Plan for Higher Education, 1960–75." *Journal of Higher Education,* 1961, *32,* 9–16.

HOLY, T. C. "The Coordinating Council for Higher Education in California: A Review of Its First Two Years." *Journal of Higher Education*, 1964, *35*, 313–322.

HOLY, T. C., AND MC CONNELL, T. R. "California Studies Its Needs and Resources in Higher Education." *Educational Record*, 1955, *36*, 291–304.

HOLY, T. C., AND SEMANS, H. H. *Summary of Efforts on Coordination of Public Higher Education in California*. Sacramento: Liaison Committee of the State Board of Education and the Regents of the University of California, 1954.

JENCKS, C., AND RIESMAN, D. "A Case Study in Vignette: San Francisco State College." *Teachers College Record*, 1962, *63*, 233–258.

Joint Committee on Higher Education. *The Academic State*. Sacramento: California State Legislature, n.d. (1967).

Joint Committee on Higher Education. *The Challenge of Achievement*. Sacramento: California State Legislature, 1969.

JOUGHIN, L. "Three Problems of the California State Colleges." *Bulletin of the American Association of University Professors*, 1967, *53*, 228–236.

JOYAL, A. E. "A New Look for California Higher Education." *School and Society*, 1960, *88*, 397–399.

KARAGUEVZIAN, D. *Blow It Up*. New York: Gambit, 1971.

KEENE, C. M. "Administration of Systemwide Faculty and Staff Affairs." *Public Administration Review*, 1970, *30*, 113–117.

KENNEDY, R. E. "An Emerging Model for Effective Decision-Making in the California State Colleges, 1862–1965." Unpublished doctoral dissertation, Claremont Graduate School and Center, Claremont, Calif., 1966.

KERSEY, V. "An Appraisal of the Carnegie Foundation Survey of State Higher Education in California." *California Schools*, 1932, *3*, 307–320.

LANE, R. E. "Faculty Unionism in a California State College." Unpublished doctoral dissertation, University of Iowa, Ames, 1967.

LANGGUTH, A. J. "San Francisco State," *Harper's*, September 1969, 99–100ff.

LARSEN, C. M. "Collective Bargaining Issues in the California State Colleges." *Bulletin of the American Association of University Professors*, 1967, *53*, 217–228.

LEASURE, W., TURNER, M., AND FLORES, R. A. *California State Colleges Deserve More Funds*. San Diego: Institute of Labor Economics, San Diego State College, ILE Bulletin 2, 1968.

LEFFLAND, N. W. "The College Administration and Faculty." Unpublished doctoral dissertation, University of Southern California, 1959.

Legislative Analyst. *Fiscal and Budget Controls for the California State Colleges*. Sacramento: State of California, 1970.

Liaison Committee of the State Board of Education and the Regents of the University of California. *The Needs of California in Higher Education*. Sacramento, 1948.

Liaison Committee of the State Board of Education and the Regents of the University of California. *The Origin and Functions of the Liaison Committee of the State Board of Education and the Regents of the University of California*. Sacramento, 1957.

Liaison Committee of the State Board of Education and the Regents of the University of California. *A Study of the Need for Additional Centers of Public Higher Education in California*. Berkeley and Sacramento, 1957.

Liaison Committee of the State Board of Education and the Regents of the University of California. *Faculty Demand and Supply in California Higher Education*. Berkeley and Sacramento, 1958.

Liaison Committee of the State Board of Education and the Regents of the University of California. *A Master Plan for Higher Education in California, 1960–1975*. Berkeley and Sacramento, 1960.

Liaison Committee of the State Board of Education and the Regents of the University of California. *Institutional Capacities and Area Needs of California Public Higher Education, 1960–1975*. Berkeley and Sacramento, 1961.

LIVINGSTON, J. C. "Collective Bargaining and Professionalism in Higher Education." *Educational Record*, 1967, *48*, 79–88.

LIVINGSTON, J. C. "Academic Senates Under Fire." In G. K. Smith (Ed.), *Agony and Response: Current Issues in Higher Education 1969*. San Francisco: Jossey-Bass, 1969, pp. 161–172.

Long Beach State College. *The First Decade of Long Beach State College, 1949–1959*. Long Beach, 1960.

Los Angeles Times, July 29, 1970.

LUCKMAN, C. "California's New State Colleges." *Architectural Record*, 1964, *136*, 200–204.

MC CALLUM, G. A. *Faculty Participation in State-Wide Policy Formulation: Progress Report*. Los Angeles: Trustees of the California State Colleges, 1962.

MC CALLUM, G. A. *Faculty Senates and Councils in the California State Colleges*. Los Angeles: Trustees of the California State Colleges, 1962.

MC CONNELL, T. R. "Restudy of the Needs of California in Higher Education." *Higher Education,* 1956, *12,* 126–129.

MC CUNN, D., AND MC GOWAN, W. N. "The California Education Coordination Committee." *California Schools,* 1954, *25,* 463–465.

MC EVOY, J., AND MILLER, A. "The Crisis at San Francisco State." In H. Becker (Ed.), *Campus Power Struggle.* Chicago: Aldine, 1970, pp. 57–77.

MC INTOSH, C. F. "Chico State College—The First 75 Years." *Diggins,* Fall 1962, 2–22.

MC INTOSH, C. W. "The Unionization of College and University Teachers." *Journal of Higher Education,* 1965, *36,* 373–378.

MC KENNEY, J. W. "Changes Expected in Colleges of California." *California Teachers Association Journal,* 1966, *62,* 38–49.

MALONE, D. H. "Testimony on Student Unrest Before California Legislative Committee." *Bulletin of the American Association of University Professors,* 1969, *55,* 91–94.

MARK, M. "Black Studies." *New Republic,* 1969, *160,* 12–13.

MATHY, L. Letter to Glenn S. Dumke, 1964.

MOELLERING, R. L. "Impasse on California's Academic Scene." *Christian Century,* 1969, *236,* 294–298.

MOORE, D. E. *Twenty Years of Higher Education: The History of Sacramento State College.* Sacramento: Associated Students of Sacramento State College, 1967.

MOORE, G. E. *History of Chico State College.* Eugene, Ore.: Unpublished master's thesis, Oregon State College, 1939.

NELSON, C. A. "Quantity and Quality in Higher Education." In R. A. Goldwin (Ed.), *Higher Education and Modern Democracy.* Chicago: Rand McNally, 1967, pp. 155–185.

NEVIN, D. "Uneasy Peace at Valley State." *Life,* 1969, *66,* 59–74.

"New State Higher Education Plan." *California Teachers Association Journal,* 1960, *56,* 36.

Office of the Chancellor. *Memorandum, The Consultative Process for Appointments to Executive Academic Positions on the Chancellor's Staff.* Los Angeles, 1966.

ORRICK, W. H., JR. *"Shut It Down!" A College in Crisis: San Francisco State College, October 1968—April 1969.* Washington, D.C.: National Commission on the Causes and Prevention of Violence, 1969.

ORRICK, W. H., JR. *College in Crisis.* Nashville, Tenn.: Aurora, 1970.

PALOLA, E. G., AND PADGETT, W. *Planning for Self Renewal.* Berkeley:

Center for Research and Development in Higher Education, 1971.

PALTRIDGE, J. G. *California's Coordinating Council for Higher Education.* Berkeley: Center for Research and Development in Higher Education, 1966.

PENTONY, D., SMITH, R., AND AXEN, R. *Unfinished Rebellions.* San Francisco: Jossey-Bass, 1971.

POSS, S. "Lawn Ordure at Fresno State." *New Politics,* 1970, *8,* 14–22.

REAGAN, R. *White Paper on Education in California.* Sacramento: Office of the Governor, n.d. (1968).

Report of the Phase I Committee to the Chancellor of the California State Colleges. Los Angeles: Office of the Chancellor, 1962.

RHOADS, H. *Report of the 1968 State College Faculty Opinion Poll.* Sacramento: California State Employees Association, 1969.

RICHFIELD, J. Letter to Glenn S. Dumke, 1970.

RIESMAN, D., AND JENCKS, C. "The Viability of the American College." In N. Sanford (Ed.), *The American College.* New York: Wiley, 1967, pp. 74–192.

ROBINSON, E. A. "The Seven State Colleges of California." *School and Society,* 1941, *53,* 649–657.

ROSENFELD, L. B. "The Confrontation Policies of S. I. Hayakawa: A Case Study in Coercive Semantics." *Today's Speech,* 1970, *18,* 18–23.

ROSSI, C. "Campus Dissidents and the Problems of Finance." *California Teachers Association Journal,* 1970, *66,* 10–12.

ROTHBART, G. S. "The Legitimation of Inequality: Objective Scholarship vs. Black Militance." *Sociology of Education,* 1970, *43,* 159–175.

ROYCE, R. *Historical Sketch of the State Normal School at San Jose, 1862–1889.* Sacramento: California State Printer, 1889.

SCHLONING, R. *Credential Reform in California.* Chicago: American Federation of Teachers, 1966.

Scope, The. A periodical published by the Academic Council of the California State Employees Association.

SEIDENBAUM, A. *Confrontation on Campus: Student Challenge in California.* Los Angeles: Ward Ritchie, 1969.

SEMANS, H. H. "Recommended Plan for Higher Education in California." *California Schools,* 1955, *26,* 215–231.

SEMANS, H. H., AND HOLY, T. C. "Areaism and Differentiation of Function in Higher Education." *California Journal of Secondary Education,* 1954, *29,* 387–392.

SHORRIS, E. "Hayakawa in Thought and Action." *Ramparts*, 1969, *8*, 38–43.

SIMPSON, R. E. "Public Higher Education in California." *California Schools*, 1955, *26*, 3–11.

SMITH, R. R. "Emerging Political Patterns in California Higher Education." *Educational Leadership*, 1969, *27*, 19–27.

SMITH, R. R. "San Francisco State Experience." In G. K. Smith (Ed.), *Agony and Response: Current Issues in Higher Education 1969*. San Francisco: Jossey-Bass, 1969, pp. 91–99.

SMITH, R. R., AXEN, R., AND PENTONY, D. *By Any Means Necessary*. San Francisco: Jossey-Bass, 1970.

State College Commission on Citizenship. *The State Colleges and Citizenship*. Sacramento, 1951.

STONE, J. C. *California's Commitment to Public Education*. New York: Crowell, 1961.

STRAYER, G. D. "California's Needs in Higher Education." *California Journal of Secondary Education*, 1948, *23*, 236–239.

STRAYER, G. D., AND OTHERS. *A Report of a Survey of the Needs of Higher Education*. Berkeley: University of California Press, 1948.

Summary. A periodical published by the Support Services Council of the California State Employees Association.

SWETT, J. *Public Education in California: Its Origin and Development*. New York: American Book, 1911.

TOOL, M. *The California State Colleges Under the Master Plan*. San Diego: Academic Senate of the California State Colleges, 1966.

"Travail of a College President." *California Teachers Association Journal*, 1969, *65*, 11–16.

U. S. Congress. *National Program of Institutional Grants*. Report No. 91–490. House of Representatives, 91st Congress, 1st Session.

U. S. Department of Health, Education, and Welfare, Financial Statistics of Institutions of Higher Education: Federal Funds 1965–66 and 1966–67, Washington Supt. of Documents, 1970.

UNRUH, J. H. "California Higher Education." In G. K. Smith (Ed.), *In Search of Leaders: Current Issues in Higher Education 1967*. Washington, D.C.: American Association for Higher Education, 1967, pp. 29–34.

UNRUH, J. H. *Sacramento Bee*, January 17, 1967, p. 86.

UNRUH, J. H. "New Management for California Higher Education." *Compact*, June 1969, 4–8.

VASCHÉ, J. B. "Our State Colleges." In *Compelling Problems and Issues in Higher Education.* San Francisco: San Francisco State College, 1954, pp. 11–15.

VASCHÉ, J. B. "The California State Colleges: Their History, Organization, Purposes, and Progress." *California Schools,* 1959, *30,* 3–25.

VASCHÉ, J. B. *The California State Colleges.* Sacramento: State Printing Office, 1959.

Voice of the Faculties, The. A periodical published by the Association of California State College Professors.

WAHLQUIST, J. T. "San Jose State College—Nine Decades of Service." *California Schools,* 1954, *25,* 57–67.

WAHLQUIST, J. T., AND THORNTON, J. W., JR. *State Colleges and Universities.* Washington, D.C.: The Center for Applied Research in Education, 1964.

WALKER, J. M. "Models of Academic Governance in Emergent Universities." Unpublished doctoral dissertation, University of California, Berkeley, 1970.

WALTER, A. "The Origin and Development of San Jose State Teachers College." Unpublished doctoral dissertation, Stanford University, 1933.

WEBB, P. E. "The Plan of the Carnegie Foundation for the Reorganization of Education in California." *California Quarterly of Secondary Education,* 1932, *8,* 53–57.

WIDMAR, K. "California: Why the Colleges Blow Up." *The Nation,* 1969, *208,* 237–241.

WILNER, H. "Zen Basketball, etc., at San Francisco State." *Esquire,* 1967, *68,* 98.

WOLK, R. A. *Alternative Methods of Federal Funding for Higher Education.* Berkeley: Carnegie Commission, 1968.

ZOOK, G. F. "California Colleges and Universities—Whither?" *Schools and Society,* 1933, *37,* 633–640.

Index

2, 15–16, 21–23, 48, 51–52,
74–75, 87, 103, 118; and organization of state colleges, 93–
94, 175; and state college budgets, 78–81; and state college
faculty, 37–39, 41, 43–45, 47–
49, 127; and University of
California, 83, 85; 1970 session of, 36, 38, 46, 73, 116,
130–131, 145, 168, 175–176,
191, 197, 201, 217
LEIFFER, D., 17
Liaison Committee of the Regents of
the University of California
and the State Board of Education, 13–15, 52. *See also*
Master Plan Survey Team
Long Beach, California State College
at, 12, 62, 151, 180n
Los Angeles, California State College
at, 12, 62, 139, 151, 180n, 192,
197
Los Angeles State Normal School,
10–11
LUCKEY, W., 10
LUCKMAN, C., 37

M

MC CUNE, E., 19
MAC QUARRIE, T., 179–180, 182
MALCOLM X, 151
MARCUSE, H., 43
MARVIN, J., 8
Master Plan for Higher Education,
5–6, 25, 48, 71–72, 103, 110,
118, 150, 156, 185, 208, 213–
216; and academic planning,
2; and coordinating council,
66, 91, 209; development of,
15–19, 21–22, 51–52, 56–57,
87–88, 90, 193, 207. *See also*
Donahoe Act
Master Plan Survey Team, 89, 184.
See also Liaison Committee
MERRIAM, T., 55
Michigan, University of, 195
Minnesota, University of, 195
MOULDER, A., 4–5, 8–9

N

National Education Association, 132–
133, 143
New College (San Jose State), 188–
189

O

Occidental College, 88

P

PACE, R., 194
Personnel Board, State, 14
Pomona, California State Polytechnic
College at, 12, 198

R

REAGAN, R., 4, 37–40, 42, 85, 99–100,
112, 216–217
Regents of the University of California: appointments to, 40;
and legislature, 44, 74; and
Master Plan, 12–13, 22, 51–
53, 88; status of, 91; terms of
office of, 16; and university
governance, 74, 100

S

Sacramento State College, 12, 180n,
198
San Bernardino, California State College at, 12, 197
San Diego State College, 10, 17, 36,
58, 138, 151, 192, 197
San Fernando Valley State College,
12, 62, 138–139
San Francisco State College: collective bargaining at, 142; and
Glenn Dumke, 17, 56; faculty
unrest at, 25; and S. Hayakawa, 123; history of, 10;
minority group students at,
62–63, 151; programs at, 58,
192, 197; strike at, 64, 100,
138–140, 148, 161–162; student government at, 167–168;
violence at, 43, 62–64
San Jose State College, 4, 62, 138–
139, 157–158, 178–189, 192,
194, 197